It's Your

LITTLE RED WAGON

*6 Core Strengths for Navigating Your Path
to the Good Life*

It's Your Little Red Wagon... 6 Core Strengths for Navigating Your Path to the Good Life.

Copyright © 2007 Sharon S. Esonis, Ph.D.

Although the author/publisher has made every effort to ensure the accuracy and completeness of information contained in this book, we assume no responsibility for errors, inaccuracies, omissions or any inconsistencies herein. Any slights of people, places or organizations are unintentional. Readers should use their own judgment or consult an appropriate healthcare professional or their own personal physician if questions arise pertaining to individual situations.

The author gratefully acknowledges permission to reprint material from "The Road to Resilience." Copyright © 2004 American Psychological Association. Adapted with permission. www.apahelpcenter.org/featuredtopics/feature.php?id=6&ch=2

First printing 2007
Published by Positive Path Publishing.
www.PositivePathLifeCoaching.com

Esonis, Ph.D., Sharon S.
    It's Your Little Red Wagon... 6 Core Strengths for Navigating Your Path to the Good Life /
    Sharon S. Esonis, Ph.D.

    ISBN 978-0-9799497-0-8

ATTENTION CORPORATIONS, UNIVERSITIES, COLLEGES AND PROFESSIONAL ORGANIZATIONS. Quantity discounts are available on bulk purchases of this book for educational or gift purposes. Specialty books or book excerpts can also be created to fit specific needs. For information, please contact Sharon S. Esonis, Ph.D., via email at ThePositivePath@cox.net. Telephone: 760-746-PATH (7284). Website: www.PositivePathLifeCoaching.com.

Set in 11-point Adobe Garamond. Cover design and layout by Kim Knoll. www.kimknoll.com

*This book is dedicated to my husband, Ray,
whose assistance on this project was invaluable,
and to my son, Patrick, who has filled my life
with humor, optimism and love.*

It's Your

LITTLE RED WAGON

*6 Core Strengths for Navigating Your Path
to the Good Life*

Sharon S. Esonis, Ph.D.

The Author

 Sharon Esonis has spent the better part of three decades helping individuals live their dreams through her work as a licensed psychologist, life coach and author. An expert in human behavior and motivation, Dr. Esonis specializes in the burgeoning field of Positive Psychology, the scientific study of optimal human functioning and the core strengths that can lead to the achievement of one's personally-defined goals – what we call "the good life."

Dr. Esonis earned her bachelor and masters degrees at Ohio University and her doctoral degree at Boston College. While at BC, she studied under a preeminent psychologist who was renowned in the field of Cognitive Behavior Therapy and was an early proponent of the Positive Psychology movement.

Dr. Esonis is licensed in psychology in Arizona and Massachusetts, and in addition to her many years of private practice as a clinician and coach, she supervised masters and doctoral students in their clinical work at Arizona State University. She has served as a hospital staff psychologist and has lectured on topics ranging from stress management, meditation and relaxation training to assertiveness and sleep management. Today, her private practice in San Diego is dedicated exclusively to personal and professional coaching.

It's Your Little Red Wagon... 6 Core Strengths for Navigating Your Path to the Good Life is Sharon Esonis' contribution to the field of Positive Psychology, presenting proven success factors and strength-building techniques that can lead individuals to a life of purpose, motivation and personally-defined happiness.

Dr. Esonis is a member of the American Psychological Association (APA), the Association for Behavior and Cognitive Therapy (ABCT), the San Diego Professionals Coaches Alliance (SDPCA) and is a Founding Member of the Centre for Applied Positive Psychology (CAPP).

Table of Contents

It's Your

LITTLE RED WAGON

*6 Core Strengths for Navigating Your Path
to the Good Life*

Introduction

"It's your little red wagon: You can push it, pull it or just stand and look at it!" That's the deal as I see it. I'm a psychologist and life coach, and I've seen many clients over the years who've presented a variety of different challenges. I don't honestly remember when I started using this metaphor, but I know it was many moons ago. My son, while growing up, heard the little red wagon bit again and again. It's probably a blessing and a curse to have a psychologist for a mother!

What this metaphor represents to me, my son and many of the clients I have had the privilege and honor to assist, is a special, shiny, vibrant red vehicle that transports our hopes, dreams, promise and passion. And in order to embark on a fulfilling journey, stay on the necessary course and ultimately reach our personally desired goals, each of us has to take and maintain control. We have to learn and accept that ultimately our wagon's progress must be engineered and navigated by the one to whom it belongs.

That's actually the good news. The fate of your little red wagon – your life as you wish it to be – is in your hands! Former Secretary of State, General Colin Powell, in his quest to help America's youth, has chosen the "little red wagon" as a symbol of hope and promise for children. I believe this is a wonderful symbol for all ages. To transform the symbol into reality, however, requires not only acceptance of the responsibilities of being in charge of your own happiness and well-being, but also a commitment to acquire the help, information and specific tools that can lead to individually-defined success.

Using this metaphor as a theme in therapy and coaching has involved two major components: First, the focus on identifying the client's goals and dreams; and second, the focus on developing the strengths that are instrumental in achieving those goals and dreams.

Six core strengths – *Optimism, Courage, Persistence, Enthusiasm, Living in the Present,* and *Resilience* – are the very means by which these people I have known so well set out and continue to journey on their special paths. I believe that tapping into and fortifying these strengths is not a difficult undertaking, as long as you're equipped with the right information and a mound of motivation, both of which I hope to provide for you here!

I remember being so touched when one client presented me with a miniature Radio Flyer red wagon. It contained flower pots with the following inscriptions: The nouns – *hope, spirit, faith, gratitude, wonder, play, adventure, harmony and balance*; the verbs – *believe, create, search and discover; and, oh yes, the sole adjective – sassy* (hmm!). Tied to the handle was a ribbon imprinted with the words *imagine, dream, inspire*, and a metal sign inscribed *Thank You*. You better believe that for a psychologist, it just doesn't get any better than that!

According to a Swedish Proverb, "God gives every bird a worm, but He doesn't throw it in the nest." If your little red wagon is not going where you want it to go, here's the good news: Psychology has taken a right turn! It's now in the business of identifying and teaching the skills that foster well-being, in addition to its longtime goal of understanding and treating psychological problems.

At last, the field is paying very special attention to the strengths that help us design and achieve a life filled with joy and purpose, a life characterized by the ability to weather storms valiantly and, in so doing, restore hope, energy and self-confidence for the ongoing adventure.

The movement is called Positive Psychology, and it's about the good life. The individual primarily responsible for igniting this is Martin Seligman, a past president of the American Psychological Association (APA), who, during his tenure in 1998, heralded this as the APA Theme of the Year. Currently there is a groundswell of energy focused on studying and teaching the techniques that enhance the good life. So very exciting!

Which brings me to why I wrote this book and what I hope to accomplish. I would like to help you in the clearest, most concise and most enjoyable way determine the strengths you want to develop, and then provide the information and guidance you need to make it happen. My goal is to appeal to a wide range of people, both hesitant and voracious readers alike. I understand that not everyone is enamored with reading motivational or self-help books. Some people have trouble concentrating or aren't in the habit of reading or don't have the time to devote to such an endeavor. And, of course, there are those who read one self-improvement book after another!

Over the years I've tried to find inspiring and helpful reading materials for all my clients, many of whom have been reluctant readers. I did this because of my belief and experience in the power of using the right materials at the right time. Reading can be a forceful adjunct in therapy, and it also can serve as a powerful resource for motivation and skill-building.

I recall suggesting to an adult client that he read Seligman's groundbreaking book, *Learned Optimism*, since we were working on that particular strength. The next time I saw him I asked how his reading was going. He said – and I'll never forget this – "He has some interesting things to say, but why doesn't he just cut to the chase?"

Trust me, Seligman's book has a lot of interesting and important things to say, but I understand that for some people brevity and "cutting to the chase" improve the likelihood that they'll find the interest, time and motivation to read and utilize the information. So I decided to write a book that gets right to the point on each of these six core strengths, telling you straightaway why each is important, what its signature elements are, and what needs to be done to make that strength a potent tool in your "take control of the good life" repertoire.

WHAT TO EXPECT

There are facets of this book I would like to explain in advance. It is all about attitude, beliefs, expectations, thinking and behavior. It's about having a choice regarding all those factors. It's about developing the necessary tools to take control and discovering your own personal path. As Carlos Castaneda tells us, "We either make ourselves happy or miserable. The amount of work is the same." And the Chinese Proverb warns, "If we do not change our direction, we are likely to end up where we are headed." Here's what you can look forward to:

QUOTES

You will find a copious selection of quotes, quotes, quotes sprinkled throughout the book. This is part of my plan to keep you interested, give you words to live by and remind you of the wisdom of the ages. For as long as I can remember I have been enamored with sayings and quotations. As a college freshman, I put a "thought for the day" on the door of my dorm room. I learned that I wasn't the only one with this fascination, because if I ever missed a day, the women on my floor voiced their disappointment loudly and clearly!

I've found quotes to be very compelling in my work as a psychologist in clinical and life coaching practice, as well as in my supervision of Masters and Doctoral students in clinical training at Arizona State University. I've encouraged clients and students alike to use a quote almost as a mantra to remind them of the new beliefs, thoughts and behaviors they want to incorporate into their lives.

For example, if a client is feeling resentment toward her boss because she was passed over for a promotion and is having a hard time getting over it, it might be helpful for her to commit to memory the quote by Malachy McCourt: "Resentment is like drinking poison and waiting for the other person to die." Or this one from Ann Landers: "Hanging on to resentment is letting someone you despise live rent-free in your head." I'm convinced that most people don't want to be that dumb!

CHARTS ON BELIEFS AND BEHAVIORS

The Charts are assessment tools to identify the beliefs and behaviors that need to be changed. These guides will help you understand the areas you need to target in order to fortify a given strength.

THE TREASURY OF MOTIVATORS

The Treasury of Motivators offers a wealth of strength-generating words and thoughts. These will be helpful in maintaining your motivation and resolve on the journey to your chosen destinations. The Treasury features several components that offer stimulating alternatives to tired old ways of thinking and believing. These include:

• Quotes to Dispute Faulty Thinking

There are beliefs or self-statements that get people into trouble again and again, diminishing their ability to master a particular strength. I have highlighted some of the negative beliefs that I've heard over the years and suggested quotes that powerfully compete with them.

- Poems, Prose, Songs

These are tools to maintain your motivation and keep your eye on the prize. Commit them to memory or carry them with you. Have them ready when "garbage thinking" descends upon you.

- Movie Synopses

This is another motivational tool to keep you on track and to provide you with alternative ways of thinking about your situation. Each movie's theme is in keeping with the chapter in which it appears.

- Motivational Quotes

This section presents powerful quotations that speak to specific subject categories such as resentment, change, security, failure/success, dreams and perfectionism. I have made suggestions on which subjects are germane to each strength. So, for example, if you have tendencies toward perfectionism, there are quotes intended to talk you out of that particular dead end way of thinking.

When you are discouraged, disenchanted or afraid, use your Treasury of Motivators to bolster your spirits and renew faith in yourself.

TOOLS & TECHNIQUES TO BUILD YOUR STRENGTHS

There are many strength-building techniques that can get you where you want to go. To do what needs to be done, you'll have to battle errant beliefs, expectations, thoughts, behaviors and habits, and find worthy, positive replacements. You'll also need to manage fear and the stress response. The tools and techniques detailed in Chapter 7 are designed to ensure an exciting, fruitful journey for you and your little red wagon!

ADDITIONAL RESOURCES: RECOMMENDED READINGS AND WEBSITES

Books, websites and audiovisual materials that are worthy of your attention are suggested for each strength. Here's to keeping your momentum going, going, going!

Chapter One

OPTIMISM

Believe You Are a Powerful Force in Your Future

"Consult not your fears but your hopes and dreams. Think not about your frustrations, but about your unfulfilled potential. Concern yourself not with that you have tried and failed in, but with what is still possible for you to do."

Pope John XXIII

With the advent of Positive Psychology, there has been a great deal of increased interest in the topic of optimism. The voluminous and robust research on optimism has brought wonderful news indeed. Not only does an optimistic approach to life provide amazing benefits, but it can be learned by anyone. Yes, an optimistic attitude can be learned – even if you happen to be one of those dyed-in-the-wool, lifelong pessimists! Find this hard to believe? Well, my pessimistic friend, I'm here to tell you that you're wrong, wrong, wrong – and I can prove it!

What would compel you to make sweeping changes in your attitude and approach to life? After all, many pessimists believe that "the devil you know is easier to take than the devil you don't know." Would it spark your interest if I presented the wide range of impressive advantages that optimism has been shown to generate, including, but not limited to, improved physical and mental health, longevity and frequent success in the attainment of goals and dreams? If I can show you these possibilities and more, would it tempt you to consider an attitude adjustment to your pervasive, moderate or even mild pessimism? Great! Not much pleases me more than converting a pessimist to an optimist!

THE BENEFITS OF OPTIMISM
Physical Health
Let's start with just what the doctor ordered. Being optimistic is very good for your

health. Martin Seligman, Ph.D., of the University of Pennsylvania, who pioneered the Positive Psychology movement, has authored several books that elucidate the findings and promise of the strength of optimism, including *Learned Optimism*, *The Optimistic Child* and, most recently, *Authentic Happiness*.

According to Seligman's research and the research of colleagues, optimists have fewer infectious diseases, are better at avoiding or delaying the chronic diseases of middle age and are more resistant to depression than pessimists. Negative psychological states, such as pessimism, depression and grieving, have a pernicious effect on health, in both the short and long term.

Several studies have found that optimists have healthier immune function and quicker recovery after surgery than those who score high on pessimism tests. Blood pressure is often lower and heart disease is less likely in optimists. In a study at the Harvard School of Public Health, 1300 men, aged 60 and over, were followed for a 10-year period; the data indicated that optimists were about half as likely as pessimists to develop heart disease and had better pulmonary function than their pessimistic counterparts.

Research at the Mayo Clinic has found that people who are pessimistic, anxious and depressed may be at a higher risk of developing dementia. In a study of 3,500 participants, those who scored high in pessimism on a standardized personality test had a 30 percent increased risk of suffering from dementia 30 to 40 years later. Participants who scored very high on both anxiety and pessimism had a 40 percent higher risk of developing this tragic brain disorder. According to Dr. Yonas Geda, the neuropsychiatrist who led the study, "There appears to be a dose-response pattern, i.e., the higher the scores [pessimism, anxiety] the higher the risk of dementia."

Cancer is a disease that affects many families. The diagnosis, as is the case with many other serious diseases, can devastate the patient emotionally, resulting in feelings of profound helplessness, fear and a sense of betrayal by one's own body. In a British study of 69 women with breast cancer, the women were followed for five years. The ones who scored high on optimism were less likely to have a recurrence of cancer and were more likely to survive longer than those who scored high on pessimism. Hope and the ability to maintain and/or renew some degree of control may be factors that offer some support in fighting this disease.

The book, *Breast Cancer? Let Me Check My Schedule*, by Donna Cedenberg, speaks directly to the role of salvaging a sense of control, even in the eye of the storm. Ten women with breast cancer relate their inspiring stories from diagnosis through treatment to the aftermath; 10 women who, in spite of cancer, devote themselves to living proactive, productive and self-directed lives. The second chapter of the book is titled, "Taking an active role: strategies and tactics for regaining control."

My point, of course, is that an optimistic attitude may work on your behalf when experiencing a life-threatening illness. I will note here that there is no study to my knowledge that suggests that optimism mitigates terminal illness. However, when the patient has control over decisions about his or her life for the time remaining, this control may well increase the quality of life – a worthy goal, indeed.

Mental Health

Mental health problems can be very debilitating and are often associated with medical complaints. In fact, many visits to primary care physicians are directly or indirectly related to issues of mental health. Optimism can be a very potent, ameliorative factor in the management of depression, stress and anxiety. It can aid in the prevention of depression, as well as play a major role in the successful treatment of an already existing depressive state. In some cases it may be more beneficial than pharmaceuticals.

Even though psychotropic medications are often effective in the treatment of mood and anxiety disorders, many people would prefer not to stay on medications any longer than they have to – often because the side effects are not well-tolerated. For example, one side effect that can occur with antidepressants is sexual dysfunction, which is unacceptable for many people. Another potential drawback of the pharmaceutical as the sole treatment agent can be a recurrence of depression or anxiety for some when the medication is terminated.

Some people find that a combination of medication and cognitive behavioral techniques, including the development of an optimistic attitude, provides very positive results, even for the most difficult cases. Others find that the cognitive behavioral/optimism strategies alone manage depression quite effectively. Some people start with the combination and then are tapered off the medication, continuing the successful management of the mood disorder with the skills they have learned. Seligman, in his book *The Optimistic Child*, asserts that depression in children and adolescents could be significantly reduced by teaching optimism skills very early on.

Anxiety and stress problems have devastating effects on many lives. I have found that teaching optimism along with anxiety/stress management techniques to clients with these challenges provides a comprehensive and powerful set of skills to manage their very distressing symptoms; this often affords them a greater sense of personal control. As is the case in depression, the combination of medication and cognitive-behavior therapy provides the most effective intervention for many people.

Longevity

With all the health advantages of an optimistic attitude, it's not surprising that there's research to indicate that this approach may very well increase how long you live. At the University of Miami in Ohio in 1975, 660 people ages 50 and older were asked five questions regarding their perceptions of aging. Twenty years later, researchers compared the answers of each participant to the length of his or her life. The subjects with an optimistic attitude toward aging lived an average of seven and a half years longer than those with a pessimistic attitude.

A supportive factor contributing to increased health and longevity may be that optimists are more likely than pessimists to seek medical advice and to follow the medical regimen recommended by their healthcare professionals. Pessimists may not be all that convinced that anything they do will improve their physical or mental health.

Performance

There are many more advantages to developing an optimistic approach. People who are optimistic have a more positive inner world, are happier, and have healthier relationships. They develop more productive behaviors and abilities, which often lead to the successful completion of goals and the realization of dreams. Christopher Peterson explains, "Optimism galvanizes people. It sets you in motion. To be optimistic in the true sense is not to wear a smile button, but to be a problem solver."

Did you know that optimism is the "breakfast of champions" – that it plays a significant role in nourishing excellence in athletic performance? Seligman and his colleagues analyzed statements by professional basketball players in an effort to predict performance success in the 1984-1985 season. His research found that optimists have a more adaptive interpretation of their behaviors, circumstances, mistakes and failures than do pessimists.

Seligman and associates applied these criteria in evaluating the statements of players for the Boston Celtics and New Jersey Nets. The Celtics were more optimistic than the Nets in their interpretations of mistakes and losses. After adjusting for team abilities, the optimistic explanatory styles of the Celtics predicted their success in the next season. The same criteria were applied to National League baseball teams, and the predictions made for winners and losers were right on the money.

In another interesting use of this approach, Seligman found that in the presidential elections between 1948 and 1984 (with the lone exception being the election of 1968), the winning presidential candidate was the more optimistic of the two contenders. He measured the optimistic language in the party nomination acceptance speeches of each candidate, and by doing so was able to posit that the optimistic approach appealed more to the voters.

Ergo

What I'm trying to tell you is that if you would like to be more in control of your life, feel better, be physically and mentally healthier, live longer, use your abilities and talents to the maximum, succeed in your goals and dreams – or run for president – then an optimism attitude adjustment may be just the ticket for you.

An optimistic style often produces courage, enthusiasm, persistence, creativity, resilience and interpersonal/emotional intelligence. These are some of the key strengths that facilitate your journey to your chosen destinations – that fill your little red wagon with abundant promise. According to Richard Devos, "The only thing between a man and what he wants from life is often merely the will to try it and the faith to believe that it is possible."

THE TRUTH ABOUT OPTIMISM

"Optimism is a strategy for making a better future. Because unless you believe that the future can be better you are unlikely to step up and take responsibility for making it so. If you assume there is no hope, you can guarantee there will be no hope. If you assume there is an instinct for freedom, there are opportunities to change things, there's a chance you may contribute to making a better world. The choice is yours."

Noam Chomsky, Professor of Linguistics
Massachusetts Institute of Technology

Okay, now that I've given you some powerful reasons why you should abandon any self-defeating, pessimistic ways, we need to talk about what optimism is and what it is not. Optimism is not about being Susie Sunshine or a Pollyanna. It is not an approach for idiots. Optimism is getting it, understanding that bad things happen to everyone in this deal called life.

When an unwanted event occurs, you have a choice; you can whine and act like a victim, you can beat yourself up, or you can understand that mistakes, failures, annoyances and downright rotten things just happen. This is not a personal attack or a punishment executed by an unknown menacing force. You need to frame this as worst case scenario, a challenge and best case scenario – a hidden treasury of opportunities. As Harry Truman said, "The pessimist is one who makes difficulties of his opportunities and an optimist is one who makes opportunities of his difficulties."

Optimism is about believing in your own power to make your life and future better. Optimism is about positive, can-do beliefs, expectations, choices and strategies, about knowing you are responsible for your life. It's about learning all you can from adversity and then propelling yourself forward toward your goals and vision. It's about taking credit for the things you accomplish, savoring these victories, and utilizing them as fuel for the ongoing journey toward dreams and discovery.

I keep mentioning dreams. As a psychologist, I have come across far too many individuals who do not have dreams. They might have had them once, but somewhere along the way their dreams got lost, defeated or forgotten. The surrender of dreams is truly sad, even tragic. If you are among those folks, take heart – because it's time to dream again! There really is nothing quite like having dreams and believing in them. Anatole France, the French author of *The Human Tragedy*, contends, "To accomplish great things, we must not only act, but also dream; not only plan, but also believe."

THE OPTIMISTIC ATTITUDE

If you're feeling that all this is beyond your capability to change, please stay with me. Remember, anyone can learn it! Each of us has an internal, ongoing conversation – we talk to ourselves. We tell ourselves why things happen, who is to blame for the darkness, who is to credit for the light, what the past means, and what might happen in the future.

I'm here to tell you that the content of your internal dialogue goes a long way in determining whether your approach is optimistic or pessimistic, whether it will serve you well or hold you back, whether it will bring you possibilities or disappointment, whether it will make you feel powerful or impotent. You get to choose. It truly is your little red wagon! In *Learned Optimism*, Martin Seligman tells us that the main differences between optimists and pessimists relate to their attitudes regarding negative and positive events.

About Negative Events
Let's look at your dialogue regarding negative events. If you make a mistake, fail at something, run into an obstacle, or encounter some misfortune, do you tell yourself that this is not going to go away or change, that this problem is permanent? Do you tell yourself that the problem, mistake, failure or cataclysmic event has been meted out by some person or force to victimize or punish you or that it was your fault? In other words, do you take it personally? And finally, do you tell yourself that this negative happening is like cancer, spreading the vicious disease to all your living parts – that it is insidiously pervasive?

Well, for openers, if that sounds like your internal dialogue, I would not want to reside in your head. The pessimist with this approach defeats himself by adopting the "three P's" in negative situations: problems are permanent, personal and pervasive. No wonder the pessimist doesn't have confidence or feel in control. How can one deal with permanent, which means forever, or personal, which means some force has it out for you, or pervasive – who wants radiation or chemotherapy for all their living parts? I'm getting exhausted and depressed just imagining the horror of thinking like this!

So let's say a pessimist goes for an important job interview. She makes it through to the last tier and is feeling pretty pumped up. The choice is between her and one other candidate. I'm sure you can guess that, in this example, she is not offered the position. What does she tell herself? "I'm a failure – I will never get a job; employers simply do not like geeky women like me. At this rate, my whole life is going down the tubes." Permanent, personal, pervasive and damn depressing, wouldn't you say? Exactly. If you think like that, your chances of becoming depressed are pretty substantial, if you're not depressed already.

Pessimism puts you on a dead-end street, often resulting in a state of helplessness. Depressed people do not think their choices and actions affect the outcome of future events. And, of course, this kind of approach can become a self-fulfilling prophecy. It's unlikely that one who feels helpless will choose a powerful course of action, or when a course is chosen, will put the necessary effort into the endeavor. Why bother to try? President Bill Clinton nails it when he surmises, "Pessimism is an excuse for not trying and a guarantee of personal failure."

So what would be the internal dialogue of an optimist when encountering a negative event? Quite frankly, it would be the diametric opposite of the pessimist's. The optimist would view the problem, setback, mistake or failure (after first smarting from the wound, of course), as something that is temporary – that is indeed changeable. She would view it impersonally, not as an indictment of her character or her abilities or the wrath of some controlling force. She would view it as particular to the given situation and not debilitating or generalized to the other aspects of her life.

In our example, when the job interviewee places second in her effort to secure the position, she would tell herself, "This was a tough interview, but I will do better next time. I've learned more about the kinds of questions that interviewers ask, and I'll be better prepared for my next big chance." The dialogue would not be about, "what a loser I am" or that "the powers that be don't want me to be employed." Rather, she'd say, "I'll think about this job situation later; for now, I'm going home to cook a great meal for my husband and son, and enjoy the evening." In other words, she won't let this affect the parts of her life that she recognizes as solid. Thus, her interpretation is not permanent, personal or pervasive. For her, this is just a bump in the road.

Lucille Ball, the famous comedienne, has this take on the subject: "One of the things I learned the hard way was that it doesn't pay to get discouraged. Keeping busy and making optimism a way of life can restore your faith in yourself." Abraham Lincoln embraces an optimistic attitude in his metaphor for life's journey: "The path was worn and slippery. My foot slipped from under me, knocking the other out of the way... but I recovered and said to myself, 'It's a slip and not a fall.'"

About Positive Events

Another very distinct difference between the optimist and the pessimist pertains to the interpretation of positive events. The pessimist believes that favorable happenings are NOT permanent, personal or pervasive – just the opposite of her interpretation of negative events.

So, when beneficial circumstances or accomplishments come her way, she thinks they're a temporary condition, that they have little or nothing to do with her abilities or behavior, and that they do not generalize to and enhance other parts of her life. She got the job by luck, this kind of luck won't last, and landing this job is not going to help her feel better about the things in her life that aren't going so well. Talk about throwing cold water on something positive! As you can see, it's damn hard and discouraging work to be a pessimist.

The sassy little optimist, of course, has a whole different approach than the ever-suffering pessimist regarding the positive event. For her, the event is indicative of more permanent, personal and pervasive factors. It will have lasting value; it's due to her abilities and effort and, in general, it will bring sunshine into her life.

I have been asked by clients if perhaps the optimist isn't somewhat delusional. The answer, according to Seligman, is yes – but in a way that apparently helps and doesn't hurt. The "delusion" is slight and seems to be a protector of the person's energy and well-being. It aids bountifully in the forward march. So – go for it! As Max More posits, "Optimism: the fuel of heroes, the enemy of despair, the creator of the future." I also like the quote by Bridget O'Donnell: "She didn't know it couldn't be done, so she went ahead and did it anyway."

What about the frightening feelings and scary thoughts that are a normal part of really tough situations? Do optimists experience them? Yes, indeed. Susan Vaughan, the psychiatrist who authored *Half Empty, Half Full*, explains that the optimist is one who knows she can handle whatever is thrown her way. She can tolerate negative feelings because of her belief in her ability to bounce back. She understands that it is okay to feel bad. So even in the midst of difficulty and emotional upheaval, she will formulate a plan for moving forward.

A Caveat Concerning Optimism

Is an optimistic approach always the way to go? No, and this is very important. There are decisions all of us face that involve serious and potentially harmful consequences. In these cases it is wise to opt for a careful and very practical plan. Seligman warns that too much optimism can erode one's sense of responsibility. If you are heavily in debt and are the only source of income for your family, quitting your current job to pursue your lifelong dream is likely a very bad idea at this time. It might be wiser to develop reality-based steps to get to the point where you can pursue your dream and still feed your family.

Flexible optimism entails anticipating and being prepared to address serious problems. It involves determining the level of risk and making judicious decisions accordingly. As with most other positive approaches in life, if taken to an extreme or applied in the wrong circumstances, an asset can be converted into to a liability. An example where a more pessimistic approach would be warranted: if you live in the southeastern United States, you may want to invest in hurricane and flood insurance.

TRAITS OF OPTIMISTIC PEOPLE

The Power of Optimism, a book by family therapist Alan Loy McGinnis, outlines 12 traits he derived from biographies of famous optimists. Optimists:

- Expect adversity
- Avoid perfectionism and divide tasks into steps
- Believe in their ability to affect the future
- Take time to reenergize themselves and associate with positive people
- Proactively change negative thinking
- Appreciate the good things in life
- Dream and imagine what their successes will be
- Are upbeat even in tough times
- Believe they are capable of more and more
- Have many loving relationships

- Spread good news
- Accept what is not changeable

DEVELOPING AN OPTIMISTIC APPROACH

"Let's see", you might be saying to yourself, "how in the world can I make these changes in interpretation and behavior when I can't even make a dent in my chocolate consumption?" The modifications you need to make are actually less difficult than you might think. The pessimist has repeated the same types of helpless, depressing statements and interpretations – what I label "garbage thinking" – over and over ad nauseam, rendering them believable and habitual. The unfortunate, programmed pessimist is often unaware of how incessant and insidious the habit has become.

The initial source of this negativity may have come from childhood, adolescence or even more recent experiences. Perhaps the pessimist followed the modeling of a significant person in his life, just repeating that person's same pathetic script. Or he listened to people who convinced him of his limited ability to control the future. Or he experienced difficult situations that made him feel helpless.

This faulty learning can become crystallized into a belief system in which the unchallenged cognitive repetition serves as a continuing reminder that you are not in control of your life or your future. Repetition of garbage thinking rules your internal domain. However, you do not have to accept this belief of no control as a foregone conclusion. You can learn, forcefully and effectively, to change the debilitating dialogue into a healthy, potent and prosperous mindset.

You have the power to create internal reasoned and motivating conversations that, by repetition, will become healthy habits. You will learn to trust the veracity of your new dialogue if you keep at it. You will learn that you can bring about desirable changes in your life. Such positive self-talk empowers and energizes the person who utilizes it. This is not about just repeating positive mantras or statements. It is about replacing "the garbage" with thoughts, beliefs and expectations that encourage planning, action, mastery and self-confidence.

WHEN MISFORTUNE OCCURS

When misfortune occurs – as it does for everyone – decide and be prepared to be proactive, not reactive. As Theodore Rubin, psychiatrist and author of *Lisa and David,* tells us, "The problem is not that there are problems. The problem is expecting otherwise and thinking that having a problem is a problem." Mike Todd, the American film producer best known for his production of *Around the World in Eighty Days,* teaches us a thing or two about the right attitude: "I've never been poor, only broke. Being poor is a frame of mind. Being broke is only a temporary situation."

In his very well-received 1990 book, *The 7 Habits of Highly Effective People,* Stephen Covey explains the difference between a proactive and a reactive approach to life. When something goes wrong, proactive people refuse to accept that nothing can be done; they believe they always have choices and that their decisions and responses will determine future outcomes.

Reactive people believe that when misfortune happens, nothing they do in the present will alter the future. The optimist is proactive, the pessimist reactive. Norman Cousins, writer, editor and holistic health advocate, explains where our choices lie: "Free will and determinism are like a game of cards. The hand that is dealt you is determinism. The way you play your hand is free will."

Being reactive is the learned helplessness, business as usual model. You do what you've always done and you get what you've always gotten. You are not the one in charge; you're allowing yourself to be manipulated by untoward circumstances or the upsetting behaviors of others. Your dysfunctional learning history sets the stage for the faulty interpretations. Examples of reactivity include blaming others for your problems, keeping score via the fairness doctrine, adopting the victim role, and catatrophizing.

The plight of the person who reacts rather than proacts reminds me of "Charlie on the MTA," with lyrics by Jacqueline Steiner and Bess Lomax Hawe and performed by the Kingston Trio. This can be found at: http://web.mit.edu/ jdreed/www/t/ charlie.html. Just in case you don't remember, the gist of it is this:

Poor 'ole Charlie says goodbye to his wife and family and heads for the Massachusetts Transit Authority (MTA) trolley at Boston's Kendall Square Station. He pays his ten cents, boards, but then gets a huge surprise when he wants to change cars for Jamaica Plain. The conductor informs him that he needs another nickel! Guess what? Charlie doesn't have another nickel! Alas, he is stuck on the train.

The ride on the subway has turned into a nightmare! He rides and rides and rides, wondering what his future will be. Will he be on this ride forever? Will he ever be able to see his relatives in Chelsea and Roxbury? His wife meets him at the Scollay Square Station every day at the same time to give him a sandwich. He obsessively laments his fate, over which he has deemed himself powerless. This is a man who never returned to his life. "He may ride forever 'neath the streets of Boston. He's the man who never returned."

Do you ever feel like you're on an endless subway ride and have no clue how to get off? If so, it's attitude adjustment time! Being proactive and optimistic in the midst of trouble involves the following:

• Step back from whatever is happening

Assess the situation with as much objectivity as you can muster. Become a problem solver. Gather the necessary information to elucidate options and search for hidden opportunities. C. Wright Mills, the American sociologist contends, "Freedom is, first of all, the chance to formulate the available choices, to argue over them, and then, to choose." Alberta Flanders believes that, "Sometimes only a change of viewpoint is needed to convert a tiresome duty into an interesting opportunity." It honestly can be quite exciting and intriguing to search for opportunities... a bit like a treasure hunt.

• Be ready, willing and able to transform dysfunctional thinking

Develop an internal conversation tempered by reason or, even better, formulate a cross-examination by an attorney who disputes all the dysfunctional garbage and determines the facts – perhaps like the Jack Webb character on Dragnet: "Just the facts, ma'am." This involves effectively disputing old reactive thoughts and their consequent behaviors, dismissing preconceptions, preoccupations and preprogramming.

In the Penn Prevention Program at the University of Pennsylvania, a school-based program that helps students cope with problems, the following skills are among those taught to promote an optimistic approach:

✓ Thought catching

The first step is to identify the thoughts that are connected to bad feelings. These thoughts, beliefs and expectations, often unrecognized by the sufferer, deflate the spirit and derail a person's forward march. Statements such as, "I'm a loser," or, "This situation will never have a happy ending," are worded in the extreme, giving a person no wiggle room at all. The gravitational pull is down, down, down. To begin to turn the tide on this self-destructive mode, write down the problematic cognitions and the concurrent feelings you experience when you talk to yourself this way. Yes, indeed – you do this to yourself!

✓ Evaluating automatic thoughts

Decide that these negative thoughts may not be correct; consider the evidence. What evidence supports your conclusion that you're a loser or that this particular situation will not have a happy ending? What evidence supports a different conclusion to these outrageous and extreme statements?

✓ Challenging automatic thoughts

Apply the information from above to formulate challenges to the pessimistic thoughts of being a loser or having no chance of a good outcome. Use accurate statements that avail you more options in terms of pro-action, statements that forcefully dispute and replace those that are decidedly permanent, personal and pervasive. For example, recall all the times you've succeeded, which contradict your conclusion about being a loser. Or repeat the reasonable deduction that even the most successful people make mistakes and experience failure. "Oh well... they keep going – that's why they're successful." Itemize what good things could come out of this situation in rebuttal to the "no happy outcome" drivel.

In Chapter 7, detailed information is provided on disputing and other strategies to arm you against dreaded and depressing pessimistic thoughts.

• Accept the things that cannot be changed

Henry Wadsworth Longfellow, the American poet, proclaims, "For after all, the best one can do when it's raining is to let it rain." Arthur Gordon emphasizes the importance of acceptance when he says, "Some people confuse acceptance with apathy, but there's all the difference in the world. Apathy fails to distinguish between what can and cannot be helped; acceptance makes that distinction. Apathy paralyzes the will-to-action; acceptance frees it by relieving it of impossible burdens."

By identifying and accepting the unchangeable, you will conserve your energy and direct it toward all the possibilities.

- Refuse to see yourself as a victim

Casting yourself as the victim in your inner world and in your public persona is a straight shot to pain and disappointment and is, of course, reactive. This misguided approach marginalizes your ability to live a fruitful, powerful and rewarding existence. Believing you are a victim and acting like one can have seriously negative effects on your relationships and can weaken your confidence in yourself.

How do people become seduced by the victim role? I can think of some possible ways. There may be increased attention from others who feel sorry for the self-anointed victim. Or feeling like a victim might serve as an excuse to avoid some circumstance that evokes fear or that's regarded as distasteful. Or perhaps, ensconcing oneself in this role is a way to feel special. Whatever the reason, it leads me to believe that we bipedal primates of the species *homo sapiens* sometimes use our high-powered brains to "snooker" ourselves.

The victim role is yet another example of thoughts gone amok. Just as in the other types of destructive self-talk, identify the thoughts, beliefs and expectations that are faulty; then counter them with an empowering, non-reactive discourse.

- Trash the misguided fairness doctrine

The misguided concept that life should be fair and all the people with whom you come in contact should treat you fairly is nothing but trouble. In therapy and coaching I call this the "you gotta be kidding me" philosophy! The person obsessed with fairness is perpetually keeping score. Gag me! Of course, what constitutes fairness in this regard is defined by each person, a thorny problem and a trap, for sure. But I have news for you: First bulletin – the world is not fair! Second bulletin – other people (surprisingly?) may not, and probably don't, see fairness the way you do. Oh, well. You don't get to make the rules or control how others think. But it will help if you understand and accept an adaptable, reasonable approach: Treat others with dignity and refuse to allow anyone to mistreat you. Define mistreatment carefully and sparingly.

Forget about fairness, which often involves unrealistic expectations of others and deems you to be the center of the universe which, of course, you are not. Remember: Expectation minus reality equals frustration. Give the nutty fairness idea the heave-ho by identifying the cognitive culprits and replacing them with more realistic thoughts, expectations and beliefs. Some people don't understand this, but it's actually quite a relief to lose the "I'm the center of the universe" bit.

• Say "no way" to the blame game

This is yet another huge detour from the path toward power. Douglas Adams tells us, "When we blame others, we give away our power to change." Albert Ellis, the famous psychologist, postulates that, "The best years of your life are the ones in which you decide your problems are your own. You do not blame your mother, the ecology, the president. You realize you control your own destiny." According to an unknown author, "If you kicked the person in the pants responsible for most of your trouble, you wouldn't sit for a month." Identify, dispute, replace this reactive garbage.

• Rope in catastrophizing and shrink it like it's a hemorrhoid

Catastrophizing is a reactive maelstrom, a depressing, slippery slope which traps one in an obsession about all the things that can go horribly wrong in the near or distant future. It can become a brain lock – pervasive and overwhelming. You have to be careful, for as Isaac Bashevis Singer, the Nobel Laureate in Literature, admonishes us, "If you keep on saying things are going to be bad, you have a good chance of becoming a prophet." Ralph Waldo Emerson believes that, "Most of the shadows of this life are caused by standing in one's own sunshine."

Imagine the man with an incontinence problem who spends hours obsessing about all the awful things that might embarrass him when he walks his daughter down the aisle on her wedding day. By the way, his daughter just turned four! What a colossal waste of his precious internal resources. He has allowed his focus to be riveted on a potential personal embarrassment many years from now – most likely to the exclusion of the wonders of the moment and the amazing possibilities of the future. Of course, it's entirely possible that he will have solved his problem by the time his daughter becomes engaged.

Use distraction techniques (discussed at length in Chapter 7), to shrink the number, strength and amount of time devoted to your own personal science fiction horror shows. Then use the disputing techniques discussed in that chapter to challenge the legitimacy of those that remain.

• Change your mind about the meaning of negative events

F. Scott Fitzgerald cautions us, "Never confuse a single defeat with a final defeat." In facing problems, develop an adaptive philosophy that "life is a work in progress." Remember the wise words of Albert Einstein: "The world we have created is a product of our thinking; it cannot be changed without changing our thinking."

George Bernard Shaw believes that, "Life isn't about finding yourself. Life is about creating yourself." If you accept that misfortune is just a part of life, that it's surmountable and can even be replete with possibilities, you will have adopted an optimistic, proactive stance. Weed out the defeatist garbage!

• Remember the good things

In the midst of your travails, keep in mind the positive things you have done, the problems you have solved, and the successes you have enjoyed. Be sure to identify the things you are doing well now and the things that are going right. It may help to write these down and read them often. Take the notebook with you and reference it whenever you can.

Make up a song, poem or a jingle that sings your praises. Memorize sayings that inspire and lead you in a positive direction. Watch a movie that has the theme of rising to the occasion and being better for it. Tell yourself that this situation is temporary and that your actions and decisions matter. These thoughts can become your contravening dialogue, a conversation in which you debate the beliefs of the helplessness mentality that paralyze you, a dialogue that frees you from the quicksand and propels you forward.

• Develop self-talk that is like a mentor or friend

In your own voice, develop internal conversations similar to those you'd have with someone who encourages you and sees you as a work in progress. Just as a mentor or true friend would question and dispute your irrational beliefs about yourself or would challenge you on destructive criticism, do the same. Just as the mentor or true friend would reinforce your positive behaviors and thinking, so should you.

Some people find it helpful in developing this voice to first utilize the "internal guide," a technique in which you choose a mentor with whom you have ongoing conversations. This guide is wise and cares about you. It can be someone you know, have known or would like to know because of your admiration and respect for his or her attitude toward life. This is a method to recalibrate your thinking process. Really imagine you're talking to this person and receiving suggestions and sage advice that compete with any garbage you throw at yourself. Some of my clients have successfully used the "internal guide" as an ongoing strategy in their quest to become optimistic.

WHEN GOOD THINGS HAPPEN

• Take credit for your accomplishments

Savor your victories; think about them often and use them as a springboard and fuel for future endeavors. Identify your personal qualities, especially the ones that were instrumental in the accomplishment. Remember when these qualities manifested in the past and connect them to the present and the future.

Repeat to yourself the impressive list of abilities and efforts that brought your goal or dream to fruition. For example, your first poem has been accepted for publication; what did it take to get it to this point? Did you exhibit creativity, persistence, courage, imagination and well-honed language skills? Was your tenacity and willingness to make sacrifices part of the mix? Think about the importance of your contributions. Consider how this achievement will affect your goals, dreams and future. Repeat to yourself: "I did it. This is going to last. This has positive ramifications on other aspects of my life."

• Consider the self-imposed limitations when a person minimizes his gifts and talents

The 1984 film, *The Last Starfighter,* is one I watched with my young son at least 20 times, many years ago. The main character, Alex Rogan (portrayed by Lance Guest), lives in a trailer park, where he plays and excels at the Starfighter Video Game. At a particularly low moment for him he is complaining to Otis, the maintenance man, that he's never had a chance to have a good time. Otis consoles him, saying "Things change. Always do. You'll get your chance! Important thing is, when it comes, you've got to grab it with both hands, and hold tight."

Enter Centauri (played by Robert Preston), a lively character who claims to represent the company that distributes the video game which Alex has mastered. Fact is, Centauri is an alien who designed the video game to locate someone with special star fighter skills to defend the frontier against Xur and the Ko-Dan armada... and that someone is Alex.

Centauri whisks Alex away to outer space so that he might join the fight to save the galaxy. Alex, overwhelmed and shocked, declines the offer and returns home. Centauri follows him back and tries to persuade him to be a hero and protect the galaxy, including earth, from an invasion. When Centauri pleads with Alex to accept this monumental, life-altering challenge, telling him how magnificently capable he is, Alex blurts out, "Centauri, I'm just a kid from a trailer park." Centauri fires back, "If that's what you think, then that's all you'll ever be." Fortunately for Alex and the galaxy, he rises to the occasion and becomes a towering hero.

- Appreciate the gifts and blessings; see them as promise for the future

Relish the fortuitous things that come your way. Spend a lot of time thinking about and appreciating the gifts. These images can be part of your repertoire of responses that compete with any pessimistic internal chatter. Develop images and thoughts of the good things so that they're strong and readily available when you need them to throw out the garbage.

YOUR VIEW OF YOURSELF

- Believe you have the ability to accomplish your dreams

Expect to succeed! Trust that you can achieve superlative things. As Ralph Waldo Emerson tells us, "Self-trust is the first secret of success." John Barton notes, "Nothing splendid has ever been achieved except by those who dared believe that something inside of them was superior to circumstance."

Josh Hinds tells us, "Set out each day believing in your dreams. Know without a doubt that you were made for amazing things." And Robert Browning's famous words ring true: "A man's reach should exceed his grasp, or what's a heaven for?" Brian Tracy says, "Winners make a habit of manufacturing their own positive expectations in advance of the event." Identify and target the thoughts and underlying beliefs that contradict the idea that you have what it takes to achieve your goals.

- Believe you deserve to be successful in your goals and dreams

It may be hard to fathom, but some people actually have difficulty believing they deserve to succeed. It doesn't take a genius to see that this could be a formidable obstacle in the journey to optimism and proaction. Assess your beliefs in this area and formulate a plan for changing the faulty beliefs and thoughts.

- Believe your choices and actions affect the outcomes in your life

As Elaine Maxwell contends, "My will shall shape the future. Whether I succeed or fail shall be no man's doing but my own. I am the force; I can clear any obstacles before me or I can be lost in the maze. My choice; my responsibility; win or lose only I hold the key to my destiny." This is an excellent mantra in your quest to become an optimist.

- Avoid perfectionism

Be alert to unrealistic expectations that you have for yourself. Remember the apt words of Evan Esar: "The closest to perfection a person ever comes is when he fills out a job application form." Or as Leonard Cohen, the Canadian poet, songwriter and novelist, writes:

> Ring the bells that still can ring
> Forget your perfect offering.
> There's a crack in everything,
> That's how the light gets in.

David Burns, the psychiatrist who wrote *Feeling Good, The New Mood Therapy,* sums it up well: "Remember that fear always lurks behind perfectionism. Confronting your fears and allowing yourself the right to be human, paradoxically makes you a far happier and more productive person."

Have a sense of humor about your limitations. We all have limitations. Rather than allowing your limitations to bring you shame or discouragement, accept the fact that you are human, be relieved you're not perfect, and see the humor. For instance, I have the world's worst sense of direction. The truth is I can get lost just about anywhere. Instead of becoming defensive when others (especially my husband), are getting such a kick out of it, I decided to join in and laugh, too. Hugh Prather explains, "Unless I accept my faults, I will most certainly doubt my virtues." Brendan Francis suggests, "Once we accept our limits, we go beyond them."

I read a really sad story about a perfectionist that I think embodies the dangers of this misguided thinking. The article, titled, "Top Surgeon kills self. Doctor treated young patients," was written by Melissa Nelson and published by the Associate Press on January 11, 2005. A summary of the article is as follows:

Dr. Jonathon Drummond-Webb, a heart surgeon at Cleveland Clinic and Arkansas Children's Hospital, performed miracles on infants and children. He was reputed to be extraordinary in his ability to save these young lives. Unfortunately, it appears that he longed to be even better than he was. Three days after saving a teen-age boy awaiting an organ transplant by using a very small heart pump, Dr. Drummond-Webb took his own life by overdosing on alcohol and drugs.

This special man, whose saga was followed in an ABC documentary in four parts, repaired tiny hearts with serious and complex defects. From what could be gathered from his suicide note, he felt that his accomplishments were not appreciated, that those around him did not care about him and his gift. He was known by other professionals as being very hard on himself. He would obsess about the few he lost rather than on the many he saved.

• Share and model optimism; spend time with optimistic people

Optimism is catching. Time spent with optimists is well spent; big things happen and excitement is generated when optimists get together. Children benefit greatly when the adults in their lives model optimism and encourage the thinking and behavior of an optimistic approach. Seligman suggests that it is important for significant adults to teach children to deal positively with failure and success. Children can learn an empowering attitude toward misfortune and can learn the techniques that will serve as potent tools throughout their lives.

NOW WHAT DO I DO?

This is an adventure of possibilities... all the wonderful possibilities that come with an optimistic approach to life. Your mission is to develop the belief that you can do what needs to be done, commit to an informed course of action, and promise yourself that giving up is not an option. The remainder of this chapter contains many strategies to help you achieve optimistic beliefs and behaviors. The tools to help you:

- The Chart on Optimism is an assessment tool to help you identify the beliefs and behaviors that need to be changed
- The Treasury of Motivators features several components that offer alternatives to tired, old ways of thinking and believing, including: Quotations to Dispute Faulty Thinking, poems, prose, movie synopses and Motivational Quotes by subject category
- Techniques and information that are applicable to developing optimism (presented in Chapter 7)
- Recommendations on additional resources

It's time for an attitude adjustment... you can do it!

CHART ON OPTIMISM – BELIEFS AND BEHAVIORS

Use the following chart to determine the beliefs and behaviors that you need to change in order to fortify your optimism. Those in the left column promote an optimistic attitude, while those in the right column deplete it. Make a list of all right column beliefs and behaviors that describe you, putting them in the order of those to be addressed first, second and so on.

How do you choose the order? There are a couple of ways. One is to start with the least threatening situation, and when that situation is under your control, target the next least threatening and then the next. Another approach is to work on the thoughts and behaviors most likely to make a difference for you. Either way gets you on the path. Your choice, your little red wagon, your life! Once you've identified what needs to be changed, review your options for modifying these, using all the tools in this book.

BELIEFS ABOUT NEGATIVE EVENTS

By Optimists

1. Mistakes are a chance for me to learn and grow.

2. Failures are temporary and, with the right attitude, provide opportunities that can lead to learning, growth and success.

3. Adversity, obstacles, disappointment are all part of life. They provide feedback and information about possibilities.

4. Change is a part of life which should be embraced and utilized. Change can be a source of energy and inspiration.

5. Negative events are temporary; circumstances will get better, and each offers a chance to find opportunities.

6. Negative events do not generalize to other parts of my life.

7. Negative events are not personal; they are not about my personal flaws or being targeted by a force that wants to make me miserable.

By Pessimists

1. Mistakes are shameful and embarrassing and should be avoided at all costs. If I make mistakes, then I'm not perfect.

2. Failures are shameful and permanently injurious. I should work strenuously to avoid failures.

3. These are negative events that I must actively avoid. They often discourage goal-setting and a proactive approach.

4. Change is to be feared and fought. It depletes energy.

5. Negative events are permanent. They will continue to affect my future negatively.

6. Negative events overflow and have a serious impact on other parts of my life.

7. Negative events are personal; they are about my personal shortcomings or about some force choosing me as a target.

BELIEFS ABOUT POSITIVE EVENTS

By Optimists

1. Opportunities and possibilities are treasures to be found, sometimes in the most unlikely of places.

By Pessimists

1. Opportunities and possibilities just happen sometimes. I have no control over them. I have to wait for a lucky break.

2. Positive events or accomplishments are due to my own efforts and abilities. It makes sense to try hard, take risks and develop my skills.

2. Positive events and accomplishments are due to external causes or luck and are not because of my efforts and abilities; so, why try so hard?

BELIEFS ABOUT THE FUTURE

By Optimists

1. The future can be better; it holds all kinds of possibilities.

By Pessimists

1. The future may get worse, not better.

2. I feel competent to make the future better.

2. I do not believe I have control over the future.

3. Dreaming about the future and having a vision are necessary and wonderful components of making my life the way I want it.

3. Dreaming is a colossal waste of my time.

BEHAVIORS AND RESPONSES

By Optimists

1. I am ready, willing and able to take risks.

By Pessimists

1. I often avoid risk-taking.

2. I choose appropriate and challenging goals.

2. I often choose unrealistic goals or goals that are a sure thing.

3. I manage negative situations by being flexible, creative; I am able to tolerate uncomfortable feelings.

3. I am overwhelmed and thwarted by misfortune; I do not change my thinking and behavior since I do not think I have the power to make a difference.

4. I have wonderful thoughts and dreams of success.

4. I am often afraid to have dreams of success because I will be disappointed.

5. I evaluate and plan my path toward the future.

5. I do not often assess or define a plan to improve the future.

6. I take responsibility for my attitude, behavior and thoughts. I assess where my control lies and enact my plan.

6. I have difficulty taking responsibility in my life since I believe that control is external.

7. I have proactive habits of thinking and behaving.

7. I have a reactive rather than a proactive approach to thinking and behaving.

8. I am interested in improving myself.

8. I may be interested in self-improvement, but I feel some degree of powerlessness.

9. I focus on my own strengths.

9. I focus on my helplessness.

10. I refuse to think and act like a victim.

10. I often see myself in the victim role.

11. I make positive comments about myself and others.

11. I make only limited positive comments about myself and others.

12. I focus on my accomplishments and not on my mistakes or failures.

12. I focus on my mistakes and failures rather than my accomplishments.

THE TREASURY OF MOTIVATORS

The Treasury of Motivators offers a wealth of optimism-generating words and thoughts. These can be helpful in maintaining your motivation and resolve on the journey to your chosen destinations. Use the treasures that are meaningful and inspirational for you. You may also enjoy your own treasure hunt for pieces that are personally energizing and encouraging.

Incorporate these into your everyday internal world. Some you can commit to memory; others can be placed in spots where you'll be reminded of what you want to believe and say to yourself. Focus on them often. Focus on "out with the garbage," and "in with your own special pep talk."

QUOTATIONS ON OPTIMISM TO DISPUTE FAULTY THINKING

This section presents harmful beliefs, expectations and thoughts that people repeat to themselves over and over again, often with strong conviction. The irrationality and toxicity of these debilitating cognitions are hardly ever questioned. These cognitions compete with the strength of optimism. You need to learn to talk back to them in meaningful and potent ways.

The goal is reduce the frequency, intensity and duration of each of them by distraction methods and to neutralize them by disputing or arguing with their content. Disputing can be done by utilizing pertinent, meaningful quotes provided for you in this chapter or by developing your own reality-based, effective retorts. Note that you may have cognitions in your repertoire that are not contained in this list of Harmful Beliefs.

Take a personal inventory of these in a separate notebook, then choose powerful quotes or other responses to question and contradict these cognitions that are holding you back. Remember, practice, practice, practice, so you're ready when they come for real! Besides increasing your readiness, practicing also decreases the potency of any noxious self-statements, aiding in your quest to be more optimistic. Distraction and disputing techniques are discussed at length in Chapter 7.

Harmful:

"When I make a mistake or fail at something, I feel ashamed, depressed hopeless and defeated."

Instead:
"Sometimes things can go right only first by going very wrong."
Edward Tenner

"Good judgment comes from experience and experience comes from bad judgment."
John F. Roed

"Never confuse a single defeat with a final defeat."
F. Scott Fitzgerald

"The way to succeed is to double your failure rate."
Henry Ford

Harmful:
"Change is so unsettling to me. I wish things would stay the same. Trying something new scares me and I don't believe taking a chance will make things better."

Instead:
"To exist is to change; to change is to mature; to mature is to create oneself endlessly."
Henri Bergson

"Change is the handmaiden that Nature requires to do her miracles."
Mark Twain

"If we can recognize that change and uncertainty are basic principles, we can greet the future and the transformation we are undergoing with the understanding that we do not know enough to be pessimistic."
Hazel Henderson

"It is not the years but the changes that make us grow."
Neal Maxwell

"Life is a process of becoming, a combination of states we have to go through. Where people fail is that they wish to elect a state and remain in it. This is a kind of death."
Anais Nin

Harmful:
"There are so many obstacles in my life. Sometimes I feel like giving up."

Instead:
"The lowest ebb is the turn of the tide."
Henry Wadsworth Longfellow

"Within the problem lies the solution."
Milto Katsela

"An adventure is only an inconvenience rightly considered."
C. K. Chesterton

"To fly we have to have resistance."
Maya Lin

"One of the secrets of life is to make steppingstones out of stumbling blocks."
Jack Penn

"Life is not a matter of holding good cards, but sometimes, playing a poor hand well."
Jack London

"When everything seems to be going against you, remember that the airplane takes off against the wind, not with it."
Henry Ford

Harmful:
"I have such bad luck. Rotten things happen to me a lot; I would say they happen to me more than they do to other people. I feel like I have a bull's eye on my chest."

Instead:
"It's hard to tell our bad luck from our good luck sometimes, and most of us have wept copious tears over someone or something when if we'd understood the situation better, we might have celebrated our good fortune instead."
Merle Shain

"All of us have bad luck and good luck. The man who persists through the bad luck – who keeps right on going – is the man who is there when the good luck comes and is ready to receive it."
Robert Collier

"Sure luck means a lot in football. Not having a good quarterback is bad luck."
Don Shula

"I find that the harder I work, the more luck I seem to have."
Thomas Jefferson

Harmful:
"Whatever accomplishments or blessings I have or will have in my life have very little to do with my talents and effort."

Instead:
"Nothing splendid has ever been achieved except by those who dared believe that something inside them was superior to circumstance."
John Barton

"Assume responsibility for the quality of your own life."
Norman Cousins

"With the exercise of self-trust new powers shall appear."
Ralph Waldo Emerson

"Your chances of success in any undertaking can always be measured by your belief in yourself."
Robert Collier

"In the long run, we shape our lives, and we shape ourselves. The process never ends until we die. And the choices we make are our own responsibility."
Eleanor Roosevelt

Harmful:
"I don't believe that things are going to get better in the future."

Instead:

"The only limit to our realization of tomorrow will be our doubt today."
Franklin Delano Roosevelt

"We must reawaken and keep ourselves awake, not by mechanical aid, but by an infinite expectation of the dawn."
Henry David Thoreau

"Far away there in the sunshine are my highest aspirations. I may not reach them, but I can look up and see their beauty, believe in them and try to follow where they may lead."
Louisa May Alcott

"The future belongs to those who believe in the beauty of their dreams."
Eleanor Roosevelt

"It's kind of fun to do the impossible."
Walt Disney

Harmful:

"Pursuing my dreams will only lead to disappointment."

Instead:

"It may be those who do most dream most."
Stephen Leacock

"There isn't a person anywhere that isn't capable of doing more than he thinks he can."
Henry Ford

"If you can dream it you can do it. Always remember this whole thing was started by a mouse."
Walt Disney

"Some men see things as they are and say 'why?' I dream of things that never were and say, 'why not?'"
George Bernard Shaw

"I have had dreams and I have had nightmares. I overcame the nightmares because of my dreams."
Jonas Salk

"Those who dream by night in the dusty recesses of their minds wake in the day to find all was vanity, but the dreamers of the day are dangerous people, for they may act their dream with open eyes, and make it possible."
T. E. Lawrence (aka Lawrence of Arabia)

"A man's dreams are an index of his greatness."
Zadok Rabinowitz

OPTIMISM IN PROSE, SONGS, MOVIES

Prose, songs and movies often touch people in ways that are motivating and inspiring. In my clinical practice I found that utilizing thematic works that resonate with an individual can be an effective and enjoyable way to keep his or her little red wagon moving along – even in the most discouraging times and circumstances.

The Treasury of Motivators contains inspirational material that might appeal to you on your quest to develop an optimistic attitude. After you've read them, choose the ones that have meaning for you, or go on your own search for a work that fits the theme of optimism. Read the prose, lyrics and movie synopsis often; think about the theme every day. When you have a chance, watch the movie. Listen to the song, sing it to yourself. When you're discouraged, disenchanted or afraid, use your Treasury Motivators to bolster your spirits and faith in yourself. These tools can help you keep your eye on the prize!

The Optimist and the Pessimist: A Tale of Two Brothers

This story of twin brothers, one an optimist and one a pessimist, has been related by many people, the most famous of whom was President Ronald Reagan. There are variations on this story, but the gist of it is this: the parents of these boys decided to enter them into a research study that was attempting to define pessimism and optimism.

One child really saw the sunny side of life and the other the doom and gloom side. In the observational part of the study, each boy was taken to a different room each with a one-way mirror. The pessimist was told that the wonderful wide array of toys in the room were his for the asking. He was observed finding something wrong with each toy, making comments such as, "I don't like to play board games; this one is an ugly color; I hate toys where you have to read the instructions." He cried and cried.

The optimist was lead to a room filled with horse manure. His instructions were only that he would be in there for half an hour. The optimist laughing and smiling immediately started playing and digging in the manure. When the puzzled researchers asked the little boy why he was so happy, he said, "I figure with all that horse manure, you were going to give me a pony if I could only find it!!!"

You Make the Call
By Rick Reilly, Sports Illustrated, August 14, 2006

This article by famed sportswriter Rick Reilly captures the essence of optimism in a little boy fighting cancer. Enter the link below into your web browser, then click on the story *Rick Reilly: You Make the Call*. http://search.sportsillustrated.cnn.com/pages/search.jsp?query=rick%20reilly%20romney

Climb Ev'ry Mountain
Lyrics by Oscar Hammerstein II and Richard Rodgers

As sung by Mother Abbess in *The Sound of Music* (1959); enter this link in your web browser. http://www.niehs.nih.gov/kids/lyrics/climbev.htm

Optimism in the Movies
If you'd like a hefty dose of optimism from the movie world, I suggest you watch the 2005 film *Elizabethtown*, featuring Orlando Bloom, Kirsten Dunst and Susan Sarandon. It's a touching and motivating road trip through a portion of one man's life that will help get your optimism juices flowing full force.

As the movie begins, we're introduced to Drew Baylor (Orlando Bloom), a wunderkind athletic shoe designer at Oregon-based Mercury Worldwide Shoe, whose latest creation – the "Spasmotica" – is about to lose the company a cool $972 million...

a total bust in the marketplace. Eight years down the drain, no job, a complete failure in his own eyes, Drew returns to his apartment, deposits all his worldly possessions on the sidewalk, and prepares to end it all.

But a persistent caller keeps his cell phone ringing and sidetracks Drew's plan; the caller is his sister Heather, and when it rains, it pours. Their father, Mitch, has died unexpectedly while visiting relatives in Kentucky, and their mother Hollie (Susan Sarandon), is incapable of dealing with the friends and family members who blame her for Dad's departure from his home: Elizabethtown. Drew, being the responsible one in the family, must go and bring their father back to Oregon for burial.

Despondent, depressed, spaced-out, Drew's life becomes almost dream-like as he goes through the motions, and emotions, of going to his father's hometown to retrieve the body. On the flight to Louisville he meets Claire Colburn (Kirsten Dunst), a quirky, effervescent, engaging flight attendant who takes an immediate liking to Drew but senses that things are not all right with this young man. Claire, who seems to know something about everyplace and everyone, draws him a map to Elizabethtown that just happens to include her name and several phone numbers where she can be reached. Drew finally arrives in Elizabethtown, but to him it might as well be another planet. Cousin Jesse, Uncle Dale, Cousin Bill, countless friends, distant relatives, people who knew his Dad all their lives but never left the homes they grew up in, descend upon Drew with condolences and offers to help with final arrangements. It all just adds to the confusion and despair that's consuming him, knowing that once it's all over, he still has his own "very dark date with destiny."

Back in his hotel room that night, Drew pleads for someone to answer his phone calls, just to hear a "normal" voice; he leaves messages with his sister, his mother, his girlfriend Ellen (whom he wants to speak to most), and even Claire – the odd flight attendant. Of course, when Ellen does return his call, it goes like this: "Drew, it's been real... it's been nice. It's been real nice." Add "dumped by the girlfriend" to the list. Luckily, though, he gets another phone call.

This time it's Claire, and over the next two days she and Drew carry on a non-stop, stream-of-consciousness cell phone conversation discussing musical tastes, places they've been to, places they'd like to go... the stuff of potential soul mates.

Claire is surprised at how little Drew knows about life as she's seen it, and she makes him promise that he'll return to Oregon by car – on a road trip across America. While Drew never forgets his impending date with the grim reaper, it's clear that Claire and the people of Elizabethtown are infusing him with something totally unexpected, an elixir that's slowly entering his body and transforming his life.

He reaches out to members of his extended family and, in so doing, finds solace in their acceptance of him as well as the warmth, sincerity and love they show toward his Dad. And Claire... she just won't give up on Drew, and she won't let him give up on himself. Surrounded by the "Chuck and Nancy" wedding party at his hotel and falling into the "lovin' life, lovin' you" theme of the happy couple, our two disparate characters at last spend a night together – under the watchful gaze of an urn containing Mitch Baylor's ashes.

"Just tell me you love me and get it over with!" exclaims Claire the next morning. But Drew isn't ready. He tells her all about the shoe fiasco, that he lost his company almost a billion dollars, and now he's supposed to be the responsible one in the family. "All I really want is not to be here," says Drew. "I have a very dark appointment with destiny!" Claire will have none of it. "That's it?? All about a shoe?" she asks incredulously. "So, you failed! You failed... you failed, you failed, you failed. Have the courage to fail big and stick around and make'em wonder why you're still smiling!"

The next day is Mitch's memorial, Drew's last day in Elizabethtown. Hollie and Heather arrive, and in a hilarious, poignant, loving testimonial to Mitch, the family and the town at last come together in celebration and remembrance of his time on Earth. Claire stops by too, with a special gift for Drew's promised road trip home – a package containing maps, music, instructions and other worldly advice, all created by Claire for a driving adventure across America. "Call me," she says to Drew, "but not before you get home. Just get into the great melancholy... it's a great map."

With the urn containing his Father's ashes strapped in the passenger seat beside him, Drew sets out per the instructions, popping CDs into the player when prompted, paying homage to an America he's never seen. When news of the disaster at Mercury Worldwide Shoe becomes public, Claire says on the CD: "You have five minutes to wallow in the delicious misery. Enjoy it, embrace it, discard it, and proceed."

Every stop she orchestrates for Drew along the way speaks to hope and optimism: the Lorraine Motel in Memphis, where Martin Luther King, Jr. was killed (and where Drew spreads a handful of Mitch's ashes); the Survivor Tree in Oklahoma City, site of the Oklahoma City bombing (more ashes).

"Sadness is easier because it's a renter," explains Claire. "I say, make time to dance alone, with one hand waving free!!" Along the way, Drew allows himself to cry – for the first time – over his Father's death, recalling the special times they spent together, dropping ashes as he drives. Life is becoming important again to Drew... important, meaningful, worth living.

In the closing scene, following Claire's instructions to stop at the "Second Largest Farmer's Market in the World," for essentials he'll need to get home, Drew gets this message: "Here you have reached a fork in the road. You can go back to your car and the instructions will take you home. Or – look for a girl in a red hat, who's waiting for you with an alternative plan." When Drew and Claire embrace again, presumably for the long haul, the film ends with Drew saying: "I recall the British Special Service Air Force motto – 'those who risk, win.' And the Pacific Northwest salmon, who beats itself bloody on its quest to swim 100 miles upstream with a single purpose... sex, of course. But also – life."

MOTIVATIONAL QUOTES THAT BUILD AN OPTIMISTIC ATTITUDE

There are several subject categories that are relevant to strength of optimism or the lack thereof. Wise quotations about a specific subject can serve to teach you topical, proactive beliefs, expectations and thoughts to replace the reactive garbage that blocks your forward progress. For example, if a lack of "belief in yourself" and its associated thinking is a particular habit of yours, find a quote that motivates you to overcome this. Repeat it to yourself often, replacing any self-defeating dialogue.

On Optimism

"No pessimist ever discovered the secrets of the stars, or sailed to an uncharted land, or opened a new heaven to a human spirit. There is no sadder sight than a young pessimist."
Mark Twain

"A cynic is not merely one who reads bitter lessons from the past; he is one who is prematurely disappointed in the future."
Sydney J. Harris

"Hope sees the invisible, feels the intangible and achieves the impossible."
Helen Keller

"A pessimist thinks nothing is so bad it can't get worse; an optimist thinks there's nothing so good it can't get better."
Author Unknown

"Optimism is a kind of heart stimulant – the digitalis of failure."
Elbert Hubbard

On Believing in Yourself
"If we did all the things we were capable of doing, we would literally astound ourselves."
Thomas Alva Edison

"Always bear in mind that your own resolution to succeed is more important than any other one thing."
Abraham Lincoln

"With the exercise of self-trust new powers shall appear."
Ralph Waldo Emerson

"In the world to come, I shall not be asked, 'Why are you not Moses?' I shall be asked, 'Why were you not Zusya?'"
Rabbi Zusya

"It's never too late to become what you might have been."
George Eliot

On Dreams
"There is nothing like a dream to create the future."
Victor Hugo

"I have learned this at least by my experiment: that if one advances confidently in the direction of his dreams, and endeavors to live the life he has imagined, he will meet with a success unexpected in common hours."
Henry David Thoreau

"Without leaps of imagination or dreaming, we lose the excitement of possibilities. Dreaming, after all, is a form of planning."
Gloria Steinem

"Hope is a waking dream."
Aristotle

On Opportunities/Possibilities
"One hundred percent of the shots you don't take don't go in."
Wayne Gretsky

"When we think positively and imagine what we want, we risk disappointment; when we don't, we ensure it."
Lana Limbert

"The best way to have a good idea is to have a lot of ideas."
Dr. Linus Pauling

"When the student is ready, the teacher will appear."
Zen Proverb

"It is always your next move."
Napoleon Hill

"Opportunity dances with those who are already on the dance floor."
H. Jackson Brown, Jr.

EFFECTIVE, PRACTICAL TECHNIQUES FOR BUILDING OPTIMISM

In order to change the beliefs and behaviors that you identified as problematic in the Chart on Optimism, you'll need to learn some specific concepts and techniques.

These include:

- ✓ Principles of Behavior Change
- ✓ The Stress Response
- ✓ Abdominal Breathing
- ✓ Imagery Relaxation
- ✓ Progressive Muscle Relaxation (PMR)
- ✓ The Relaxation Response
- ✓ Systematic Desensitization
- ✓ Assertiveness
- ✓ Disputing
- ✓ Distraction

These techniques are discussed in detail in Chapter 7.

ADDITIONAL RESOURCES: RECOMMENDED READINGS AND WEBSITES

Recommended Readings:

Peterson, C. and Bossio, L. (1991), *Health and Optimism*

Seligman, M.E.P. (1990, 1998), *Learned Optimism: How to Change Your Mind and Your Life* (1996), *The Optimistic Child: Proven Program to Safeguard Children From Depression and Build Lifelong Resilience* (2002), *Authentic Happiness*

Vaughan, S. (2000), *Half Empty, Half Full: Understanding the Psychological Roots of Optimism*

Websites:

http://www.authentichappiness.org
http://www.positiveway.com

OPTIMISM ENDNOTES

Pg. 7   Seligman, M. (2002) *Authentic Happiness.* New York: The Free Press
           Seligman, M., Reivich, K., Jaycox, L. and Gillham, J. (1995) *The Optimistic Child.* New York: Houghton-Mifflin
           Seligman, M. (1991) *Learned Optimism.* New York: Knopf

Pg. 7   Seligman, M. and Buchannan, G. "Learned Optimism Yields Health Benefits." APA Help Center: Get the Facts. Mind/Body Connection, 1995-96. American

Segerstrom, S.C. (2006) *Breaking Murphy's Law: How Optimists Get What They Want from Life and Pessimists Can Too.* New York: Guilford.

Segerstrom, S.C., Taylor, S.E., Kemeny, M.F. and Fahey, J.L. "Optimism is associated with mood, coping and immune change in response to stress." *Journal of Personality and Social Psychiatry.* 1988, 74, 1646-1655

Kubzansky, L., Wright, R.J., Cohen, S., Weiss, S., Rosner, B. and Sparrow, D. "Breathing easy: a prospective study of optimism and pulmonary function in the normative aging study." *American Journal of Cardiology* (2000) July 15, 1986, (2), 145-149

Kubzansky, L.D., Sparrow, D., Vokonas, P. and Kawachi, I. "Is the glass half empty or half full? A prospective study of optimism in the normative aging study." *Psychosom.* Med 2001, Nov-Dec; 63(6): 910-916

Miller, M.C. "The Benefits of Positive Psychology." *Harvard Mental Health Letter,* 2002, 18, 6

Geda, Y. "Pessimism and depression increase dementia risk." *Amer. Academy of Neurology,* April 14, 2005

Pg. 8   Cedenberg, D. (1997) *Breast Canter? Let Me Check My Schedule.* USA: Westview Press

Pg. 9   Seligman, M., Reivich, K., Jaycox, L. and Gillman, J. (1995) *The Optimistic Child.* New York: Houghton-Mifflin

Pg. 9   Duenwald, M. "The Power of Positive Thinking extends, it seems, to aging." *New York Times,* Nov. 19, 2002. Review research Levi and Kunkel

Pgs. 10, 12 Seligman, M. *Learned Optimism.* New York: Knopf

Pg. 15   Vaughan, S. (2000) *Half Empty, Half Full.* Orlando, FL: Harcourt

Pg. 15   McGuire, P. "Seligman touts the art of arguing with yourself." APA Monitor, 1998, Vol. 29, #10 McGinnis, A.L. (1990) *The Power of Optimism.* Harper Collins

Pg. 15   McGinnis, Alan Loy (1993) *The Power of Optimism.* Harper Torch.

Pg. 17   Covey, S. (1989) *The 7 Habits of Highly Effective People.* New York: Simon & Schuster

Pg. 19   Gillham, J.E., Reivich, K.J., Jaycox, L.H. and Seligman, M.E.P. (1995) Prevention of Depressive Symptoms in schoolchildren: two-year follow up. *Psychological Science*, 6, 343-351

           Pikes, T. and Daniels, V. (2000) Listen to us! Voices of Despair. *Reaching Today's Youth.* Vol. 4, No. 4, 6-8.

Pg. 27   Seligman, M., Reivich, K., Jaycox, L. and Gillham, J. (1995) *The Optimistic Child.* New York: Houghton-Mifflin

Chapter Two

COURAGE

Face Your Fears, Take Risks

"You gain strength, courage, and confidence by every experience in which you really stop to look fear in the face... you must do the thing which you think you cannot do."

Eleanor Roosevelt

Courage is a towering strength, one that has earned the revered status of a virtue over the ages. To many it may represent something quite daunting, but in reality, it's not nearly as elusive as many people might believe. Courage propels a person from powerless to robust and increases exponentially the ability to transform an impossible dream into a mission accomplished. Walt Disney, the great dream maker, believes that, "All our dreams can come true, if we have the courage to pursue them."

I get such a kick out of helping people who either advertently or inadvertently have allowed themselves to be frozen out of their hopes and dreams because they're afraid to be courageous. I remember being asked by an assistant in my office how in the world I could see so many depressed, stressed and anxious clients and still profess to enjoy my work. I paused to formulate my response and said, "Because they get better!"

I love watching the 150 watt light bulb go on during their journey forward, the epiphany that facing your fears and refusing to be helpless makes you a mighty force for enacting your vision and ensuring the quest to become the best you can be. The process of learning to take risks and act boldly is truly an awesome experience, the gift that keeps on giving. This is the gift you give to yourself and the one you offer to others by your example. Children reap enormous benefits when parents and other adults express the belief that courage is profoundly important and then act in accordance with that belief again and again.

TYPES OF COURAGE

Courage manifests in a number of ways. Physical courage is the type that generally comes to mind first: Putting oneself in harm's way to save another or to fight for a beloved cause. The man who does not know how to swim yet jumps in the river to save a child is a model of physical courage. Then there is moral courage, which involves standing up for beliefs when doing so may well lead to aversive personal consequences such as decreased security, comfort or popularity. Whistle-blowers in corporations and government exemplify moral courage.

Psychological courage, the focus of this book, is about being hale and hardy in your internal world, making choices for yourself and converting them into behavioral expression. It is exemplified by proactively dealing with situations such as: Facing psychological, emotional and medical problems, making difficult and bold choices, ending unhealthy interpersonal situations, making important habit changes, welcoming and using change as an ally instead of an adversary, and becoming the person you want to be by pursuing your goals and dreams to a fare-thee-well. The three types of courage often interact and strengthen one another.

THE ROLE OF FEAR

What is the common bond among the three types of courage? Quite simply, FEAR. As Senator John McCain posits in his book, *Why Courage Matters*, "There is only one thing we can claim with complete confidence is indispensable to courage, that must always be present for courage to exist – FEAR. You must be afraid to have courage." Mark Twain declares, "Courage is resistance to fear, mastery of fear, not the absence of fear." Ambrose Redmoon proclaims, "Courage is not the absence of fear, but rather the judgment that something else is more important than fear." And according to John Wayne, "Courage is being scared to death and saddling up anyway."

I have to say this concept of what constitutes courage appears to be foreign to many folks in my world. Clients, relatives and friends have painfully confessed experiencing fearfulness with the misguided conclusion that fearfulness connotes personal weakness. This is truly an irrational belief with remarkably negative consequences! Chastising yourself for experiencing fearful feelings and physical symptoms is like telling yourself you're a pig because you have hunger pangs. Useless, deflating and damn dumb in my book!

Fear, like hunger, is nature's way of insuring survival of the species. It is a distinct part of human wiring, not something that should be a source of shame. What counts is your attitude and behavior when faced with the uncomfortable feelings of the fear response, which can range in intensity from mild to extreme. What do you tell yourself and what do you do? Do you believe that owning your own life is more important than retreating from the fearful situation? And are you willing to do what it takes to shape your life in the direction of your goals in spite of fear? Ben Johnson asserts, "No greater hell than to be a slave to fear."

THE BENEFITS OF PSYCHOLOGICAL COURAGE

What do you have to gain by becoming psychologically courageous? Yourself! There is a wonderful freedom that comes from being brave and facing your fears. Robert Frost maintains that, "Freedom lies in being bold."

Unchallenged fear is a prison that progressively depletes your world of choices as you comply repeatedly with its dictates. A slippery slope indeed! Avoidance leads to more avoidance, becoming a debilitating detour from a fulfilling, fruitful life. Anais Nin, the French author famous for her diaries, contends that, "Life shrinks or expands in proportion to one's courage." With courage you have a greater opportunity to be the person you want to be.

Courage fosters creativity, happiness, integrity and social connections. It is a potent, integral variable in the growth of persistence, optimism, passion and resilience. Without the "red badge of courage," the other strengths weaken and fade. Sir Winston Churchill trumpets, "Courage is rightly esteemed the first of human qualities... because it is the quality that guarantees all others." Remarkably, courage turns change from a fear stimulus to a "field of dreams," helping in the discovery of the power within. It is super fuel for your little red wagon!

Self-Empowerment

Courage nourishes self-confidence, self-respect, self-efficacy and personal growth. You say "NO" to the path of avoidance, the alluring, deceptive path of least resistance, and choose the path of forward motion, facing fear straight away. Lao-Tzu, the founder of the Chinese philosophy Taoism, believes, "A man with outward courage dares to die. A man with inward courage dares to live." Seneca, the wise Roman philosopher, captures the difficulty of many people who struggle: "Sometimes even to live is an act of courage."

Abraham Maslow, the famous psychologist, declares, "You will either step forward in growth or you will step back in safety." The common misconception regarding security is addressed by Alan Cohen when he says, "It takes a lot of courage to release the familiar and seemingly secure, to embrace the new. But there is no real security in what is no longer meaningful. There is more security in the adventurous and exciting, for in movement there is life and in change there is power." Helen Keller professes, "Security is mostly a superstition. It does not exist in nature... Life is either a daring adventure or nothing."

Soren Kierkegaard, the Danish existential philosopher, asserts, "To dare is to lose one's footing momentarily. To not dare is to lose oneself." Norman Mailer, the American novelist, playwright and film director, points out, "There was that law of life, so cruel and so just, which demanded that one must grow or else pay more for remaining the same."

Self-empowerment is about choosing. Peter Senge, the author of *Wrote Presence: Human Purpose* and *The Field of the Future*, contends, "Personal mastery teaches us to choose. Choosing is a courageous act; picking the results and actions which you will make into your destiny." Seneca, the Roman philosopher, advises, "It is not because things are difficult that we do not dare, it is because we do not dare that things are difficult."

Self-confidence often soars like the eagle with keen eyes and powerful wings when one takes the path of courage. How so? As Jack Gibb, a pioneer of humanistic psychology informs us, "Self-confidence is the result of a successfully survived risk." And William Jennings Bryan, an early U.S. Secretary of State, is convinced that, "The way to develop self-confidence is to do the thing you fear."

Acting with courage contributes to a healthier life. In their book, *How You Feel is Up To You*, psychologists Gary McKay and Don Dinkmeyer conclude that, "Courage and risk-taking are central elements in coping with stress." Stephen Covey, author of *The 7 Habits of Highly Effective People*, declares, "It takes courage to realize that you are greater than your moods, greater than your thoughts and that you can control your moods and thoughts." People with stress, anxiety and depression can improve their mental and physical health by facing their fears rather than retreating.

Horace, the Roman poet, contends, "It is courage, courage, courage that raises the blood of life to a crimson splendor. Live bravely and present a brave front to adversity." The French poet, Guillaume Appollinaire, heralds the possibilities garnered by courage:

Come to the edge.
We can't. We're afraid.
Come to the edge.
We can't. We will fall.
And they came.
And he pushed them.
And they flew.

Annie Besant, an English social reformer, recommends the attitude of personal power: "Never forget that life can only be nobly inspired and rightly lived if you take it bravely and gallantly, as a splendid adventure in which you are setting out into an unknown country, to meet many a joy, to find many a comrade, to win and lose many a battle."

Creativity
Creativity requires courage, courage, courage. It requires the willingness to take leaps into the unknown; it requires the fortitude to continue to believe in yourself and your creation when others offer only discouragement. According to Albert von Szent Gyorgy, Nobel Laureate in Medicine, "Discovery consists of seeing what everybody else has seen and thinking what nobody has thought." Maxwell Maltz suggests that, "we must have courage to bet on our ideas, to take the calculated risk, and to act…"

Creativity requires managing the fear of failure and sometimes the fear of success. Joseph Chilton Pearce, the author of *Magical Child*, tells us, "To live a creative life, we must lose our fear of being wrong." Erich Fromm believes, "Creativity requires the courage to let go of certainties." According to Doc Childre and Bruce Cryer in their book *From Chaos to Coherence*, "Any jazz musician knows, it takes flexibility and adaptability for improvisation to create beauty." Adaptability requires the courage to change, the courage to go where the flow takes you.

Erica Jong, American author and educator, points out, "Everyone has talent. What is rare is the courage to follow that talent to the dark place where it leads." Neil Simon, the American playwright, gets right to the heart of it when he concludes, "If no one ever took risks, Michelangelo would have painted the Sistine floor."

Creativity is born of adventurousness – flirting with the impossible – which so often takes mountains of courage. Thomas Disch believes that "Creativity is the ability to see relationships where none exist." The Dalai Lama asserts that, "Great love and great achievement require great risk." Rollo May contends "Creativity is neither the product of neurosis nor simple talent, but an intense encounter with the gods." And Henri Matisse, the 20th century French painter and artist, warns, "An artist must never be a prisoner. Prisoner? An artist should never be a prisoner of himself, prisoner of style, prisoner of reputation, prisoner of success, etc."

Happiness

Courage and happiness go hand in hand. According to Holbrook Jackson, the British journalist, writer and publisher, "Happiness is a form of courage." Seneca tells us, "Where fear is, happiness is not." When fear controls you, choices and the gifts of life become very elusive. George Sheehan explains that, "Happiness is different from pleasure. Happiness has something to do with struggling and enduring and accomplishing."

Dan Baker, a psychologist, and Cameron Stauth, in their book *What Happy People Know*, advise "We need to be willing to charge headlong into the inferno of our most horrific fears – eyes open, intellect and spirit at the ready – even as our survival instincts are screaming, 'Run! Run! Get out!' That takes courage, and that's why courage is one of the prerequisites for happiness." And further they conclude that uncontested fear is the "greatest enemy of happiness…"

Friedrich Nietzsche, the German philosopher, advises, "The secret of harvesting from existence the greatest fruitfulness and the greatest enjoyment is – to live dangerously! Build your cities on the slopes of Vesuvius! Send your ships into uncharted seas." Walter Bagehot, the 19th century British journalist believes, "The great pleasure in life is doing what people say you cannot do."

Alexander Dumas, the French writer, explains, "Happiness is like those palaces in fairy tales whose gates are guarded by dragons; we must fight in order to conquer it." Robert Anthony, author of *How to Make the Impossible Possible* and *Doing What You Love – Loving What You Do*, suggests, "Most people would rather be certain they're miserable, than risk being happy." How sad is that?

Success

I probably don't have to work too hard to convince you that courage and success are highly interactive; that is, each goes a long way in promoting the other. Ralph Waldo Emerson, the American author and philosopher, makes the connection, "Whatever you do, you need courage. Whatever course you decide upon, there is always someone to tell you that you are wrong. There are always difficulties arising that tempt you to believe your critics are right. To map out a course of action and follow it to an end requires some of the same courage that a soldier needs..."

Terence, the Roman playwright, clamors, "Fortune favors the brave." Johann Wolfgang von Goethe, the German poet and humanist, urges, "Whatever you can do or dream you can, begin it. Boldness has genius, power and magic in it. Begin it now." And James Bryant Conant, the former Harvard University President, says, "Behold the turtle. He makes progress only when he sticks his neck out." Phillip Adams points out, "A lot of successful people are risk-takers. Unless you are willing to do that, to have a go, to fail miserably, and have another go, success won't happen." Frederick Wilcox warns, "Progress always involves risk; you can't steal second base and keep your foot on first."

Courage leads the way. Marcel France confides, "The secret of life is this: when you hear cannons, walk toward them." H. Jackson Browne, Jr., maintains, "Don't be afraid to go out on a limb. That's where the fruit is." Robert F. Kennedy, former United States Senator and Attorney General, posits, "Only those who dare to fail greatly can ever achieve greatly." And George Sheehan tells us, "Success means having the courage, the determination, and the will to become the person you believe you were meant to be."

A Gift to Others

Courage is the gift we give to others by our example. In a moving tribute to her husband, Eleanor Clift, the political commentator and contributing editor to *Newsweek* magazine, told of her husband's courage and its effect on others in his battle with kidney cancer. This article, published on April 1, 2005, can be accessed at http://www.msnbc.msn.com/id/7357718/site/newsweek/.

Her husband, Tom Brazaitis, died one day before Terry Schiavo. Imagine the irony of a political columnist seeing her husband slip away as the world watches the Schiavo news story. What Eleanor Clift wants you to know is how bravely he faced his struggle with cancer. Diagnosed in 1999 with kidney cancer, the pernicious disease had spread to his lungs within a year. The dire diagnosis evoked his journalist instincts, leading him down a path of researching and subjecting himself to grueling interventions.

Tom continued to write for the *Cleveland Plain Dealer* about politics and his medical status throughout the ordeal. Eleanor points out that he eschewed self- pity and refused to complain. He thought of his struggle as a sports event in which he was playing defense. As she states, he faced this disease "with a clarity of mind and spirit that made him an inspiration to others." He talked her into joining him in an interview with Diane Rehm on her radio program. By this time the cancer had invaded his brain. The courage he displayed in his answers affected many people in the radio audience. Courage is contagious.

THE RESULTS OF PSYCHOLOGICAL COWARDICE

In the event that you allow yourself to be governed by fear, lacking the courage to proactively live the life that is congruent with your vision, there are many negative consequences you can anticipate. The likelihood of getting what you want is markedly reduced. As Nora Roberts asserts, "If you don't go after what you want, you'll never have it. If you don't ask, the answer is always no. If you don't step forward, you'll always be in the same place." This positions you to assume the helpless role, a self-debasing role that evokes disrespect and sometimes abuse from others while fostering conformity.

The psychological coward sooner or later experiences disappointment and haunting regrets about numerous lost opportunities. Mark Twain warns that, "Twenty years from now you will be more disappointed by the things you didn't do than the ones you did do. So throw off the bowlines. Sail away from the safe harbor. Catch the trade winds in your sails. Explore, dream, discover."

Regrets pile up and before you know it all you can think about is what you have lost and cannot regain. Your growth has been stunted; you keep paying dearly for your fear of fear. And sadly, this defeatist, fear-driven approach is often passed from generation to generation. The character Victor Fox in the movie *Unconditional Love* draws a quirky, but accurate, conclusion: "A life lived in fear is no fun." Indeed. Psychological cowards are controlled from without, not from within, and their ability to garner what is resplendent in this life is severely limited.

THE ELEMENTS OF PSYCHOLOGICAL COURAGE

Managing Fear Instead Of Letting It Manage You

"Fear is the cancer of the human spirit."

Rick Beneteau

What is malignant to the human spirit is not fear alone, but the capitulation to fear. Dealing with fear in proactive, healthy ways is the primary element of psychological courage. Fear is one of the emotional/physical pathways set into gear when the old, non-thinking part of the brain perceives that a situation is life-threatening. The other pathway is aggression. The fear reaction sets the body in motion to run or escape from the threat, while the aggression reaction sets the body in motion to fight. This "fight or flight response" is essential in truly dangerous circumstances to decrease the chance of injury or death.

The key word here is "perceives." The perception that a situation is life-threatening does not mean it is. And therein lies the rub. Most of us have experienced fear in circumstances that do not threaten our safety. But our body is acting like a big old bear is chasing us down a mountain! The response is the same as in the days of the cavemen. It is, however, our interpretation of the situation – what we tell ourselves about the potential consequences – instead of a real threat of danger that has become the trigger.

As Dean Koontz tells us in his novel, *Seize the Night:*

> With higher intelligence comes an awareness of the complexity of the world, and from this awareness arises a sense of mystery, wonder. Superstition is the dark side of wonder. Creatures with simple animal intelligence fear only real things, such as their natural predators. But those of us who have higher cognitive abilities are able to torture ourselves with an infinite menagerie of imaginary threats: ghosts and goblins and vampires and brain-eating extraterrestrials. Worse, we find it difficult not to dwell on the most terrifying two words in any language, even monkey-talk: what if...

What are these fears that paralyze us needlessly? Some people fear making mistakes, or even more catastrophic, failing in any way. Just the thought can generate a panic attack. Others will do just about anything to avoid disapproval or embarrassment. Then there is fear of the unknown. Whoa, how overwhelming is that, since there are so many unknowns in this life?

The one I love is fear of success. Imagine what an action-stopper that can be; some people are afraid of both failure and success! Fear of change and the possible loss of control that can accompany it, even if for a short time, can profoundly intimidate some people. And on and on it goes....

These non life-threatening possibilities are often interpreted as being dire. They have much to do with our learning and the ways in which we talk to ourselves about how bad things might get if such and such happens. For example, you might tell yourself that it would be devastating if people laughed at you because of some goofy thing you said when giving a speech, or that you might disappoint someone if you had a lame answer to an intelligent question from a member of the audience.

For many years, from childhood through graduate school, I was horrified by public speaking. I realized on a rational level that this was a very common fear, but I still believed beyond a doubt that my case was special, that for some reason I was more terrorized by this prospect than anyone in history. Just the thought of presenting in front of a group made me feel incredibly sick. Now that I've worked for so many years with clients who are fearful, I realize many people feel like their reactions are beyond the usual human experience. Okay, I'm not special!

Anyway, I was compelled to overcome this fear because professors are not very understanding of graduate students with this problem (or any other problem for that matter). The real day of reckoning came when my supervising professor assigned me to give a lecture to a psychology association membership.

On the way to the talk, I actually thought how being in a minor car accident might be preferable to showing up! Not that I would intentionally do such a ridiculous thing, but how crazy is that? Think about it. I imagined how great it would be to have some sort of acceptable excuse to avoid my fear rather than stand and talk to people who had no reason to hurt me! When I work with clients I reflect on that day; the very vivid memory keeps my empathy flowing.

I am delighted to tell you that fear is very treatable and, in most cases, without a therapist. The principles and tools are pretty straightforward. Keep in mind that you are dealing with the "fight or flight response." Abundant research and clinical work have availed strategies that can empower you to confront your fear and manage it quite well. This is true even if you have an anxiety disorder that may make this response potentially more challenging. I learned these strategies, and some time ago I conquered any fear of giving public talks... a relief indeed! I will be getting into effective strategies later in the book.

People with anxiety disorders generally have a heightened reaction to certain fear-evoking situations. The reaction may be triggered more quickly, may last longer, or may be greater in intensity than would be the effect on the rest of us. You bet – that's not fair! The same strategies are used for managing these heightened reactions with a significant success rate. So for those of you with anxiety disorders, realize that it is far better to spend your energy utilizing effective methods than to waste energy wondering "why me?" It is what it is. Confucius believes, "It is better to light a candle than to curse the darkness." People with anxiety disorders often need professional help to manage the condition optimally.

Making Difficult or Bold Choices and Taking Risks
Rollo May, the American psychologist and author of *The Courage to Create*, has this to say about the importance of choosing:

The acorn becomes an oak by means of automatic growth; no commitment is necessary. The kitten similarly becomes a cat on the basis of instinct. Nature and being are identical in creatures like them. But a man or woman becomes fully human only by his or her choices and his or her commitment to them. People attain worth and dignity by the multitude of decisions they make from day to day.

Making bold choices involves learning to tolerate, even enjoy, the prospect of unknown results. It is an attitude of wonder, not fear of the unpredictable. Making difficult or bold choices teaches us to look at the plethora of possibilities. And with each choice that's made, we're rewarded with strength and self-confidence, even if the choice does not work out as well as we had hoped. According to Harvey Mackay, author of *Swim With the Sharks Without Being Eaten Alive*, "There are lots of ways to become a failure, but never taking a chance is the most successful."

Taking risks and making courageous decisions are integral in paving the path to your personally-defined destiny. As one of my very favorite authors, Dr Seuss explains, "If you want to catch beasts you don't see everyday, you have to go out-of-the-way. You have to go places no others can get to. You have to get cold and you have to get wet, too."

Taking risks can alert the brain to engage its alarm system. But keep in mind that when you are not held hostage by this primitive system, you become the engineer of your existence. Anais Nin declares, "It takes courage to push yourself to places you have never been before, to test your limits, to break through barriers. And the day came when the risk it took to remain tight inside the bud was more painful than the risk it took to blossom." Andre Gide observes that, "One does not discover new lands without consenting to lose sight of the shore." And Mario Andretti suggests, "If things seem in control, you are not going fast enough."

Being Ready, Willing and Able to Face Conflict
Interpersonal conflict can have a chilling, incapacitating impact on many people. Once a person starts avoiding or retreating from conflict, this pattern of avoidance and escape gets a heavy dose of negative reinforcement. The concept of negative reinforcement/avoidance learning is important in understanding and changing behavior. Left unaddressed, it wields a destructive influence on your ability to succeed in your goals and dreams. Bottom line, whatever you avoid due to fear detours your little red wagon.

When you avoid something that evokes the fear response, the physiological, cognitive and emotional symptoms generally subside. Avoidance is reinforced by the removal or curtailing of these symptoms. You feel better when the symptoms decrease so in the future you'll be more likely to use this same approach. All types of reinforcement increase the probability of the behavior they follow. The reinforcement here is symptom decrease. The behavior is avoidance or escape from conflict.

A husband hates getting into arguments with his wife. She's much quicker at comebacks and can be quite the bully. As a child he hated hearing his parents argue and then came the disturbing silence for what seemed like an eternity to a small boy. The husband has learned to keep his mouth shut regarding opinions that dissent with his wife's views. In this way he avoids the discomfort of conflict and silence and spares his child from the fear and sadness he felt growing up. His avoidance is reinforced by peace at home.

Sound okay? No way. This husband has convinced himself that psychological cowardice is his best course. It's not. He is not standing up for himself. He has adopted a role of emotional impotence that almost always fosters resentment and difficulty in relationships. As Barbara De Angelis, Ph.D., maintains:

> Living with integrity means: Not settling for less than what you know you deserve in your relationships. Asking for what you want and need from others. Speaking your truth, even though it might create conflict or tension. Behaving in ways that are in harmony with your personal values. Making choices based on what you believe, and not what others believe.

To add to the dysfunctional effects, the husband is setting an unhealthy example for his child, an example of acquiescing again and again. Milton R. Sapirstein, author of *Paradoxes of Everyday Life*, contends that, "To observe people in conflict is a necessary part of a child's education. It helps him to understand and accept his own occasional hostilities and to realize that differing opinions need not imply an absence of love."

I stipulate that conflict is best handled with fair fighting skills and rules. The husband and his wife in my example need to learn assertiveness and conflict resolution. Ann Landers subscribes to the belief that, "All married couples should learn the art of battle as they should learn the art of making love. Good battle is objective and honest – never vicious or cruel. Good battle is healthy and constructive and brings to a marriage the principal of equal partnership."

Abraham Maslow, the American psychologist believes that, "Conflict itself is, of course, a sign of health as you would know if you ever met really apathetic people, really hopeless people, people who have given up hoping, striving, coping."

Developing a Proactive Attitude Toward Difficulties in Life

A person's attitude about failure and difficulties has a commanding effect on the vim and vigor of psychological courage. If you believe that failure is shameful or unfair and difficulties are something to cry over, then courage will be sadly compromised in your repository of strengths.

After all, you can choose to allow life's stuff to beat you down and depress you, or you can take to heart the words of Leonardo Da Vinci: "Obstacles cannot crush me; every obstacle yields to firm resolve." It takes courage to keep moving in spite of life's "to be expected" arduous downturns and troubles.

Who in the world told you that goal achievement was supposed to come easily, quickly and without some bruises and cuts – sometimes deep cuts? If that's the assumption you have, it would serve you well to give that irrational belief the heave ho. Instead of feeling sorry for yourself, refuse to be discouraged by failures, delays, difficulties, mistakes and other prickly interruptions. Change your internal dialogue. Rethink what it means to propel your little red wagon – your goal and dream machine.

Tell yourself that it won't do any good to wish that your little red wagon had its own engine, maintenance-free, no refueling necessary, and that the route is direct and without potholes, detours or steep inclines. Courage is born of understanding and accepting that life, with its dreams and goals, is often messy, difficult and painful. But for goodness sakes, take heart in what Christopher Robin said to Pooh, "Promise me you'll always remember you're braver than you believe, and stronger than you seem, and smarter than you think."

Some difficulties, of course, are more stinging than others. Courage is a major component of the strength of resilience. When terrible things happen or when many difficulties occur simultaneously, courage will be a significant strength in helping you bounce back, in helping you persist. Mary Ann Rodmacher-Hersh believes, "Courage doesn't always roar. Sometimes courage is the quiet voice at the end of the day saying, 'I will try again tomorrow.'"

Facing Psychological, Emotional and Medical Problems

I have spent a great portion of my professional career treating individuals with psychological problems. I can tell you that facing one's psychological and emotional demons requires profound courage. Whether it's the woman with panic disorder who feels like she's having a heart attack each time she drives her children to school; or the person with bipolar disorder who's on a roller coaster ride of mania followed by deep depression; or the little boy who hears voices; or the man who was abused as a child and still suffers from the trauma, courage is mandatory for these people in their quest for mental health.

Committing to treatment and doing what needs to be done invariably present monumental challenges that so often evoke sheer terror. I take my hat off to anyone who finds the courage for such an important endeavor. Those of us who have not been plagued with these conditions cannot really understand the magnitude of courage that one must muster to do what needs to be done.

Facing medical problems, too, often presents gargantuan challenges that require enormous courage and resolve. Undergoing painful and frightening procedures, taking medications that have untoward side effects, experiencing physical limitations, waiting for what seems like an eternity for potentially life-altering answers, or receiving a frightening prognosis exemplify only some of the experiences in which one's courage will be put to the test.

Mother Theresa states, "To have courage for whatever comes in life – everything lies in that." Courage is facing these challenges and at the same time continuing to live each day to the fullest. Alice M. Swain reminds us that, "Courage is not the flowering oak that sees storms come and go; it is the fragile blossom that opens in the snow."

Ending Unhealthy Interpersonal Situations

Eleanor Roosevelt said, "You gain courage and confidence by every experience in which you really stop to look fear in the face. You are able to say to yourself, 'I have lived through this horror. I can take the next thing that comes along.' You must do the thing you think you cannot do." Many people find themselves in complicated, abusive relationships where fear and uncertainty are pervasive, where the choice to end the situation is fraught with unknown, potentially negative consequences.

The woman without financial options whose husband beats her and the children has to look long and hard for the backbone to leave. Her problems are overwhelming; after all, how will they survive without an income? What if he comes after them in a rage? Or the teenager who was lonely and embarrassed not to have a boyfriend; she believes something is wrong with her if she's not involved in a relationship. Her current partner is kind now and then, but most of the time he tells her she's a loser and too fat. She wonders, "isn't any kind of boyfriend better than no boyfriend at all?"

And then there's the man whose father has criticized him since childhood. He has tried every way he knows to please and impress this man — painfully, to no avail. If his father cannot love him, he thinks maybe he is unlovable. These are the relationships that need to be modified, even terminated. They are toxic. It takes tremendous courage to do what needs to be done. Professional help is often warranted in cases such as these.

Making Important Habit Changes

Habits are not, in and of themselves, negative. Many of the habits we have serve us well. It's not possible, and definitely not convenient, to have to think about everything we do day in and day out. Brushing your teeth in the morning and after each meal is done automatically; it has become a habit. There are some habits, however, that do not serve us well.

Some are pesky, little habits like nail biting that we would prefer to eliminate; some are bad habits that have a moderately negative effect on our health, well-being and goal achievement, such as eating more food than we need or working too much or not getting enough exercise. Then there are some habits that are highly destructive in our lives and in the lives of those close to us. It takes courage, in some cases, huge quantities of courage, to do what needs to be done to change or eliminate these habits.

Most addictions (other than to chocolate, of course), would fall into the category of needing more help than simple habit change. And often just following guidelines spelled out in a book simply is insufficient. More support and/or treatment are indicated. Conquering addictions requires great courage.

Abraham Lincoln declares, "Always bear in mind that your own resolution to succeed is more important than any other one thing." Do NOT be discouraged if you have met with little or no success in building new positive habits or reforming old negative habits. To be courageous in this context often requires specific information and a persistent attitude to get the job done. I love that commercial about smoking cessation. A kind voice says, "All those other times you tried, maybe they were just practice."

Making Change Your Ally Instead of Your Adversary
You have a choice in how you view, react to and utilize change. You can be afraid, hoping that very little will be different from what you have come to expect, or you can welcome change as one of your best friends. Either way, change will come, whether you like it or not. Outside factors just don't stay the same!

Anne Morrow Lindbergh, the American aviator and author, points out, "Only in growth, reform and change, paradoxically enough, is true security to be found." John Cage, the American composer and author, shares with us his view: "I can't understand why people are frightened of new ideas. I'm frightened of the old ones."

Eric Hoffer, author of *The Ordeal of Change*, tells us, "In times of change, learners inherit the Earth, while the learned find themselves beautifully equipped to deal with a world that no longer exists." Change is our ally. Mark Twain announces, "Change is the handmaiden that Nature requires to do her miracles." Price Pritchett believes, "Change always comes bearing gifts."

Hazel Henderson, evolutionary economist and author of *Building a Win-Win World*, suggests, "If we recognize that change and uncertainty are basic principles, we can greet the future and the transformation we are undergoing with the understanding that we do not know enough to be pessimistic." President John Fitzgerald Kennedy advises, "Change is the law of life. And those who look only to the past or present are certain to miss the future."

Becoming the Person You Want to be by Pursuing Your Goals and Dreams
Courage fosters your belief in yourself and your belief in all the possibilities within your reach. As e.e. cummings, the American poet and playwright, surmises, "It takes courage to grow up and turn out to be who you really are." Erma Bombeck, the beloved humorist and author of *At Wit's End*, says it so well:

> There are people who put their dreams in a little box and say, 'Yes, I've got dreams, of course I've got dreams.' Then they put the box away and bring it out once in a while to look in it, and yep, they're still there. These are great dreams, but they never even get out of the box. It takes an uncommon amount of guts to put your dreams on the line, to hold them up and say, 'how good or bad am I?' That's where courage comes in.

What gets in the way of goals and dreams? Plenty of things: Fear of failure, fear of success, fear of the critical opinions of others regarding your choices, preoccupation with today's obligations or yesterday's disappointments, addiction to comfort and security, inadequate attention to what your goals and dreams really are, or whatever the "excuse de jour" happens to be.

Timothy Luce proclaims, "The brave don't live forever, but the cautious don't live at all." Pursuing your goals and dreams involves a belief system that renders courage a necessity in the pursuit of a fulfilling existence. You must believe in the importance and accessibility of your most treasured aspirations, and you must be daring and determined in the chase. Dreams flourish when one has the right kind of internal conversation. You must become your own coach and cheerleader, repeating, "It can be done, and I'm just the one who will prove it!"

DEVELOPING COURAGE

Spend Time With Positive, Supportive, Courageous People
Be aware of folks in your world who discourage you in your important quest. Develop ways to neutralize their dissuasions. Assertiveness skills can be helpful in preparing you to stand up to those who attempt to deter you from your path of courage. Practice disputing the slings and arrows of others, both the ones you anticipate in your head and the ones actually hurled at you. These skills are discussed in Chapter 7.

Follow the lead of hardy people like Oprah Winfrey, who says she surrounds herself with people who say "Why Not?" to her ideas. Find those folks who have demonstrated their courage and who enjoy watching others succeed. Assume the role of modeling courage for those you care about.

Ask Yourself Three Questions Regarding Fear of Failure

Steven Scott, author of *Simple Steps to Impossible Dreams,* suggests answering the following:

a. What's the worst thing that can happen?
b. What's more likely to happen?
c. What's the best possible outcome?

Once you've defined the worst case scenario and have developed strategies to decrease the probability of the catastrophe, then use distraction and disputing techniques (discussed in Chapter 7) to reduce the time and energy usurped by these pernicious thoughts. Replace the catastrophic imagery with the internal pictures and words that are associated with the best outcome.

Remember That the Journey Can Be Divided Into Steps

This is an ongoing journey that unfolds in a step-by-step progression. According to Lao-Tzu, the Chinese philosopher, "The journey of a thousand miles begins with one step." This is especially true in terms of managing fear. Try measuring the intensity of your fear on a one to 10 scale, with 10 being the most extreme; then formulate steps, step one being the mildest fear response, then the next mildest and so on. You'll be amazed at how manageable fear really is! A more detailed explanation of desensitization (exposure) is presented in Chapter 7.

Believe That You Are Able to do What Needs to be Done

Develop a mantra that encourages you in this regard. There are quotes in the "Treasury of Motivators" later in this chapter that will be meaningful in refuting or replacing what I call "garbage thinking." Garbage thinking includes thoughts and beliefs which do nothing but discourage and dissuade you from your forward march. You also have the option of developing your own powerful slogan. Place this slogan in spots where you'll see it often, such as on your refrigerator, desk, bathroom mirror, your car visor, briefcase or purse. Commit to repeating this 10 or more times a day.

Don't Talk Yourself Out of Action

Senator John McCain, in *Why Courage Matters*, recommends the following:

> If you do the things you think you cannot do, you'll feel your resistance, your hope, your dignity, and your courage grow stronger every time you prove it. You will someday face harder choices that very well might require more courage. You're getting ready for them. You're getting ready to have courage. And when those moments come, unbidden but certain, and you choose well, your courage will be recognized by those who matter most to you. When your children see you choose, without hesitating, without remark, to value virtue more than security, to love more than you fear, they will learn what courage looks like and what love it serves, and they will dread its absence.

It's time to stop procrastination. As David Mahoney suggests, "There comes a moment when you have to stop revving up the car and shove it into gear."

Practice, Practice, Practice

You can make courage a habit by doing it again and again and again. Plan to do at least one act a day that requires courage. Ruth Gordon tells us, "Courage is very important. Like a muscle, it is strengthened by use." And Aristotle explains, "We are what we repeatedly do. Excellence, then, is not an act, but a habit."

Stop Thinking of Yourself as a Victim

Identify instances in your thinking and imagery in which you have ordained yourself the victim. Use distraction and disputing techniques described in the last chapter to challenge these clearly counterproductive thoughts and images. In this world, the victim mentality is an impediment to productive self-control, and certainly to the strength of courage. Develop visual imagery and a dialogue in which you are powerful, determined, brave and successful.

Learn to Manage the Stress Response

The more control you have over your body and its emergency gear, the more likely you are to face your fears and make bold choices. In the last chapter of this book, you'll find a description of the stress response and techniques to bring it under control.

Spend Time Dreaming; Control Catastrophizing

Find a comfortable place where you won't be disturbed. Start with a relaxation exercise such as the Relaxation Response (meditation), 10 minutes of diaphragmatic breathing or a guided imagery technique described in Chapter 7. Don't allow any form of distractions to interfere with your dream session. Let your mind go to the very best possibilities. Dream away! Passively let problems and obstacles go. Concentrate on the fun part.

Identify Cognitions That Feed Fear and Block Forward Progress

Use cognitive techniques, such as distraction and disputing, to reduce, eliminate or replace the fear cognitions. For a week, keep a record of fear and negatively based thoughts and images. Identify their frequency, duration and the circumstances under which they occur. Circumstances or triggers can include times of day, interactions with others, situations where things do not go your way, and so on.

NOW WHAT DO I DO?

This is an adventure of possibilities… all the wonderful possibilities that come with being courageous on your own behalf. Your mission is to develop the belief that you can do what needs to be done, commit to an informed course of action and promise yourself that giving up is not an option. The remainder of this chapter contains many strategies to help you achieve courageous beliefs and behaviors:

- The Chart on Courage is an assessment tool to help you identify beliefs and behaviors that need to be changed
- The Treasury of Motivators features components that offer alternatives to tired, old ways of thinking and believing including: Quotations to Dispute Faulty Thinking, poems, songs and movie synopses
- Techniques and information that are applicable to developing courage (presented in Chapter 7)
- Recommendations on additional resources

CHART ON COURAGE – BELIEFS AND BEHAVIORS

Use the following chart to determine the beliefs and behaviors that you need to change in order to fortify your courage. Those in the left column promote courage, while those in the right column deplete it. Make a list of all right column beliefs and behaviors that describe you, putting them in the order of those to be addressed first, second and so on.

How do you choose the order? There are a couple of ways. One is to start with the least threatening situation, and when that situation is under your control, target the next least threatening and then the next. Another approach is to work on the thoughts and behaviors most likely to make a difference for you. Either way gets you on the path. Your choice, your little red wagon, your life! Once you've identified what needs to be changed, review your options for modifying these, using all the tools provided in this book.

BELIEFS

Beliefs That Foster Courage

1. My dreams are valuable and I can make them come to fruition.

2. Courage counts in big ways. It is instrumental in achieving self-confidence, productivity and health.

3. Being afraid does not mean I am weak and lacking in courage.

4. Taking charge of my life is more important than avoiding the uncomfortableble feelings of fear. When I give in to fear, I have less control of my life. I have fewer choices.

5. I am powerful, not helpless, in determining the outcomes in my life.

Beliefs That Hinder Courage

1. Dreams are something beyond my reach and their pursuit is a waste of my time and energy. I should be focusing on more important things.

2. Courage is not so important and I can have a good life without it.

3. Courage and fear cannot coexist. When I am afraid, I am personally weak, which is shameful.

4. Fearful feelings should be avoided. I think personal control is doing whatever I have to in order to prevent the discomfort of being afraid.

5. Most of what happens to me is beyond my control.

6. It is better to try something that might not work out than to wonder what might have happened and have regrets. "I'd rather be sorry for something I did than for something I didn't do." (Kris Kristofferson)

6. It is better to avoid things that may not work out. I'll deal with regrets later.

7. I believe that mistakes, failures, setbacks are just part of the way things are, and if I handle them in smart ways I can use them to my advantage.

7. I am horrified by the prospect of mistakes, failures and setbacks. Nothing good can come from them.

8. I do not fear the unknown; actually it can be exciting and challenging to think about the possibilities.

8. The unknown is to be feared and avoided when possible. I believe what works best for me is to pick predictable outcomes, even if they are less than what I really long for.

9. It is important for me to stand up for myself when I am having disagreements or conflict with others. Conflict can promote growth. Handling conflict builds my self confidence.

9. Conflict with others is very uncomfortable and I believe I'm better off avoiding it.

10. Taking risks is an essential part of getting what I want in life. Being secure and staying in my comfort zone may well get in the way of goals that matter to me.

10. Having security and staying in my comfort zone is far more important than taking chances that might lead to something better.

11. I understand that to achieve my goals there will be plenty of obstacles, that it may take more time than I would like and it may involve some suffering.

11. I believe that the path to my goals should be quick, easy and obstacle and pain free.

12. If something knocks me down flat, I will be able to get back up. Courage is a major factor in being resilient.

12. If something very deflating or traumatic happens to me, I don't know if I have what it takes to get back up.

13. I believe that achieving a fulfilling life is my right and responsibility. Others can give me input but it is my choice; I will not be unduly influenced by the opinions and feedback of others.

13. I believe that others often know what is better for me than I do. I do not want to disappoint people I care about.

14. When something goes wrong in my life, I refuse to see myself as a victim.

14. I feel like a victim when I am plagued by negative events in life. People tend to take care of me when I have been hurt or disappointed.

15. I believe that change brings many positive gifts and I am not afraid of it.

15. Change is very frightening; I think it is better when things stay the same.

BEHAVIORS

Behaviors That Foster Courage

1. I manage fear proactively; I do not avoid situations that scare me. I use appropriate techniques to approach fear stimuli.

Behaviors That Hinder Courage

1. I avoid people, places, challenges, etc., that evoke fear or discomfort.

2. I develop, commit to and execute a plan to take risks. I make bold and difficult choices part of an ongoing stragegy/habit.

2. I am conscientious about detecting all choices that might lead to uncertain outcomes. I make it a habit to opt out of or avoid such undertakings.

3. I make stress management an integral, daily component of my courage toolbox.

3. I use stress management skills only when my life is spinning totally out of control, or not at all.

4. I identify the cognitive, behavioral and physiological triggers that deplete courage. I make a plan to manage these triggers. I practice and stick to the plan.

4. I have no plan. I allow the triggers to control all levels of my functioning.

5. I am assertive. I stand up for myself. I choose which situations are appropriate for this and which ones do not need a response.

5. I avoid conflict. I do not tell others what I think and feel.

6. I get help for mental health challenges when needed.

6. I handle mental health problems on my own. I keep repeating, "I can do this by myself. All I have to do is buck up. It would be catastrophic for anyone else to know that I have psychological problems."

7. I target habits that stand in the way of goals, dreams and health. I learn behavioral and cognitive strategies to reduce or eliminate these obstructions. I get help when necessary.

7. I avoid any attempts to change negative habits that fill the voids. This can be too upsetting and it can be difficult to replace them.

8. I evaluate and develop a plan to set boundaries or remove myself from unhealthy personal situations. I get help if needed.

8. I stay the course in relationships, no matter how dysfunctional. I believe "the devil you know is better than the devil you don't know.

9. I dream, dream, dream. I take time to enjoy and cultivate my dreams.

9. I avoid dreaming. It leads to disappointment.

| 10. In the quest for a fulfilling life, I try new experiences. I use this information to broaden my path. | 10. I do the same things over and over. I don't vary my routine. I avoid anything out of the ordinary. |

THE TREASURY OF MOTIVATORS

The Treasury of Motivators offers a wealth of courage-generating words and thoughts. These can be helpful in maintaining your motivation and resolve on the journey to your chosen destinations. Choose the treasures that are meaningful and inspirational for you.

You may also enjoy your own treasure hunt for pieces that are personally energizing and encouraging. Incorporate these into your everyday internal world. Some you can commit to memory; others can be placed in spots where you'll be reminded of what you want to believe and say to yourself. Focus on them often. Focus on out with the garbage, and in with your own special pep talk.

QUOTATIONS ON COURAGE TO DISPUTE FAULTY THINKING

The following statements are harmful beliefs, expectations and thoughts that people repeat to themselves over and over again, often with strong conviction. The irrationality and toxicity of these debilitating cognitions are hardly ever questioned. These cognitions compete with the strength of courage. You need to learn to talk back to them in meaningful and potent ways.

The goal is reduce the frequency, intensity and duration of each of them by distraction methods and to neutralize them by disputing or arguing with their content. Disputing can be done by utilizing pertinent, meaningful quotes provided for you in this chapter or by developing your own reality-based, effective retorts. Note that you may have cognitions in your repertoire that are not contained in this list of Harmful Beliefs.

Take a personal inventory of these in a separate notebook, then choose powerful quotes or other responses to question and contradict these cognitions. Remember, practice, practice, practice, so you are ready when they come for real! Besides increasing your readiness, practicing also decreases the potency of any noxious self-statements, aiding in your quest to be more courageous. Distraction and disputing techniques are discussed in Chapter 7.

Harmful:
"I'm scared to death to take risks that could change my life in unexpected ways."

Instead:
"There would be nothing to frighten you if you refused to be afraid."
Stephen Covey

"Behold the turtle. He only makes progress when he sticks his neck out."
James Conant Bryant

"Isn't it amazing how many people tip-toe cautiously through life hoping to make it safely to death?"
Carl E. Hiebert

"I believe that one of life's greatest risks is never daring to risk."
Oprah Winfrey

"Progress always involves risk; you can't steal second base and keep your foot on first."
Frederick Wilcox

Harmful:
"I'm afraid of what might happen or how I might feel if I make the wrong decision, suffer a setback or fail."

Instead:
"Whenever you see a successful business, someone once made a courageous decision."
Peter Drucker

"You've got to get to the stage in life where going for it is more important than winning or losing."
Arthur Ashe

"Only those who do nothing... make no mistakes."
Joseph Conrad

"In any moment of decision the best thing you can do is the right thing, the next is the wrong thing, and the worst thing you can do is nothing."
Theodore Roosevelt

"Be bold. If you're going to make an error, make a doozy, and don't be afraid to hit the ball."
Billie Jean King

Harmful:
"I want to stay in my comfort zone. Why should I take chances? What's so important about having courage?"

Instead:
"Never forget that life can only be nobly inspired and rightly lived if you take it bravely and gallantly, as a splendid adventure in which you are setting out into an unknown country, to meet many a joy, to find many a comrade, to win and lose many a battle."
Anne Besant

"It takes courage to grow up and turn out to be who you really are."
e.e.cummings

"Don't be afraid to go out on a limb. That is where the fruit is."
H. Jackson Browne

"Act boldly and unseen forces will come to your aid."
Dorothea Brande

"Courage is rightly esteemed the first of human qualities... because it is the quality which guarantees all others."
Winston Churchill

Harmful:
"Security is the most important thing in life. I don't want to give up the things I have worked so hard for at the outside chance life might get better."

Instead:

"Life shrinks or expands in proportion to one's courage."
Anais Nin

"It takes a lot of courage to release the familiar and seemingly secure to embrace the new. But there is no real security in what is no longer meaningful. There is more security in the adventurous and exciting, for in movement there is life and in change there is power."
Alan Cohen

"A ship in the harbor is safe, but that is not what a ship was built for."
William Shedd

"Security is mostly a superstition. It does not exist in nature... life is either a daring adventure or nothing."
Helen Keller

"You will either step forward in growth or you will step back into safety."
Abraham Maslow

Harmful:

"What if other people think I'm crazy to make such a risky move with an unknown outcome?"

Instead:

"Dance like no one is watching. Sing like no one is listening. Love like you've never been hurt and live like it's heaven on earth."
Mark Twain

"The great pleasure in life is doing what people say you cannot do."
Walter Bagehot

"One good measure of ego-strength and inner confidence is the degree to which a person can risk unpopularity when the occasion demands."
Martin Luther King, Jr.

"Whatever you do, you need courage. Whatever course you decide upon, there is always someone to tell you that you are wrong. There are always difficulties arising that tempt you to believe your critics are right. To map out a course of action and to follow it to an end requires some of the same courage that a soldier needs. Peace has its victories, but it takes brave men and women to win them."
Ralph Waldo Emerson

"It is not the critic who counts, not the man who points out how the strong man stumbled, or where the doer of deeds could have done better. The credit belongs to the man who is actually in the arena, whose face is marred by dust and sweat and blood, who strives valiantly, who errs and comes short again and again, who knows the great enthusiasms, the great devotions, and spends himself in a worthy cause, who at best knows achievement and who at worst if he fails at least fails while daring greatly so that his place shall never be with those cold and timid souls who know neither victory nor defeat."
Theodore Roosevelt

Harmful:
"I'm just not as brave as other people; there must be something different about me."

Instead:
"Courage is very important. Like a muscle, it is strengthened by use."
Ruth Gordon

"Courage is sometimes frail as hope is frail: a fragile shoot between two stones that grows brave toward the sun though warmth and brightness fail, striving and faith the only strength it knows."
Frances Rodman

"It's not the size of the dog in the fight, it's the size of the fight in the dog."
Mark Twain

"It was high counsel that I once heard given to a young person, always do what you are afraid to do."
Ralph Waldo Emerson

"Whoever said anybody has a right to give up?"
Marian Wright Edelman

Harmful:
"I'm afraid of change. Why can't things stay the same?"

Instead:
"The important thing is this: To be able at any moment to sacrifice what we are for what we could become."
Charles Dubois

"The only way to make sense of change is to plunge into it, move with it, and join the dance."
Alan Watts

"There are some things one can only achieve by a deliberate leap in the opposite direction."
Franz Kafka

"There was that law of life, so cruel and so just, which demanded that one must grow or else pay more for remaining the same."
Norman Mailer

"If we can't change, we can't grow. If we don't grow, we really are not living. Growth demands a temporary surrender of security."
Gail Sheehy

Harmful:
"I don't really believe that I can make my dreams come true. I am too afraid to try."

Instead:
"There are people who put their dreams in al little box and say, 'Yes, I've got dreams, of course I've got dreams.' Then they put the box away and bring it out once in a while to look in it, and yep, they're still there. These are great dreams, but they never even get out of the box. It takes an uncommon amount of guts to put your dreams on the line, to hold them up and say, 'How good or bad am I?' That's where courage comes in."
Erma Bombeck

"Whatever you can do or dream you can, begin it. Boldness has genius, power and magic in it. Begin it now."
Johann Wolfgang Von Goethe

"When I dare to be powerful to use my strength in the service of my vision, then it becomes less and less important whether I am afraid."
Andre Lorde

"The only limit to our realization of tomorrow will be our doubts of today."
Franklin Delano Roosevelt

"Discouragement is not the absence of adequacy but the absence of courage."
Neal A. Maxwell

Harmful:
"I don't know how to be brave enough to take control of my life."

Instead:
"To fight fear act. To increase fear – wait, put off, postpone."
David Joseph Schwartz

"It takes courage to realize that you are greater than your moods, greater than your thoughts and that you can control your moods and thoughts."
Stephen Covey

"When you can't choose between two evenly balanced courses of action to take, choose the bolder."
General W.J. Slim

"Do the thing you fear and the death of fear is certain."
Ralph Waldo Emerson

"I have learned over the years that when one's mind is made up, this diminishes fear; knowing what must be done does away with fear."
Rosa Parks

Harmful:
"I think it is wise to avoid conflict. Conflict with others is very uncomfortable."

Instead:
"Conflict is the beginning of consciousness."
M. Esther Harding

"Peace is not the absence of conflict, but the ability to cope with it."
Author Unknown

"Never be bullied into silence. Never allow yourself to be a victim. Accept no one's definition of your life, but define yourself."
Harvey Fierstein

"Be who you are and say what you want, because those who mind don't matter and those who matter don't mind."
Dr. Seuss

"The only tyrant I will accept in this world is the 'still, small voice within me.'"
Mahatma Gandhi

COURAGE IN POEMS, SONGS, MOVIES

Poems, songs and movies often touch people in ways that are motivating and inspiring. In my clinical practice I found that utilizing thematic works that resonate with an individual can be an effective and enjoyable way to keep his or her little red wagon moving forward – even in the most discouraging times and circumstances.

The Treasury of Motivators for courage contains poems, songs, motivational quotes and a movie synopsis that might appeal to you on the quest to free yourself from the ravages of fear. After you've read them, choose the ones that have meaning for you, or go on your own search for a work that fits the theme of courage.

Read the poems, lyrics and movie synopsis often; think about the theme every day. When you have a chance, watch the movie. Listen to the songs, sing them to yourself. When you are discouraged, disenchanted or afraid, use your Treasury Motivators to bolster your spirits and faith in yourself.

OH! The Places You'll Go!
by Dr. Seuss
Go to: members.tripod.com/~techbabe/places.html
(If this web site is unavailable, use your favorite search engine to find the poem)

The Journey
By Mary Oliver
Go to: www.panhala.net/Archive/The-Journey.html
(If this web site is unavailable, use your favorite search engine to find the poem)

The Road Not Taken – The story behind the poem by Robert Frost
From Selected Letters of Robert Frost, edited by Lawrence Thompson

Robert Frost had a very close friend, Edward Thomas, who walked with Frost in the English countryside. Thomas made it his goal to show Frost something special on each walk. Many times as the walk proceeded, Thomas would lament his choice and suggest an alternative that might have been more special. Frost often chided his friend about his longing and wasted regrets. Frost conjectured that "we should not look back." Upon returning to the United States, Frost wrote The Road Not Taken, and sent a copy to his friend.

The Road Not Taken
By Robert Frost
Go to: www.bartelby.com/119/1.html
(If this web site is unavailable, use your favorite search engine to find the poem)

Courage
By Anne Sexton
Go to: www.duke.edu/~sss7/courage.htm
(If this web site is unavailable, use your favorite search engine to find the poem)

I'd Rather Be Sorry

Lyrics by Kris Kristofferson

Go to: www.poemhunter.com/song/i-d-rather-be-sorry/

(If this web site is unavailable, use your favorite search engine to find the lyrics)

Taxi

Lyrics by Harry Chapin

Go to: www.sing365.com/music/lyric.nsf/taxilyrics-Harry-Chapin/3d86a

A song about not pursuing your dreams.

(If this web site is unavailable, use your favorite search engine to find the lyrics)

Courage in the Movies

I've discussed how courage comes in various forms, from physical to moral to psychological, and surely there have been myriad examples of each portrayed in film throughout the years. One of my particular favorites, however, examines courage in a way that's both poignant and whimsical – and teaches us that when we face our fears, there's no limit to what we can accomplish.

I'm referring to the 1991 film *Defending Your Life,* with Albert Brooks, who not only wrote and directed the movie, but also plays the main character, Daniel Miller. If you're familiar with Albert Brooks and his cinematic work, you know that he never fails to deliver intelligent, thought-provoking commentaries on life (and in this case, the afterlife), where a potent mixture of offbeat comedy and tragedy usually leave the viewer with food for thought long after the film has ended. And such is the case with this movie, whose message is the perfect antidote for anyone poisoned by fear.

When we're introduced to Daniel, he's celebrating a lonely 40th birthday and recent divorce by purchasing a shiny new BMW automobile. Soon after leaving the dealership, however, he drives head-on into a city bus and immediately finds himself in… well, we don't know exactly where he finds himself, and neither does he. Turns out that Daniel, having died in the accident, has been transported to "Judgment City," a utopian-like destination – neither Heaven nor Hell – where all recently deceased adults go for a short length of time in order to "defend their lives." Those who are successful in their defense are allowed to move forward in their journey through eternity. Those who are not are required to return to Earth in an attempt to "get smarter, use more of their brain and learn how to conquer fear."

Daniel meets his appointed defender, Bob Diamond (wonderfully portrayed by Rip Torn), who says gleefully, "people on Earth use only three to five percent of their brains because they spend most of their life dealing with fear... that's what 'little brains' do!" Bob continues, "I'm just like you, but I grew – I advanced, moved on, got smarter and got over my fear. Fear is like a giant fog... it sits on the brain and blocks everything – real happiness, true joy."

Daniel Miller, along with his defender, the prosecutor Lena Foster (played by Lee Grant), and the judges who'll make a final decision on his fate, are about to get a bird's eye view of several episodes from Daniel's life to see just how well he dealt with fear.

Judgment City is more than just defenders, prosecutors and judges, though. It's a paradise where the weather is always sunny and clear, the food is superb and plentiful (you can eat as much as you want and not gain weight!), and entertainment options abound. One evening Daniel visits the resident Comedy Club and finds himself seated near one of the few people his age in Judgment City – and who also happens to be a beautiful woman. Her name is Julia (portrayed by Meryl Streep), and she's about to enter Daniel's "life" in a most important way.

During the daytime, however, Daniel must concentrate on his trial, and he has nine days of it to look forward to; that is, they will look at nine episodes from his lifetime that illustrate his ability – or inability – to deal with fear. Daniel is shocked when they show him actual events that occurred during his life, as a toddler, a young child, an adolescent and finally an adult, all of which are being examined for some indication of courage in the face of fear. As Lena Foster states, "I intend to prove that Daniel Miller is still held back by the fear that has plagued him from lifetime to lifetime."

The episodes we witness from Daniel's life are vintage Albert Brooks comedy: understated, touching, funny and eminently relatable – we've all been there, and how we've dealt with it determines who we are. For instance, a nine-year-old Daniel is punched and verbally abused by a bully on the playground, but he refuses to fight back; cowardly or simply restrained?

As an adult, Daniel is about to apply for a terrific new job, and to hone his interviewing skills he practices at length with his wife the night before, insisting with determination and conviction, "I'm sorry, but I can't accept the position for anything less than $65,000. Sorry." The next day, at the end of the actual interview, his boss says, "Daniel, I'm prepared to offer you $49,000." Daniel replies without hesitation, "I accept." Why didn't Daniel stand up for what he believed, as he had done the night before??

As more episodes are revealed, it becomes clear that Daniel's life is defined by fear, which he is incapable of overcoming. But outside the tribunal, a loving bond is being forged with Julia, like nothing either has experienced before. Of course, Julia is the polar opposite of Daniel, someone whose courage shines through and who, according to her defender, can expect to be "moving on." Daniel's prospects are not nearly as rosy.

On the eve of judgment day, Julia and Daniel express their love for each other; Julia invites him to spend their final night together, in her hotel room. Of course, Daniel wants to, more than anything... but he's afraid. "I want to," says Daniel, "but I'm afraid I'll just screw it up. I've been defending myself so much lately...I'm tired of being judged." Daniel returns to his own room, alone, once again defeated by fear.

But back at his hotel, Daniel has a change of heart. He tries to reach Julia by phone but is unsuccessful. He's certain he's blown it again. And sure enough, when his trial concludes the next day and the decision is handed down, Daniel is going back to Earth – to get smarter, to conquer his fear. "Don't kick yourself forever," Bob Diamond consoles him. "Just take the opportunities when they come... follow what's in here," touching his heart.

As Daniel sullenly boards the tram that will return him to another lifetime on Earth, he hears Julia yelling his name from the other side of the huge tarmac, from a tram filled with those who are moving on! Daniel breaks free from his seat belt and forces open the doors, screaming, "I love you, I won't let you go, I won't let you go!" Daniel jumps from the moving tram, stung by a bolt of electricity, then stumbling across the tarmac, dodging oncoming vehicles, shouting Julia's name and at last reaching her, both of them frantically trying to pry open the door. "Hold on, hold on," exhorts Julia through the window. "Wait for me, I love you, I love you!" cries Daniel.

Unbeknownst to our two heroes, however, this all unfolds under the omnipresent view of Judgment City's hierarchy. "Well, brave enough for you?" asks Bob Diamond. Prosecutor Lena Foster responds with a wry smile and a simple nod. As the judge says "let him go" into his microphone, Daniel forces himself through the door of the tram and into Julia's waiting arms.

The English philosopher Bertrand Russell once said, "To conquer fear is the beginning of wisdom."

MOTIVATIONAL QUOTES TO BUILD COURAGE

On Courage
"To have courage for whatever comes in life – everything lies in that."
Mother Theresa

"The strangest, most generous and proudest of all virtues is true courage."
Michel Ey Quem Montaigne

"Courage is its own reward."
Plautus

"The secret of harvesting from existence the greatest fruitfulness and the greatest enjoyment is – to live dangerously! Build your cities on the slopes of Vesuvius! Send your ships into uncharted seas."
Friedrich Nietzsche

"Courage, it would seem, is nothing less than the power to overcome danger, misfortune, fear, injustice, while continuing to affirm inwardly that life with all its sorrows is good; that everything is meaningful everything is meaningful even if in a sense beyond our understanding; and that there is always tomorrow."
Dorothy Thompson

On Avoidance
"Weep for the lives your wishes never led."
W. H. Auden

"The dangers in life are infinite, and among them is safety."
Goethe

"Do you know what happens when a procrastinator gets a good idea? Nothing!"
Donald Gardner

"An infallible method of conciliating a tiger is to allow oneself to be swallowed."
Konrad Adenauer

"No appeasement will avoid the necessary battles. It only makes them more costly and lengthy."
Gustave le Bon

On Fear
"Whoever said anybody has a right to give up?"
Marian Wright Edelman

"Fear defeats more people than any one thing in the world."
Ralph Waldo Emerson

"Fear is not the opposite of courage. Fear is the catalyst of courage."
Joan D. Chittister

"An inferiority complex is a conviction by your fears."
Author Unknown

"Do the thing you fear and the death of fear is certain."
Ralph Waldo Emerson

EFFECTIVE, PRACTICAL TECHNIQUES FOR BUILDING COURAGE

In order to change the beliefs and behaviors that you identified as problematic in the Chart on Courage, you'll need to learn some specific concepts and techniques. These include:

- ✓ Principles of Behavior Change
- ✓ The Stress Response

- ✓ Abdominal Breathing
- ✓ Imagery Relaxation
- ✓ Progressive Muscle Relaxation (PMR)
- ✓ The Relaxation Response
- ✓ Systematic Desensitization
- ✓ Assertiveness
- ✓ Disputing
- ✓ Distraction

These techniques are discussed in detail in Chapter 7.

ADDITIONAL RESOURCES: RECOMMENDED READINGS AND WEBSITES

Recommended Readings:

Alberti, R. and Emmons, M. (1995), *Your Perfect Right*

Bourne, E. (2001), *The Anxiety and Phobia Workbook*

Bourne, E. (2001), *Beyond Anxiety and Phobia*

Davis, M., Eschelman, E. R. and McKay, M. (1988), *The Relaxation and Stress Reduction Workbook*

Jeffers, S. (1996), *Feel the Fear and Do It Anyway*
Phelps, S. and Austin, N. (1997), *The Assertive Woman*

Websites:

Basic Guided Relaxation: Advanced Technique by L. John Mason, Ph.D.
http://www.dstress.com/guided.htm

Panic, Anxiety Education Management Services
http://www.healthyplace.com/communities/anxiety/paems/index.html

Systematic Desensitization, by R. Richmond, Ph.D.
http://www.guidetopsychology.com/sysden.htm

COURAGE ENDNOTES

Pg. 47   McCain, J. (2004) *Why Courage Matters.* New York: Random House

Pg. 50   McKay, G. and Dinkmeyer, D. (2002) *How You Feel is Up to You.* Atascadero, CA: Impact Publishers

Covey, S. (1989) *The 7 Habits of Highly Effective People.* New York: Simon and Schuster

Pg. 51   Baker, D. and Starth, C. (2003) *What Happy People Know.* USA: Rodale, Inc.

Pg. 53   Clift, E. "Dying with Courage: A personal tribute to Tom Brazaitis, a husband who endured his final days with a clarity of mind and spirit." *Newsweek.* April 1, 2005

Pg. 55   Koontz, D. (1998) *Seize the Night.* USA: Bantam Books

Pg. 64   Scott, S. (1998) *Simple Steps to Impossible Dreams.* New York: Fireside

Pg. 65   McCain, J. (2004) *Why Courage Matters.* New York: Random House

Chapter Three

PERSISTENCE
Develop Patience, Discipline and Endurance

"The big shots are the little shots that kept shooting."
Christopher Morley

It's great fun working with clients on the strength of persistence… or, maybe not! When I introduce this strength to clients, it's as if I had suggested they take part in a 48-hour Candy Land marathon – boring, boring, boring. I have to cautiously reference its components of patience, discipline and endurance, risking reflexive yawns, heavy eyelids and serious inattention. Okay, I get it; this is not the most titillating of subjects. However, persistence is a strength that is indispensable to your plans for self-fulfillment and success. And yes, believe this: it can be an inspiring strength that often brings unexpected and special gifts.

The fact is you may be strongly tempted to turn the page to something more captivating or you might be thinking that by comparison, the leftover carryout from last night is starting to sound pretty exciting. I don't blame you, but before you skip out on this one, understand something hugely important – that in navigating your little red wagon on the path to your deeply desired destinations, powerful key strengths include optimism, passion, courage, living in the present, and resilience, while persistence is the one that holds them all together for the length of the journey.

Yes, indeed, you will not be achieving your goals and dreams without persistence. Without tenacity you won't have the opportunity to measure up to the person you are capable of being, the person you want to be.

THE REWARDS OF PERSISTENCE

Persistence plays a critical role in the quest for victory, wisdom, achievement, success, fulfillment, self-confidence and character. Most of the eventualities we long for require our focused, vigilant attention, ingenuity, patience, flexibility and stick-to-it-ness. Persistence involves setting a goal, committing to a course of action, making the necessary sacrifices, overcoming obstacles, mistakes, setbacks, failures, criticism, and all the while maintaining your focus, motivation, energy and faith in yourself.

It requires adaptability in a wide variety of "challenges" – all those predictable and unpredictable variables that make life so interesting! It requires reviewing and altering expectations. Persistence keeps you on a trail of possibilities that sustains you when you hit a wall with one course of action; this resolute approach enables you to reenergize yourself so that you continue exploring creative options.

Have you ever worked so hard on one plan, got stymied amid your efforts, and then fortuitously found another way that was so much more productive and rewarding? If you had given up, where would you have been? Defeated, lost, crestfallen. And how long does it take to get up when you've let yourself down?

The words of President Calvin Coolidge tell us of the unique importance of this strength: "Nothing in the world can take the place of persistence. Talent will not; nothing is more common than unsuccessful men with talent. Genius will not; unrewarded genius is almost a proverb. Education alone will not; the world is full of educated derelicts. Persistence and determination alone are omnipotent."

Success
Achieving success in your goals and dreams requires persistence. John D. Rockefeller, the American industrialist and founder of Standard Oil, shares his belief on this subject: "I do not think there is any quality so essential to success of any kind as the quality of perseverance. It overcomes everything, even Nature." Conrad Hilton, founder of the Hilton hotel chain, surmises, "Success seems to be connected with action. Successful people keep moving. They make mistakes, but they don't quit."

Bertrand Russell, the British philosopher and social critic, reminds us, "No great achievement is possible without persistent work." Thomas Alva Edison advises that, "Our greatest weakness lies in giving up. The most certain way to succeed is always to try just one more time." Benjamin Franklin asserts, "Energy and persistence conquer all things."

George Allen contends that, "People of mediocre ability sometimes achieve outstanding success because they don't know when to quit. Most men succeed because they are determined to." Former Secretary of State, Colin Powell, believes "There are no secrets to success. Don't waste your time looking for them. Success is the result of perfection, hard work, learning from failure, loyalty to those for whom you work and persistence."

Dr. A. B. Meldrum advises, "Bear in mind, if you are going to amount to anything, that your success does not depend upon the brilliance and impetuosity with which you take hold, but upon the everlasting and sanctified bull doggedness with which you hang on after you have taken hold." John Rennie says, "All achievement is the triumph of persistence."

Performance Excellence

Performance has much to do with persistence. Martha Graham, the American choreographer and dancer who was a major force in pioneering modern dance, declares, "Dancing appears glamorous, easy, delightful. But the path to paradise of the achievement is not easier than any other. There is fatigue so great that the body cries, even in its sleep. There are times of complete frustration, there are daily small deaths."

James A. Michener, the American author, discloses, "I have never thought of myself as a good writer. Anyone who wants reassurance of that should read one of my first drafts. But I'm one of the world's great rewriters." Marabel Morgan contends, "Persistence is the twin sister of excellence. One is a matter of quality; the other a matter of time."

Athletic performance and winning, of course, depend on persistence of the highest degree. Paul "Bear" Bryant, one of the most successful college football coaches of all time, maintains that, "It's not the will to win, but the will to prepare to win that makes the difference."

Vince Lombardi, the Green Bay Packers coach with five NFL championships and the epitome of persistence, says emphatically, "All right Mister, let me tell you what winning means…you're willing to go longer, work harder, give more than anyone else." He also said, "The Green Bay Packers never lost a football game. They just ran out of time."

James Keller relates the dedication, determination and sacrifice of one of the most famous women golfers: "When Babe Didrickson Zaharia, often called the athletic phenomenon of all time, won the British Women's Golf Tournament, people said of her what they said many times before. 'Oh, she's an automatic champion, a natural athlete.' When Babe started golfing in earnest … she hit as many as 1,000 balls in one afternoon, playing until her hands were so sore they had to be taped."

Grit

Mahatma Gandhi, the spiritual and political leader of India, tells us, "Strength does not come from physical activity. It comes from an indomitable will." Mark Twain asserts that, "The miracle or the power that elevates the few is to be found in their industry, application, and perseverance under the prompting of a brave, determined spirit." We build the ability to endure by developing the habit of persistence.

A genesis of strength grows in the person who manifests true grit. In a study at the University of Pennsylvania called "The GRIT Study," GRIT was defined as perseverance toward an ambitious goal, a goal that could take years to reach often requiring the ability to overcome discouragement, obstacles and difficulties.

The research found that the Penn undergraduates who had high scores on a self-report questionnaire designed and validated to assess GRIT, achieved grade point averages above and beyond their Scholastic Aptitude Scores and high school Grade Point Averages. Low GRIT scores also predicted which cadets would drop out during the first summer at West Point.

Louis Pasteur, the French chemist and microbiologist famous for his discovery of pasteurization, discloses, "Let me tell you the secret that has led to my goal: my strength lies solely in my tenacity." Indira Gandhi, the former Prime Minister of India, recaps the sage advice she lived by: "My grandfather once told me that there were two kinds of people: those who do the work and those who take the credit. He told me to be in the first group; there was much less competition."

Jack Dempsey had true grit. He held the world heavyweight boxing title for seven years. For him, "A champion is someone who gets up, even when he can't." Roger Banister tells us, "The man who can drive himself further once the effort gets painful is the man who will win."

Genius and Talent

Staying with a task or goal no matter what the intervening obstacles has much to do with what we identify as talent and genius. H. Jackson Browne, Jr., the author of *Life's Little Instruction Book,* waxes philosophic when he suggests, "Talent without discipline is like an octopus on roller skates. There's plenty of movement, but you never know if it's going to be forward, backward or sideways."

Honore de Balzac, the French novelist, contends "There is no such thing as great talent without great willpower." Stephen King, master of the macabre, doesn't mince words when he says, "Talent is as cheap as table salt. What separates the talented individual from the successful one is a lot of hard work." Sir Noel Coward, English actor, composer and playwright, is of the conviction that "Thousands of people have talent. I might as well congratulate you for having eyes in your head. The one and only thing that counts is – do you have staying power?"

Charles Schultz was an academic disaster in junior high and high school, a lonely child who was socially awkward, a man who had many rejections along the way in his career of drawing cartoons. Also known as "Sparky," Charles Schultz believed he was a loser. He was Charlie Brown. And yet he persisted and presented us with his profound talent, a source of enjoyment, entertainment and enrichment for people the world over.

Eric Hoffer, the American social writer who authored *The Ordeal of Change* explains, "Those who lack talent expect things to happen without effort. They ascribe failure to a lack of inspiration or ability, or to misfortune, rather than to insufficient application. At the core of every true talent there is an awareness of the difficulties inherent in every achievement, and the confidence that by persistence and patience something worthwhile will be realized. Thus talent is a species of vigor."

"Genius," in the words of Benjamin Franklin "is nothing but a greater aptitude for patience." One of my favorite geniuses, Mark Twain, is of the opinion that, "It usually takes three weeks to prepare a good impromptu speech." Sir Isaac Newton, the much celebrated English scientist and philosopher, reflects, "If I have ever made any valuable discoveries, it has been owing more to patient attention, than to any other talent."

Thomas Alva Edison became deaf at 12 years of age. Instead of allowing this loss to compromise his genius in inventing, he looked at it as an advantage – he could concentrate better! He shares with us his idea of genius: "Genius is one percent inspiration and ninety-nine percent perspiration. I make more mistakes than anyone else I know, and sooner or later, I patent most of them." Michelangelo talks of his persistence: "I saw an angel in the marble and carved until I set him free."

Albert Einstein confesses, "It's not that I am so smart, it's that I stay with problems longer." Alexander Hamilton, the American politician who founded the Federalist Party, discloses, "Men give me credit for some genius. All the genius I have lies in this: when I have a subject in hand, I study it profoundly. Day and night it is before me. My mind becomes pervaded with it. Then the effort that I have made is what people are pleased to call the fruit of genius. It is the fruit of labor and thought."

Maturity and Character
"Stick-to-it-ness" plays a significant role in the development of maturity and character. Ann Landers, the advice columnist who helped so many people with problems over the years, believes, "Maturity is perseverance, the ability to sweat out a project or a situation in spite of heavy opposition and discouraging setbacks. Maturity is the capacity to face unpleasantness and frustration, discomfort and defeat, without complaints or collapse." Joshua Liebman suggests, "Maturity is achieved when a person postpones immediate pleasures for long-term values." Napoleon Hill, the writer, teacher and lecturer, posits, "Persistence is to character what carbon is to steel." James A. Michener suggests, "Character consists of what you do on the third and fourth tries."

Self-Respect and Confidence
Self-respect is being proud of who you are and what you have accomplished. Confidence is believing you have what it takes to get things done. George Bernard Shaw, winner of the Nobel Prize for Literature, notes, "No man who is occupied in doing a very difficult thing, and doing it very well, ever loses his self-respect." Brian Tracy posits, "When you engage in systematic, purposeful action, using and stretching your abilities to the maximum, you cannot help but feel positive and confident about yourself."

Thomas A. Bennett, the artist in residence for the North Carolina Museum of Natural Sciences, implores us, "Having once decided to achieve a certain task, achieve it at all costs of tedium and distaste. The gain in self-confidence of having accomplished a tiresome labor is immense." Richard Kline, an American actor and director suggests, "Confidence is preparation. Everything else is beyond your control."

Alexander Graham Bell, scientist and inventor of the telephone, maintains, "What this power is I cannot say; all I know is that it exists and becomes available only when a man is in that state of mind in which he knows exactly what he wants and is fully determined not to quit until he finds it." William Blake surmises, "If the fool would persist in his folly he would become wise."

Happiness

Persistence is a variable of happiness. According to the research of Nancy Cantor, Distinguished Professor of Psychology at Syracuse University, and Catherine Sanderson, Associate Professor of Psychology at Amherst College, individuals who take part in a sustained task of personal or cultural value have a greater likelihood of experiencing well-being or happiness. Norman Vincent Peale says, "The really happy people are those who have broken the chains of procrastination, those who find satisfaction in doing the job at hand. They're full of eagerness, zest, productivity…"

Brutus Hamilton, the Olympic Decathlete, suggests, "It is one of the strange ironies of this strange life that those who work the hardest, who subject themselves to the strictest discipline, who give up certain pleasurable things in order to achieve a goal, are the happiest men. When you see 20 or 30 men line up for a distance race in some meet, don't pity them, don't feel sorry for them. Better envy them instead."

Theodore Rubin, the American psychiatrist and author, is of the opinion that, "Happiness does not come from doing easy work but from the afterglow of satisfaction that comes after the achievement of a difficult task that demanded our best."

THE CHALLENGE OF BEING PERSISTENT

What is so elusive about persistence? What makes it so difficult to learn and convert into a habit? This is a haunting question for anyone who made a New Year's resolution and blew past it by January 3rd. How does procrastination become a way of life, often resulting in self-loathing? If persistence eludes you and you've labeled yourself lazy, a procrastinator, one of life's losers, you may want to rethink your conclusions so that you can effectively develop goals and the habits that bring them to fruition. You can resign from the "I couldn't change a habit if my life depended on it" club. Unfortunately, this club has many, many members, so if you resign, you probably won't be missed!

Persistent people have some common characteristics. They display autonomy and self-control, look for challenging goals, expect positive results and, most importantly, explain negative events in a way that does not defeat them. The persistent person believes that a pitfall merely means a challenge to try harder, get more information or be flexible about evaluating, and fine tuning the goal and its concomitant strategies. In other words, the persistent person is very much like the energizer bunny with purpose; he or she just keeps on going, going, going.

Persistent people understand that it is highly probable that there will be course alterations along the way; this is not a calamity, but just the way things usually work out. They get it – that keeping one's expectations in line with reality regarding the potholes likely to be encountered is smart, proactive and supports success. A persistent person knows intuitively that it's his or her little red wagon, and believing that is a very good thing.

Procrastination: Enemy of Persistence, Thief of Time

To many people, it's a mystery "why" they're stuck in the procrastination trap. They realize that it makes no sense to berate themselves endlessly for repeating the same tired, old avoidance behaviors; nor does it make sense to label themselves lazy and worthless; and it becomes crazy to keep promising to reform their self-defeating ways, when they unwittingly continue to get deeper and deeper in the sludge.

I'm not so big on the "why" question; it's an elusive query that distracts attention from the meat of the matter. It's far too easy to spend inordinate amounts of time reviewing childhood issues and other past influences, attempting to connect them to the current state of paralysis. And even if the conclusions sound reasonable and appropriate, they could be wrong and even more likely useless. Too many people spend too much time trying to understand "why," when it would be so much more productive to determine what needs to be modified and what factors play a continuing role in the procrastination trap.

Effective assessment involves the identification of cognitive and behavioral factors that are relevant in promoting procrastination. These would entail variables that are currently operative.

Aversion/Boredom

You might procrastinate because the job is distasteful, boring or at the moment seems rather inane. Something else might be so much more appealing to you, competing with the less attractive alternative. In other words, you put off one thing to do something that you find more interesting or enjoyable now.

Fear

Another reason for this bad habit is fear; you might feel inadequate and may not want to have this inadequacy confirmed for all to see. Or you may be fearful of an unpredictable outcome, once you commit your time and energy to the goal. Fear of success can be a powerful variable as well. If you succeed, you or someone else might expect you to maintain that level of functioning. If you have perfectionist tendencies, you may fear taking on an endeavor that could manifest in a flawed result. Heaven forbid!

Pressure From Others

Feeling pressure from others to perform can produce resentment and resistance which, more often than not, are action stoppers. Due to someone else's expectations, you "cut off your nose to spite your face." By the way, who is in charge of your life, anyway? Are you going to let someone else dictate your path?

Expectation Problems

You might feel entitled to have your dream today without all the wear and tear – a desire and expectation of quick, easy results. Or you might be beating yourself up for not following through on expectations you had for yourself. There are people who make this self-abuse a mantra. True action stoppers!

Learned Helplessness

Another action stopper is learned helplessness, the state in which a person feels that no matter what he or she does, it won't make much of a difference in the final result, so why bother? David Burns, M.D., in his book, *Feeling Good, the New Mood Therapy*, notes that you may talk yourself out of action because of a helplessness mindset. For example, you may magnify the problem so it seems impossible; you may conclude that you have to do everything at once instead of in steps; you may tell yourself that you are not capable of doing what needs to be done or that the end result will not be worth the effort. This kind of internal dialogue is utterly paralyzing and often connected to depression. Persistence is just too hard to maintain in this mindset.

The Avoidance Trap

How does procrastination become a strong pattern of functioning, in effect taking on a life of its own? Behaviorally, it's an avoidance trap. When you avoid something that scares you, those fearful feelings and the accompanying physical symptoms often diminish or disappear. When you avoid something that is distasteful or boring, the absence of the negative or boring situation reinforces the avoidant behavior.

Because the behavior of avoiding or escaping is so powerful in halting what's distressing, distasteful or boring, it becomes more likely that you'll use this response again when the same situation or a similar one presents itself. Avoidance has gained strength, and you are in backward motion. Avoidance leads to more avoidance. When this is the case, you have limited or lost your control in this area. It's not that you're lazy or good-for-nothing; you're simply caught up in a cognitive and behavioral state of turbulence and confusion.

Let's say you're afraid of public speaking. You've agreed to give a talk, but just the thought of standing in front of a large audience gives you heart palpitations, gas, sweaty palms and thoughts of moving to Australia. You put off practicing the speech because even practicing makes you feel ill. You make a phone call to cancel or reschedule your commitment with the lame excuse of having a disease one can only contract in a remote village in Africa.

When you hang up from the call, your heart palpitations and gas disappear, your sweaty palms become dry, and your thoughts are focused on what you're going to have for lunch. Avoidance in the moment has aborted your fearful symptoms. The avoidant behavior has gained the upper hand, and in the future the likelihood of using this course of action has increased, sometimes markedly. Avoidance controls you. In the arena of your public speaking fear, persistence has been dealt a blow. It's like drinking alcohol in the morning to treat your hangover. This intervention may reduce your symptoms, but I can guarantee you are not in control – the alcohol is in control.

The same applies for avoidance of the distasteful. You hate going to your mother-in-law's house for dinner on Sunday, a precious day off, especially when she's fixing her liver and egg concoction. You tell your husband that the boss called asking you to help him prepare the schedule for next week. Your husband believes you, and you go shopping instead of dealing with the dreaded liver and boring conversation.

Upon making your escape, your feelings of fatigue, mild depression and frustration magically evaporate into thin air. The thought enters your mind, "I wonder if this will work the next time?" Avoidance has saved the day, and the probability of searching for an escape mechanism the next time has increased. Avoidance controls you.

So what's wrong with strategies that make you feel better, if even for just the short term? What's so wrong about managing fear and aversive situations in this way? The answer is important. Your behavior is reactive, not proactive, and in both these cases, patently dishonest. You are not being true to yourself or to other people, and you are not in control of your internal and external behavior in this area. You are not going toward your power, you are moving away from it. You have decidedly limited your choices.

This backward spiral may take on a life of its own. It can become infectious, spreading or generalizing to other aspects of your life. I have seen the far-reaching effects of avoidance many, many times. These effects can result in one's own personal prison. Avoidance promotes procrastination and is antithetical to persistence. Fortunately, this pattern can be turned around. You can become proactive and regain control and be true to your values.

DEVELOPING PERSISTENCE, TERMINATING PROCRASTINATION

"Watch your thoughts, for they become words.
Watch your words, for they become actions.
Watch your actions, for they become habits.
Watch your habits, for they become character.
Watch your character, for it becomes your destiny."

Patrick Overton

The author of this quote has captured the importance of your decisions concerning what you think and what you do. To become persistent and to eliminate procrastination, you need to know what works and what doesn't. By identifying cognitive and behavioral factors that are germane in your procrastination or lack of persistence, you can begin the process of developing this. Start by identifying your beliefs, expectations, thoughts, feelings and behaviors connected to the following aspects of persistence:

Have a Vision

"Cherish your visions and your dreams, as they are the children of your soul, the blueprints of your ultimate achievements."

Napoleon Hill

Persistence starts with a vision of the desired results. Seneca, the Roman philosopher and statesman, maintains, "Our plans miscarry because they have no aim. When a man does not know what harbor he is making for, no wind is the right wind." Lewis Carroll, the English author and mathematician, believes, "If you don't know where you are going, you'll probably end up somewhere else."

Stephen Covey explains, "How different our lives are when we really know what is deeply important to us, and keeping that picture in mind, we manage ourselves each day to be and do what really matters most." Joel Barker points out, "Vision without action is merely a dream. Action without vision just passes the time. Vision with action can change the world."

When you want to pursue a goal or build a dream, do you start with an unfettered vision or do you think of all the problems, sacrifices and effort that it's going to take to get where you want to go? The latter reminds me of a terrific response Ann Landers wrote to a man who was considering becoming a lawyer. In his letter, he lamented the fact that he was 36 years old and that he would be 40 by the time he completed Law School. Ann Landers asked him how old he would be in four years if he didn't go to Law School!

By an unfettered vision, I mean taking time to relax, close your eyes, and imagine all the wonderful gifts you will be choosing to pursue. Do not allow the garbage to come in, those upsetting thoughts that make you fearful and unsure of yourself; just tell yourself that you will work out the details at another time. Consider all the possibilities. Let loose that part of your brain that loves to dream.

I recommend to clients that they focus on the vision as often as possible, carving out time for this rewarding activity. The vision can sustain you when the going gets tough, boring, scary or frustrating. Your passion can help you keep your eye on the end game, as well as ensure that the journey of you and your little red wagon is very gratifying.

Transform Trouble into Opportunity
Albert Einstein's three rules of work:

- Out of clutter find simplicity
- From discord, find harmony
- In the middle of difficulty lies opportunity

Your attitude toward obstacles, criticism, setbacks, mistakes and failure is paramount in the development of the strength of persistence, as it is in so many of the strengths. Being afraid of encountering any of these, avoiding them whenever possible, is an entirely counterproductive approach. Victor Frankl, author of *Man's Search for Meaning*, explains, "What a man needs is not a tensionless state but rather the striving and struggling for some goal worthy of him. What he needs is not the discharge of tension at any cost, but the call of potential meaning waiting to be fulfilled by him."

I can promise you that 95% of the time when you are working toward a goal, you will experience at least one, but more likely many, of the above. It's your job in becoming persistent to normalize these, that is, see them as an inevitable part of the process, not a catastrophe. They are as common as inclement weather for you, me and everyone!

To reverse the deleterious effects of your response to any problem, first identify specifically the beliefs, thoughts, feelings and behaviors that manifest when each of these occurs. For example, what do you tell yourself and how do you feel after you've made a mistake? What are your beliefs about mistakes, failures and other problems? How does your behavior change in response to the occurrence?

It often helps to record these data. When you keep records of this sort, you're able to find less obvious and less familiar cognitions and behaviors that stand in your way. Next, you can address the ineffectual elements in your repertoire with techniques that empower you to make the necessary changes.

The person who really learns persistence is the one who views difficulties as challenges replete with all sorts of possibilities. Thus, it would be to your advantage to change your self-talk from that of the defeatist to that of the conquering hero. Use a compelling quote or your own strong statement to dispute the cognitions that immobilize your plans and dreams. The instructions for both cognitive and behavioral techniques are presented in Chapter 7.

1. Find the feedback in criticism

Elbert Hubbard, American philosopher, publisher and writer, warns us, "To avoid criticism, do nothing, say nothing, be nothing." Fear of criticism, a powerful antidote to persistence is, of course, attached to caring entirely too much about what others think about your performance and worth; it is also connected to an interpretation of the criticism as a personal indictment. This fear is a major impediment to stead-fastly moving through the steps en route to your goals and dreams.

Others have their own reasons for critiquing you or your plan. Some folks have your best interest at heart and will give you honest, constructive feedback. Such feedback can be very valuable. On the other hand, some people may not be best served by your success and tenacity, having perhaps an agenda that competes with yours.

Thus, it makes sense to evaluate the feedback and the motives of the person sending it your way; view it objectively as information that is worthy/not worthy of your assessment. And for heaven's sake, do not take it personally! William James, American psychologist and philosopher, says, "The art of being wise is the art of knowing what to overlook."

President Theodore Roosevelt, in an eloquent speech delivered at the Sorbonne in Paris in April, 1910, declares:

> It is not the critic that counts; not the man who points out how the strong

man stumbles, or when the doer of deeds could have done better. The credit belongs to the man who is actually in the arena, whose face is marred by dust and sweat and blood, who strives valiantly; who errs and comes short again and again; because there is no effort without error and shortcomings; but who does actually strive to do the deed; who knows the great enthusiasm, the great devotion, who spends himself in a worthy cause, who at best knows in the end the triumph of high achievement and who at worst, if he fails at least fails while daring greatly. So that his place shall never be with those cold and timid souls who know neither victory nor defeat.

2. Be undaunted by mistakes on the path to persistence

The Austrian psychiatrist, Alfred Adler, reminds us of a lesson to ponder:

What do you first do when you learn to swim? You make mistakes, do you not? And what happens? You make other mistakes, and when you have made all the mistakes you possibly can without drowning – and some of them many times over – what do you find – that you can swim? Well – life is just the same as learning to swim! Do not be afraid of making mistakes, for there is no other way of learning how to live!

I continue to find it curious that so many people expect to achieve their small and big dreams without making mistakes. Mistakes are a huge part of the learning curve of persistence. Be clear: mistakes are opportunities to learn. Everyone makes them. What counts most is your view of how they impact the situation. If you interpret a mistake as a personal shortcoming or a sign that you're pursuing the wrong dream, or that it's time to make a u-turn, it will likely result in the blunting or curtailing of your efforts to fortify yourself and keep moving.

Sure, you want to understand where you went wrong so you will not make the mistake even one more time, but interpreting it as a sign of your incompetence or a sign that you're barking up the wrong tree is absurd. Normalize mistakes in your belief system. James Joyce, the Irish writer and poet, proclaims, "A person's errors are his portals of discovery."

Choose an appropriate quote or make up your own statement to stealthily debate your thoughts and feelings of inadequacy; re-evaluate mistakes as critical information in the shaping of your path. Shakespeare got it right all those years ago: "There is nothing good or bad, but thinking makes it so."

3. View obstacles to persistence as normal and surmountable
Frank A. Clark concludes, "If you find a path with no obstacles, it probably doesn't lead anywhere." John Quincy Adams, the nation's sixth President, states, "Patience and perseverance have a magical effect before which difficulties disappear and obstacles vanish."

Obstacles are to be expected; don't be afraid of them. Think of them as availing you important information on the path to your chosen vision. They often present the opportunity to reevaluate your plan and recharge your battery. If you do not expect them, you'll spend a lot of time being frustrated. If you do expect them, you'll be way ahead of the game. Expectation minus reality = frustration!

Christopher Reeve, the late actor who battled back after a tragic horseback accident, explains, "I think a hero is an ordinary individual who finds the strength to persevere and endure in spite of overwhelming obstacles."

4. Treat failure as just another step on your way to the prize
Some people fear and avoid failure as if it is the ultimate catastrophe. It's not failure, but fear of failure that ravages a person's life and relegates one to the procrastination/ inaction trap. The most impressive success stories are of those folks who failed again and again, but who did not let failures affect their persistence, passion and optimism. They embraced flexibility and adaptability; they beat the odds by expecting to eventually triumph and by continuing to do whatever was necessary to prevail.

Truman Capote, the American writer of novels, non-fiction and plays, sees the bright side of failure: "Failure is the condiment that gives success its flavor." Lao-Tzu instructs us. "Failure is the foundation of success, and the means by which it is achieved." Abraham Lincoln counsels, "My great concern is not whether you have failed, but whether you are content with your failure." Michael Larser believes that, "Failure is the path of least persistence."

Thomas A. Edison lets us know, "Many of life's failures are people who did not realize how close they were to success when they gave up." And according to John

Christian Bovee, "A failure establishes only this, that our determination to succeed was not strong enough." In other words. a true failure occurs only when you allow yourself to quit. Most so-called failures are merely part of the learning curve in progress.

TAKE CONTROL OF THE JOURNEY TO YOUR DREAMS

It truly is your little red wagon. You can push it, pull it or just stand and look at it! When it comes to navigating your dream machine, you are the only one who can decide the destination and itinerary. Lao-Tzu tells us, "At the center of your being you have the answer; you know who you are and you know what you want."

Ditch the victim/self-pity mentality

Seeing yourself as a victim, as restricted in the options and the ability to make things go your way, obstructs the path to persistence. It is a form of self-pity. Helen Keller warns that, "Self-pity is our worst enemy and if we yield to it, we can never do anything wise in this world." Dr. Megan Reik, the Scottish philosopher, explains, "There are few human emotions as warm, comforting and enveloping as self-pity. And nothing is more corrosive and destructive. There is only one answer; turn away from it and move on."

Stop thinking and acting like a victim; no matter what has happened to you or who has done you wrong, it will not serve your goals to have the victim mentality. A victim, by definition is one who has been injured, destroyed, tricked or duped, and thus is on the reactive not proactive end of the equation.

Victims are often poisoned by resentment of others and/or self-denigration. If you have been seriously abused, physically or mentally, and cannot get past your injuries, I would recommend you seek professional help. This can be tough territory to go alone. Otherwise, get past it by looking at it from the power point. Power comes from letting these things go. Confucius reminds us that, "To be wronged is nothing unless you continue to remember it." Malachy McCourt asserts, "Resentment is like drinking poison and waiting for the other person to die."

Refuse to make excuses or use alibis

Excuses and alibis lead you down a seductive and thorny path to impotence. Don Wilder and Bill Rechin believe that, "Excuses are the nails used to build a house of failure." Ben Franklin notes that, "He that is good for making excuses is seldom good for anything else." Alan Cohen explains, "There are two kinds of people in the world; those who make excuses and those who get results. An excuse person will find any excuse why a job was not done and a results person will find any reason why it can be done."

Eric Hoffer enlightens us about alibis:

> There are many who find a good alibi far more attractive than an achievement. For an achievement does not settle anything permanently. We still have to prove that we are as good today as we were yesterday. But when we have a valid alibi for not achieving anything, we are fixed, so to speak, for life. Moreover, when we have an alibi for not writing a book and not painting a picture and so on, we have an alibi for not writing the greatest book and not painting the greatest picture. Small wonder that the effort expended and the punishment endured in obtaining a good alibi often exceed the effort and grief requisite for the attainment of a most marked achievement.

Excuses and alibis are tools of avoidance. You talk yourself out of facing the difficult, the fearful, the unknown, the boring; you grant yourself a pass citing specific reasons, and often quite persuasively so. Remember, in this excuse/alibi mentality, avoidance can be insidious and addictive. When you avoid something negative, you feel momentarily better and the excuse/alibi gets reinforced; it's about as easy as becoming hooked on chocolate or ice cream!

When you excuse yourself from an endeavor, check the excuse to see if your motives are connected to negative physical, mental or emotional manifestations that signal you to avoid rather than approach the situation. Be honest. In the milieus of therapy and coaching, I initiate these questions and then teach clients to ask themselves what is really operating here.

If your response uncovers some form of avoidance, figure out the precipitants such as fear, lack of confidence, an aversion to boredom or any other reason you might have for talking yourself out of action. Divide the task into smaller forward steps that improve the probability of your following through. Don't be concerned with how small your steps are. Abraham Lincoln discloses, "I am a slow walker but I never walk backwards."

Get rid of the idea of entitlement

Do you believe that the world owes you your dreams in short order and without sacrifice? Do you have the idea that things should be "fair" according to your self-serving definition? Do you think you are special and therefore different rules should apply to you? If your answer to any of these questions is yes, I have good news and bad news. The good news is that beliefs can be changed. The bad news is that your beliefs are out in left field, promoting ineffectiveness and probably great angst for you and others close to you.

It isn't really important how you arrived at this debilitating philosophy about your standing in the world and how things should be; what is important in pursuing persistence is that you overhaul this mentality. As in the other misguided cognitive approaches, you will need to determine general and specific cognitions and behaviors that support this debilitating dogma. Counter them with thoughts that are more in line with reality, thoughts that require that you act on your own behalf.

As teenagers say, "get a clue." Or as one of my clients once chose for her mantra, "Don't get stuck on stupid." Maurice Seitter tells us, "Too many people miss the silver lining because they are expecting gold."

Work on your belief system

Faulty belief systems confuse people and often prevent forward movement. In this chapter you'll find two supplements: the Chart on Persistence and Quotes to Dispute Faulty Thinking. Use these to identify self-defeating thoughts and beliefs. Then formulate a plan to make the appropriate changes. The information presented in Chapter 7 will be helpful in this undertaking.

Be deliberate about your plan of action

"Action is eloquence."

William Shakespeare

Once you have adjusted and fine tuned your attitude so that the garbage thinking has been replaced by your own positive pep talk, then it's prime time for the development of an action plan. There are a number of components in planning that will increase the probability of your becoming persistent. First, set clear, measurable goals; decide how many goals you can handle at any given time and the order in which you will address them. Consider a time frame that is reasonable and flexible.

Next, outline the steps you will be taking to reach your goal. The steps should be small enough not to overwhelm you, yet big enough to challenge you and reinforce your efforts as you complete them. Keep in mind that there will be times when it seems as if you're moving at a snail's pace. So be it. Keep records of your progress. Set up a quick, easy way to do this. Keeping records has been shown to be very helpful in the behavior change process.

Identify any behaviors in your repertoire that may compete with your forward march. Decide on ways to neutralize or change the behaviors which can trip you up. Remember, conventional wisdom suggests that if you can do a new behavior for three weeks, you may well have developed a habit. Of course, we all know that some habits take longer.

Consider what external factors might increase the probability of success. Do you need training in one area or another? A support system often makes a big difference. Spending time with positive people helps you maintain your energy and enthusiasm. Read supportive, motivational materials.

Each day, make a list of the activities you will accomplish toward your effort. My dad taught me to do the least appealing assignment first and then the next least appealing... and so on. By the middle of the day you're doing the fun stuff. Reward yourself for completed steps. Register your efforts, accomplishments and strengths in your internal dialogue. Be as supportive of yourself as you would of someone else you love.

NOW WHAT DO I DO?

This is an adventure of possibilities... all the wonderful possibilities that come with being persistent on your own behalf. Your mission is to develop the belief that you can do what needs to be done, commit to an informed course of action and promise yourself that giving up is not an option. The remainder of this chapter contains many strategies to help you achieve persistent beliefs and behaviors:

- The Chart on Persistence is an assessment tool to help you identify the beliefs and behaviors that need to be changed

- The Treasury of Motivators features several components that offer alternatives to tired old ways of thinking and believing including: Quotations to Dispute Faulty Thinking, poems, prose, songs, movies, and Motivational Quotes by subject category
- Techniques and information that are applicable for developing persistence (presented in Chapter 7)
- Recommendations on additional resources

It's time for an attitude adjustment… you can do it!!

CHART ON PERSISTENCE – BELIEFS AND BEHAVIORS

Use the following chart to determine the beliefs and behaviors that you need to change in order to fortify your persistence. Those in the left column promote persistence, while those in the right column deplete it. Make a list of all right column beliefs and behaviors that describe your repertoire, putting them in the order of those to be addressed first, second and so on.

How do you choose the order? There are a couple of ways. One is to start with the least threatening behavior change or the belief you think is the least difficult to change, and when the behavior change or belief is under your control, target the next behavior or belief on that scale, and so on. Another approach is to work on the thoughts and behaviors most likely to make a difference for you. When that one is stable, go to the next and so on. Your choice, your little red wagon, your life! Once you've identified what needs to be changed, review your options for modifying these, using all the tools in this book.

BELIEFS

Beliefs That Foster Persistence

1. Mistakes, disappointments, failures and obstacles are normal happenings in the course of seeking goals. Encountering these does not suggest incompetence, a reason for self-recrimination or a sign that the goal should be abandoned.

Beliefs That Hinder Persistence

1. Negative events mean that there is something wrong with me or my goal. I should give up if things get too tough.

2. I am capable of achieving my goals and dreams. I am not helpless.

2. No matter how hard I work, I do not believe I'm in control of my future.

3. I am responsible for my thoughts and behaviors; I have the ability to control my internal dialogue and habits. Learning new skills can help, even in the midst of difficulty.

3. I believe that I do not have control nor can I learn to have control over my thoughts and behaviors.

4. Goals and dreams take time, work and patience. No big deal.

4. If success does not come to me easily and in a time I think is reasonable, I should cut my losses and abandon the goal.

5. Criticisms, opinions and expectations of others should not have undue sway. Others cannot make me feel bad unless I allow it. I am responsible for my choices.

5. What others think of me is very important. I do not want to be criticized or embarrassed. I do not want to disappoint people who are important in my life.

6. Dreams and passion are very important to my health and happiness.

6. Dreams and passion are not necessary for health and happiness. Security makes me healthy and happy.

7. Strength comes from facing my fears and not using excuses to avoid what I find difficult or frightening. Facing fear is one way to take responsibility for my life.

7. Avoidance is often my best choice. Fear overwhelms me.

8. I refuse to believe I am a victim, even when others have treated me badly. The role of a victim is counterproductive to my goals and dreams.

8. If something bad happens to me, I need to find who is to blame. I am entitled to feel angry and resentful.

9. Boredom is inevitable in seeking goals; it's important to learn to tolerate it.

9. Boredom makes me miserable; I think I should avoid it whenever possible.

10. I don't believe in luck; I must make things happen myself.

10. Luck plays a major role in success and failure. If I'm not lucky, I won't achieve my goals and dreams.

11. Taking risks and committing to a course of action leads to success.

11. I am afraid to take risks and commit to a plan because the whole thing could end in failure.

12. It's better to think of possibilities instead of limitations.

12. It's too late or I am too old or the task is too big to start now.

BEHAVIORS

Behaviors That Foster Persistence

1. I have unfettered vision.

Behaviors That Hinder Persistence

1. I use most of my energy to worry about what could go wrong, what the negatives are about the vision.

2. I set clear, measurable goals and determine the steps needed to achieve those goals.

2. I wing it.

3. I commit to a course of action.

3. I focus on my fears. I choose to do nothing.

4. I make the necessary sacrifices to achieve my goals.

4. I keep score, obsess and resent the work that's necessary to reach my goals.

5. I identify behaviors and thoughts that compete with my progress. I make a plan to challenge these responses.

5. I keep thoughts and behaviors as usual. I believe "the devil you know is easier to take than the devil you don't know."

6. I am willing to delay gratification or reinforcement.

6. I give up if I have to wait too long.

7. I figure out positive ways to assess and react to criticism.

7. I am defensive, insulted and hurt by criticism. Criticism affects my choices.

8. I am creative about overcoming obstacles, mistakes and failures.

8. I let obstacles, mistakes and failures overwhelm me. I don't try to find methods for solving these difficulties.

9. I spend time with positive, supportive, proactive people.

9. I spend time with people who are negative, afraid and who would be upset if I succeeded.

10. I seek out information and help when I need it.

10. I am skeptical about seeking new information and help.

11. I recognize avoidance and procrastination patterns and set up manageable

11. I give myself a free pass on avoidance.

12. I maintain confidence in myself and do not take problems personally.

12. I keep asking myself, "why me?" when things go wrong.

13. I avoid an all or nothing, black or white approach. I consider a number of ways to view my strategies and expected results.

13. I stick by my perfectionism. There is only one way to do things and one acceptable outcome.

THE TREASURY OF MOTIVATORS

The Treasury of Motivators offers a wealth of persistence-generating words and thoughts. These can be helpful in maintaining your motivation and resolve on the journey to your chosen destinations. Choose the treasures that are meaningful and inspirational for you. You may also enjoy your own treasure hunt for pieces that are personally energizing and encouraging. Incorporate these into your everyday internal world. Some you can commit to memory; others can be placed in spots where you'll be reminded of what you want to believe and say to yourself. Focus on them often. Focus on "out with the garbage" and "in with your own special pep talk."

QUOTATIONS ON PERSISTENCE TO DISPUTE FAULTY THINKING

The following statements are harmful beliefs, expectations and thoughts that people repeat to themselves over and over again, often with strong conviction. The irrationality and toxicity of these debilitating cognitions are hardly ever questioned. These cognitions compete with the strength of persistence. You need to learn to talk back to them in meaningful and potent ways.

The goal is to reduce the frequency, intensity and duration of each of them by distraction methods and neutralize them by disputing or arguing with their content. Disputing can be done by utilizing pertinent, meaningful quotes provided for you in this chapter or by developing your own reality-based, effective retorts. Note that you may have cognitions in your repertoire that are not contained in this list of Harmful Beliefs.

Take a personal inventory of these in a separate notebook, then choose powerful quotes or other responses to question and contradict these cognitions. Remember, practice, practice, practice, so you're ready when they come for real! Besides increasing your readiness, practicing also decreases the potency of any noxious self-statements, aiding in your quest to build persistence. Distraction and disputing techniques are discussed in Chapter 7.

Harmful:

"Failures and disappointment mean there is something wrong with me or my goal. I should give up if things get too tough or discouraging."

Instead:

"Sure I am of this, that you have only to endure to conquer."
Sir Winston Churchill

"Through perseverance many people win success out of what seemed destined to be certain failure."
Benjamin Disraeli

"Disappointment should always be taken as a stimulant and never viewed as a discouragement."
C. B. Newcomb

"Whoever said you had a right to give up?"
Marian Wright Edelman

Harmful:

"I believe that if success does not come to me easily and in the time period that I expect, I should cut my losses and abandon my goal or dream."

Instead:

"Once you quit, it becomes a habit."
Vince Lombardi

"Your persistence is your measure of your faith in yourself."
Author Unknown

"It took me twenty years to become an overnight success."
Eddie Cantor

"Beware of the fury of a patient man."
Publius Syrus

"Quit now, you'll never make it. If you disregard this advice, you'll be halfway there."
David Zucker

Harmful:
"Mistakes are shameful and may mean I am not capable or suited to pursue this goal."

Instead:
"Mistakes are the portals of discovery."
James Joyce

"She had an unequalled gift of squeezing big mistakes into small opportunities."
Henry James

"Strong people make as many mistakes as weak people. The difference is strong people admit their mistakes, laugh at them, learn from them. That is how they become strong."
Richard Bach

"I have learned throughout my life as a composer chiefly through my mistakes and pursuits of false assumptions, not by my exposure to founts of wisdom and knowledge."
Igor Stravinsky

Harmful:
"I should be able to succeed without any real difficulties or obstacles."

Instead:
"History has demonstrated that the most notable winners usually encountered heart breaking obstacles before they triumphed. They refused to become discouraged by their defeats."
B. C. Forbes

"Every path has its puddle."
English Proverb

"It is the constant and determined effort that breaks down all resistance and sweeps away all obstacles."
Claude M. Bristol

"Every worthwhile accomplishment, big or little, has its stages of drudgery and triumph; a beginning, a struggle and a victory."
Mahatma Gandhi

"In the confrontation between stream and rock, the stream always wins – not through strength but by perseverance."
H. Jackson Brown, Jr.

Harmful:
"I have put so much into this goal. What if it doesn't pay off? Maybe I should cut my losses."

Instead:
"Many of life's failures are people who did not realize how close they were to success when they gave up."
Thomas Alva Edison

"Paralyze resistance with persistence."
Woody Hayes

"All right Mister, let me tell you what winning means… you're willing to go longer, work harder, give more than anyone else."
Vince Lombardi

"Others can stop you temporarily – you are the only one who can do it permanently."
Zig Ziglar

Harmful:
"No matter how hard I work and how long I stay at it, I do not believe I am in control of how things turn out."

Instead:
"When nothing seems to help, I go and look at the stonecutter hammering away at his rock perhaps a hundred times without as much as a crack showing in it. Yet at the hundredth and first blow it will split in two, and I know it was not that blow that did it – but all that had gone before."
Jacob Riis

"The Dictionary is the only place that success comes before work. Hard work is the price we pay for success. I think you can accomplish anything if you are willing to pay the price."
Vince Lombardi

"The mighty oak was once a little nut that stood its ground."
Author Unknown

"Spectacular achievements are always preceded by painstaking preparation."
Roger Staubach

"The miracle, or the power, that elevates the few is to be found in their industry, application, and perseverance under the prompting of a brave, determined spirit."
Mark Twain

Harmful:
"It's too late or I am too old or the task is too big to start now."

Instead:
"Vitality shows in not only the ability to persist but the ability to start over."
F. Scott Fitzgerald

"Don't tell me how rocky the sea is, just bring in the ship."
Vince Lombardi

"Don't say you don't have enough time. You have exactly the same number of hours per day that were given to Helen Keller, Pasteur, Michelangelo, Mother Theresa, Leonardo da Vinci, Thomas Jefferson and Albert Einstein."
H. Jackson Browne, Jr.

"It is a shameful thing for the soul to faint while the body still perseveres."
Marcus Aurelius Antonius

"It's a little like wrestling a gorilla. You don't quit when you're tired, you quit when the gorilla is tired."
Robert Strauss

Harmful:

"I believe that luck plays a major role in success and failure. No matter how persistent I am in pursuing my goal, if luck's not on my side, things won't happen the way I want them to."

Instead:

"Diligence is the mother of good luck."
Benjamin Franklin

"Half of life is luck; the other half is discipline – and that's the important half, for without discipline you wouldn't know what to do with luck."
Carl Zuckmeyer

"Good luck is another name for tenacity of purpose."
Ralph Waldo Emerson

"The only good luck many great men ever had was being born with the ability and the determination to overcome bad luck."
Channing Pollock

"I am a great believer in luck and I find the harder I work, the more I have of it."
Thomas Jefferson

Harmful:

"I am afraid to set goals, afraid to commit to something that will take so long and may end unsuccessfully."

Instead:

"You must have long-term goals to keep from being frustrated by short-term failures."
Charles C. Noble

"How different our lives are when we really know what is deeply important to us, and keeping that picture in mind, we manage ourselves each day to be and do what really matters most."
Stephen R. Covey

"The tragedy in life doesn't lie in not reaching your goal. The tragedy lies in having no goal to reach."
Benjamin Ways

"Give me a stock clerk with a goal and I will give you a man who will make history. Give me a man without a goal and I will give you a stock clerk."
J.C. Penney

"Goals allow you to control the direction of change in your favor."
Brian Tracy

PERSISTENCE IN POEMS, SONGS, MOVIES

Poems, songs and movies often touch people in ways that are motivating and inspiring. In my clinical practice I found that utilizing thematic works that resonate with an individual can be an effective and enjoyable way to keep his or her little red wagon moving forward – even in the most discouraging times and circumstances.

The Treasury of Motivators for persistence contains poems, motivational sayings, and a movie synopsis that might appeal to you on the quest to free yourself from the factors that prevent tenacity. After you've read them, choose the ones that have meaning for you, or go on your own search for a work that fits the theme of persistence.

Read the poems, sayings and movie synopses often; think about the theme every day. When you have a chance, watch the movie. When you are discouraged, disenchanted or afraid, use your Treasury of Motivators to bolster your spirits and faith in yourself.

Perseverance
By Sarah Orne Jewett

This wonderful poem can be accessed at http://www.public.coe.edu/~theller/soj/poe/persev.htm.

Polly is a child who is tenacious about finding a four-leaved clover. She searches an entire hayfield for this sign of luck. But the narrator tells her that bad luck does not come to one who works so hard. Her patience will serve her well in all circumstances.

The Rose
Lyrics by Amanda McBroom
Go to http://www.azlyrics.com/lyrics/bettemidler/therose.html

This song, beautifully performed by Bette Midler, was featured in the 1979 movie, *The Rose,* about the life of Janis Joplin. The words tell us of the many metaphors of love, such as it is a river, it is a hunger, it is a heart afraid of breaking, a dream afraid of waking that never takes the chance. But alas when you think there is no hope for you, "Just remember in the winter far beneath the bitter snows lies the seed that with the sun's love in the spring becomes the rose."

Persistence in the Movies – #1

If persistence were a man, his name would be Andy Dufresne. Actually, Andy is a movie character, but that's not important. What is important, and ultimately inspiring, is the utter persistence with which Andy pursues – and completes – a quest that most of us would have never begun.

Maybe you recognize Andy Dufresne. He's the main character (portrayed by Tim Robbins) in the 1994 Academy Award-nominated film *The Shawshank Redemption.* In the movie, Andy is a nondescript New England banker who's wrongfully convicted of murdering his wife and her lover. Sentenced to two life terms in Maine's Shawshank prison, Andy suffers the horrors of sadistic inmates, brutal guards and an immoral warden.

But soon it becomes clear that Andy has a special gift, a powerful characteristic that none of these forces can break down – and that's Hope. The conviction that better things lie ahead. Andy is convinced that, given his dire circumstances and Shawshank's deplorable conditions, he has a choice: either "get busy livin", or "get busy dyin." Andy chooses the former.

Once Andy decides to get busy living, he lets nothing prevent him from reaching his goal. He needs to get out of that prison and resurrect his life. Realizing that the walls at Shawshank are old and porous, he procures a small rock hammer, no bigger than a soup spoon, through the prison's bartering system. To everyone else, it's a tool he'll use to carve out chess pieces; to Andy, it's the key to his freedom.

Night after night, alone in his cell after lights out, Andy uses his diminutive rock hammer to dig at the wall of his cell, eventually creating a hole through which a man can crawl and concealing it with an oversized poster of that era's most desirable woman – Rita Hayworth. He crumbles the broken rock and transports it out to the prison yard in his pants pockets, slowly discarding it as he strolls the grounds.

Andy is allowed to keep his rock hammer because the thought of using it to tunnel out of Shawshank is preposterous – it would take a man "600 years," he's told by a fellow inmate. But Andy Dufresne is more than a man. He's a metaphor for what a man can accomplish when hope, ingenuity and courage are wrapped together in an impenetrable sheath of persistence. For without persistence, none of his other heroic traits can lead him to freedom.

Wearing that rock hammer down to a nub, it takes Andy close to 20 years to tunnel through Shawshank's wall, cleverly covering the opening with new posters of Rita Hayworth's successors: Marilyn Monroe and, in the end, Raquel Welch. At last, finished, Andy crawls through the wall and descends into a putrid sewer pipe the length of three football fields to eventual freedom.

The next time you want to achieve an important goal in life but think you face seemingly impossible odds, with obstacles you can't possibly overcome, take a moment to remember Andy Dufresne.

Persistence in the Movies – #2

Google the word persistence and you'll probably find a photo of Daniel E. Reutigger. Who is Daniel E. Reutigger? Does "Rudy" Reutigger ring any bells? Okay, let's drop the last name altogether. How about simply Rudy, which, you may recognize, is the nickname of a boy who has a crazy dream of playing football for the Fighting Irish of Notre Dame. Fact is, it's more than a dream… it's a quest. And when it comes to persistence, Rudy is someone to whom we should all pay close attention.

Yes, Daniel Reutigger is *Rudy*, whose larger than life story is captured in the emotional 1993 film of the same name, featuring actor Sean Astin in the title role. As a boy growing up in a steelworker town in rural Illinois, Rudy is the youngest member of a family that idolizes the University of Notre Dame and its storied football program. Rudy gets caught up in the fervor, and then some. Football and Notre

Dame become his passions. He memorizes the famous pep talks of legendary coach Knute Rockne. He fantasizes about stepping on that field in South Bend some day and suiting up for the blue and gold of Notre Dame.

Trouble is, no one else – parents, teachers or friends (save one, whom we'll get to) – even remotely shares his dream or offers any encouragement. And on top of that, Rudy is hardly a standout either on his high school football team or in the classroom. Athletically and academically, Rudy is not Notre Dame material; a career in the steel mill awaits, alongside his father and two older brothers.

But Rudy isn't ready to settle for a life in the steel mill. His dream continues to simmer below the surface, suddenly percolating one day when Pete, his best friend from high school and now a fellow steelworker, presents him with an authentic Notre Dame jacket. "You're the only one who took me seriously," Rudy tells Pete. "Having dreams is what makes life tolerable," replies Pete.

But it takes a tragic event for Rudy to bring his dream back to a full boil. Pete is killed in a mill accident, and Rudy is devastated. But instead of succumbing to the pain of losing his best friend, Rudy uses Pete's death as motivation to get back to the dream, to pursue his rightful place on the University of Notre Dame football team.

The next two years of Rudy's life epitomize what a person can accomplish when he persists! He doesn't have the high school grades to gain admission to the University, but he's given an opportunity by Notre Dame officials to prove his scholastic abilities by enrolling at nearby Holy Cross Community College. He introduces himself to the Notre Dame head football coach, the renowned Ara Parshigian, but fails to make an impression. He attempts to join booster clubs at Notre Dame but is turned away because he isn't enrolled. He lobbies for a job with the grounds crew at the football stadium just so he can stay close to the action. He strives to improve his grades at Holy Cross but still doesn't qualify for entry into Notre Dame.

Finally, after three semesters, Rudy is accepted by the University, and tries out for the football team as a non-scholarship walk-on player. "Walk ons" who are fortunate enough to even make the squad rarely suit up for a game, and they never play. But as we know by now, Rudy is just a little different. He's going to make the team, and he's going to get into at least one game before his playing days are through. During practice sessions, Rudy proves his mettle time and time again to the coaching staff and teammates, personifying what it means to have "heart", and shaming some of the gifted athletes who don't possess his passion and dogged persistence.

In the end, with the coaches and teammates solidly in his corner, Rudy defies all possible odds when new head coach Dan Devine puts him into the final play of the final game of the season against Georgia Tech – while Rudy's parents, brothers and friends cheer wildly from the stands. What an unbelievable (but believe it because it's true) testament to the incredible power of persistence!

MOTIVATIONAL QUOTES THAT BUILD A PERSISTENT ATTITUDE

Wise quotations about a specific subject can serve to teach you topical, proactive beliefs, expectations and thoughts to replace the reactive garbage that blocks your forward progress. For example, if believing in yourself needs work, find a quote that motivates you to look at yourself in a more positive way. Repeat it to yourself often, replacing your self-defeating mumbo jumbo.

On Persistence

"The difference between persistence and obstinacy is that one often comes from a strong will and the other from a strong won't."
Henry Ward Beecher

"In the confrontation between stream and rock, the stream always wins—not through strength but by perseverance."
H. Jackson Browne, Jr.

"Diligence is the mother of good luck."
Benjamin Franklin

"The measure of success is not whether you have a tough problem to deal with, but whether it is the same problem you had last year."
John Foster Dulles

"Everything comes to him who hustles while he waits."
Thomas Alva Edison

On Expectations

"You begin by always expecting good things to happen."
Tom Hopkins

"The definition of insanity is doing the same thing over and over and expecting different results."
Benjamin Franklin (among others)

"The problem is not that there are problems. The problem is expecting otherwise and thinking that having problems is a problem."
Theodore Rubin

"Expectation minus reality = frustration."
Author Unknown

On Failure/Success

"Most of us look at our successes in the same positive way. It's how we deal with our failures that determines what we get out of life."
Daniel Amen, M.D.

"I have missed more than 9000 shots in my career. I have lost almost 300 games. On 26 occasions I have been entrusted to take the game winning shot... and missed. And I have failed over and over and over again in my life. And that is why... I succeed."
Michael Jordan

"Rock bottom is good, solid ground, and a dead end street is just a place to turn around."
Buddy Buie and J.R. Cobb in their song, "Rock Bottom"

"Disappointment should always be taken as a stimulant and never viewed as a discouragement."
C. B. Newcomb

"Men succeed when they realize that their failures are the preparation for their victories."
Ralph Waldo Emerson

On Perfection

"Even the best needles are not sharp at both ends."
Chinese Proverb

"When you aim for perfection, you discover it's a moving target."
George Fisher

"Striving for excellence motivates you; striving for perfection is demoralizing."
Harriet Braiker

"Aim for success not perfection. Never give up your right to be wrong, because then you will lose the ability to learn new things and move forward with your life."
David Burns, M. D.

"Remember that fear always lurks behind perfectionism. Confronting your fears and allowing yourself the right to be human can, paradoxically, make you a far happier and more productive person."
David Burns, M.D.

EFFECTIVE, PRACTICAL TECHNIQUES FOR BUILDING PERSISTENCE

In order to change beliefs and behaviors that you have identified as problematic in the Chart on Persistence, you'll need to learn some specific concepts and techniques. These include:

- ✓ Principles of Behavior Change
- ✓ The Stress Response
- ✓ Abdominal Breathing
- ✓ Imagery Relaxation
- ✓ Progressive Muscle Relaxation (PMR)
- ✓ The Relaxation Response
- ✓ Systematic Desensitization
- ✓ Assertiveness
- ✓ Disputing
- ✓ Distraction

These techniques are discussed in detail in Chapter 7.

ADDITIONAL RESOURCES: RECOMMENDED READINGS AND WEBSITES

Recommended Readings:

Allen, D. (2001) *Getting Things Done: The Art of Stress-free Productivity*

Claiborn, J. and Pedrick, C. (2001) *The Habit Change Workbook*

Emmett, R. (2000) *The Procrastinator's Handbook: Mastering the Art of Doing it Now*

Fiore, N. (1989) *The Now Habit. A Strategic Program for Overcoming Procrastination and Enjoying Guilt-free Play*

Website:

http://www.authentichappiness.org

PERSISTENCE ENDNOTES

Pg. 90   Doskoch, P. "The Winning Edge." *Psychology Today,* Nov/Dec 2005.

Pg. 93   Cantor, N. and Sanderson, C.A.(1999) "Life task Participation and Well-Being: The Importance of Taking Part in Daily Life." In Kahlneman, Diener and Schwartz (eds), *Well-Being: The Foundations of Hedonic Psychology*

Pg. 95   Burns, D. (1980) *Feeling Good, The New Mood Therapy*. New York: Harper Collins Publishers

Chapter Four

ENTHUSIASM
Get Excited, Get Very Excited!

"The most powerful weapon on earth is the human soul on fire."

Field Marshall Ferdinand Foch
French author and military educator

I have a magnificent gift for you; call this strength enthusiasm, passion, vitality, zest or exuberance – whatever word means a quest in which you are on fire, delighted, deeply engaged, energetic, loving the pursuit, and actively taking your talents and emotions to their outer limits. The Latin *enthusiasmus* literally means "to be inspired by a god."

Some of you may have already embraced this gift. If passion is an integral and compelling part of your life, I extend my heartiest congratulations! You have discovered pure gold. For those who have missed out on this gift, it's never too late to start mining. Richard Chang tells us the welcome news: "Passion is not a privilege of the fortunate few; it is a right and a power that we all possess."

Passion is about living deeply, finding what inspires you, what sets your creative soul and emotional world ablaze, what brings purpose and meaning to your life. William Wallace, in the movie *Braveheart,* clamors, "Every man dies. Not every man really lives." The person with overflowing enthusiasm embraces the belief of Helen Keller that, "Life is a daring adventure or nothing at all," and thus makes it a mission to seize the incredible opportunity to live life to the fullest.

The importance of passion and enthusiasm as forces in the world has received much attention from those who have achieved greatness. Tennessee Williams, the distinguished American playwright, believes, "Enthusiasm is the most important thing in life." Federico Fellini, one of the finest film directors of all time declares, "There is no end. There is no beginning. There is only the infinite passion of life."

The British Prime Minister, Benjamin Disraeli, proclaims that, "Man is only truly great when he acts from his passions." And Ralph Waldo Emerson, the American poet, author and philosopher ardently maintains that, "Enthusiasm is the mother of effort, and without it nothing great was ever achieved."

I believe it is imperative for each of us to answer honestly the question posed by Friedrich Nietzsche, the Prussian philosopher: "Is life not a hundred times too short to bore ourselves?" If you agree with Nietzsche, the next step is to accept and follow the counsel given in the Hasidic saying: "Everyone should observe which way his heart draws him, and then choose that way with all his strength."

Sometimes pursuing your passion may seem like a preposterous and embarrassing undertaking. In the movie *Serendipity,* the main character, Jonathon Trager, follows his heart when it makes no sense at all. At a point when the effort appears to have come to a deeply disappointing dead-end, his friend, Dean Kansky, who writes obituaries for *The New York Times,* consoles him with these words of wisdom: "You know the Greeks didn't write obituaries. They only asked one question after a man died: Did he have passion?" Yes, passion is that important – important enough to risk looking like a damn fool!

THE REWARDS OF ENTHUSIASM AND PASSION

Enthusiastic, passionate people live well. They frequently experience excitement, success in attaining their visions and dreams, creativity, happiness and confidence. They are undaunted by obstacles and challenges, suffer few regrets and every now and then even accomplish the impossible. Paul Meyer tells us, "Whatever you vividly imagine, ardently desire, sincerely believe, and enthusiastically act upon must inevitably come to pass." Aeschylus announces, "When a man is willing and eager, the gods join in."

Success
Enthusiasm and passion promote success. Success, of course, is personally defined by each of us, just as the experience and source of our passion is distinctly individual.

Andrew Wood tells us that, "When Mark Twain was asked to explain his success in life he said, 'I was born excited.'" Passion is an energizer that goes a long way toward goal attainment, whatever the goal or dream happens to be, because we enjoy it and do not tire of it. It sustains us when the going gets tough, serving as high-test fuel for our journey of discovery, revving up the engine of our little red wagon so we can navigate the bumps and steep inclines.

George Washington Doane, the inspirational writer and poet, declares, "Enthusiasm is the element of success in everything. It is the light that leads and the strength that lifts people on and up in the great struggles of scientific pursuits and of professional labor. It robs endurance of difficulty, and makes pleasure of duty." Will Rogers, the American humorist and social commentator, suggests that, "If you want to be successful, it's just this simple. Know what you are doing. Love what you are doing. And believe in what you are doing."

In his book, *The Passion Plan*, Richard Chang explains, "Only when people are in touch with their passions do they use their heads to give shape and substance to their dreams. By linking the two in a process of self-evaluation and action, 'passioneers' use their greatest strengths to achieve their greatest goals." The term he has coined, "passioneers," refers to people who "are actively engaged in building their lives by pursuing their passion; they know no other way."

Genius, Creativity, Talent

Genius, creativity, talent and a consummated vision are the prolific progenies of those who follow their passions. Isaac Disraeli, the father of a British Prime Minister and author of *Curiosities of Literature* surmises, "Enthusiasm is that secret and harmonious spirit which hovers over the production of genius." Aldous Huxley, social critic and author of *Brave New World*, fervently declares, "The secret of genius is to carry the spirit of the child into old age, which means never losing your enthusiasm." And Eric Hoffer, a self-educated longshoreman, who rose to fame with the publication of many books, including *The True Believer* and *The Passionate State of Mind*, explains, "It sometimes seems that intense desire creates not only its own opportunities, but its own talents."

Creativity is nurtured and heightened by passion and enthusiasm. Leonardo da Vinci, often referred to as the "Renaissance Man," is convinced that, "Where the spirit does not work with the hand, there is no art." Ludwig van Beethoven captures the essence of the enthusiasm/creativity connection in his experience: "From the glow of enthusiasm I let the melody escape. I pursue it. Breathless, I catch up with it. It flies again, I seize it. I embrace it with delight. I multiply it then by modulations, and at last triumph in the first theme. The whole symphony."

Happiness

And then there is happiness. Psychologists Christopher Peterson and Martin Seligman tell us that vitality is one of the five strengths most highly correlated with happiness; it promotes positive emotions, energizes others, and contributes to physical and mental wellness. What a great and enjoyable elixir for body and mind! Albert Greenfield says, "Enthusiasm is mental sunshine that keeps everything in us alive and growing…"

Happiness is promoted when one is deeply involved in an activity. Earl Nightengale believes, "We are our very best, and we are the happiest when we are fully engaged in work we enjoy on the journey toward the goal we've established for ourselves. It gives meaning to our time off and comfort to our sleep. It makes everything in life so wonderful, so worthwhile."

Mihaly Csikszentmihalyi, the psychologist famous for his work on the concept of "flow," informs us that, "The happiest people spend much time in a state of flow – the state in which people are so involved in an activity that nothing seems to matter; the experience itself is so enjoyable that people will do it even at great cost, for the sheer sake of doing it." Sound a lot like passion? Yes, indeed. You can look forward to more on the intriguing concept of "flow" later in this chapter.

Energy

In their comprehensive book, *Character Strengths*, Christopher Peterson and Martin Seligman tell us the following about the strengths of vitality and energy:

Individuals with a high level of vitality would strongly endorse such statements as these:

- I feel alive and vital
- I have energy and spirit

- I nearly always feel awake and alert
- I feel energized
- I feel full of pep
- I rarely feel worn out

A person who is vital is energetic and fully functioning.

Do you feel these statements apply to you? What would you be willing to do to have this level of energy and spirit?

Effective Parenting

Passion plays an important role in parenting. Modeling passion, providing opportunities for exploration of many kinds, and encouraging a child's enthusiasm go a long way in preparing a child for life's journey. Rachel Carson, biologist and author of *Silent Spring*, believes, "If a child is to keep alive his inborn sense of wonder without any such gift from the fairies, he needs the companionship of at least one adult who can share it, rediscovering with him the joy, excitement and mystery of the world we live in."

The energy and excitement of the passion pursuit fortifies a child's ability to persist in the midst of life's twists and turns. Peter Duscoch, former editor of *Psychology Today*, explains that success in lofty goals is often more a result of passion-sustaining persistence than talent. Since passion is so important in producing success in children, parents should be exposing their kids to many types of activities to find what excites and engages them. Duscoch purports that finding their passions may even be more significant in long-term triumphs than remediating any educational challenges. Don't forget, Bill Gates dropped out of Harvard University – to start a company called Microsoft.

A DEARTH OF ENTHUSIASM AND PASSION

There are many folks in this world who live a safely dispassionate life. Their thinking goes something like this: "Feeling safe is the most important thing in the world to me. So what if I don't test the limits of my existence or take risks? Look what can happen when a person tries to follow his passion. My friend who loves music formed a band and he is as poor as the proverbial church mouse. That's just not how I see my life." Any guesses on which man is fulfilled and happy? My money is on the man in the band.

Some people allow themselves to be divorced from their passion by the metaphorical "golden handcuffs" of the corporate world because of financial security, stock options, a 401k, etc. If you hate your job, corporate or otherwise, but fear losing all the goodies that tie you to that existence, the ones that make you feel safe and secure, then eight or so hours of your day, five or more days a week, may be sadly devoid of this wonderful stimulant.

I have worked with many people in the corporate world and have heard too many times, "I only have five or 10 years to hold on and then I'll be free to enjoy my life." Good grief! There has to be much more to life than feeling safe. What often results from this capitulation to security is regret, disillusionment, a sense of helplessness and frustration. H.W. Arnold declares, "The worst bankruptcy in the world is the person who has lost his enthusiasm." And as Charles Kingsley says, "We act as though comfort and luxury were the chief requirements in life, when all we need to make us really happy is something to be enthusiastic about."

Many folks believe that their choices in life should be made almost entirely by appealing to reason and logic. Trouble indeed! Ray Bradbury warns us, "If we listened to our intellect, we'd never have a love affair. We'd never have a friendship. We'd never go into business, because we'd be cynical. Well, that's nonsense. You've got to jump off the cliffs all the time and build your wings on the way down." H. Jackson Browne affirms, "Sometimes the heart sees what's invisible to the eye."

A dearth of enthusiasm can make you cranky, tired, frustrated, bored, confused and overwhelmed with regret. For some this may result in a state of depression, often characterized by feelings of helplessness. You may be tempted to believe that the fault lies with others for whatever chagrin you are experiencing. Big mistake! It's your little red wagon, and if it's stuck in the mud, you're the only one who can rescue it, wash it, make it shine and get it moving with flair – whistling and chortling again.

If fear is the cold water extinguishing your passion and keeping you immobilized, keep in mind that fear is strengthened by the avoidance of whatever scares you, but is conquered by taking action toward the desired goal. This is the case even if your forward steps are measured and small. The person who lacks enthusiasm has to adopt the belief that she can make a difference for herself; then, she must find the courage to develop and execute a potent action plan. If fear is your Achilles heel, please believe that your life doesn't have to be controlled by this action stopper. You will not regret learning how to beat fear!

DEVELOPING ENTHUSIASM AND PASSION

One of the real joys of my profession is helping people identify and pursue what makes them feel alive. It's amazing to behold their discovery that with passion, they can have their cake and eat it, too! Passion and practicality do not have to be mutually exclusive entities; in fact, they actually enhance one another. You can follow your dreams and still support you family, spend time with loved ones, prepare for retirement, etc. What a deal!

I've come to relish that special look a person gets when identifying a true area of passion. There is only one other time I see that facial expression – when someone is thinking about or proclaiming profound love for another person or a beloved pet. I love that look! It's a countenance that expresses excitement and peace at the same time. It's as if the person has forged a deep connection with the life force within – that vital energy that continually circulates, that's seldom noticed and very rarely embraced whole-heartedly. What does it take to reach so deeply within?

ASK YOURSELF THE RIGHT QUESTIONS: AN INWARD LOOK

Spend time answering these questions as completely as you can. Answer them today, and again in a week. Explore your thoughts and feelings about the questions during the time in between.

- What are your strengths and gifts? Which ones do you enjoy the most? The 1–10 rating scale may be helpful here. One=no interest, enjoyment, 10=the ultimate interest, enjoyment.
- What activities or pursuits most interest you now? Use the 1-10 scale.
- What activities or pursuits most interested you in the past? Start with early childhood, followed by each succeeding stage; allow yourself to reminisce freely. What passions did you leave behind that might still excite and fulfill you? Any

idea why you left them behind?

- What gives meaning and purpose to your life right now?
- What would give meaning and purpose to your future? What would you like your legacy to be?
- What rejuvenates you when you are out of energy?
- What does success mean to you? What successes have you had in the past that really impressed you and made you feel alive?
- What are your values? What role do your values and beliefs play in your life of passion and purpose?
- What are your needs? Distinguish between needs and wants. Needs are those thing we must have to live; wants are not necessities, but desires.
- What factors get in the way of your passion pursuit: insecurity, perfectionism, discouragement from others, practical concerns?
- What exciting situations do you daydream about?
- What activities bring you abounding energy before, during and after?

DREAM, DREAM, DREAM AND DEVELOP A VISION

Dreaming and imagining what you want to accomplish and where you want to go – allowing your heart and mind to entertain all possibilities culminating in your vision – is profoundly important in achieving fulfillment and well-being. Sound a lot like optimism? Exactly. This facet of passion and enthusiasm pertains to the future; the hopes and beliefs about your ability to attain what you want out of life.

Soren Kierkegaard, the Danish philosopher and theologian, captures the essence of passion's gifts: "If I were to wish for anything, I should not wish for wealth or power, but for the passionate sense of potential – for the eye which ever young and ardent sees the possible. Pleasure disappoints possibility never."

Jonas Salk, discoverer of the polio vaccine, discloses that, "It is always with excitement that I wake up in the morning wondering what my intuition will toss up to me, like gifts from the sea, I work with it and rely on it. It is my partner." George Bernard Shaw believes, "Imagination is the beginning of creation. You imagine what you desire; you will what you imagine, and at last you create what you will."

Unleashing your imagination and its accompanying feelings helps you define the dream and believe the future belongs to you. And if you don't have a dream, where does that leave you? Think for a minute about the simplicity and wisdom in the following from the song "Happy Talk" in the movie, *South Pacific*. The Polynesian character Bloody Mary sings to Lieutenant Cable: "You got to have a dream; if you don't have a dream, how you gonna have a dream come true?"

No dreams, no vision. Helen Keller, the blind and deaf activist was asked, "Is there anything worse than being blind?" to which she answered, "Yes, a man with sight and no vision."

Gloria Steinem explains the importance and relevance of dreaming: "Without leaps of imagination or dreaming, we lose the excitement of possibilities. Dreaming, after all, is a form of planning." T. E. Lawrence posits that, "Those who dream by night in the dusty recesses of their minds wake in the day to find all was vanity, but the dreamers of the day are dangerous people, for they may act their dream with open eyes, and make it possible."

And Steven Spielberg confesses, "I don't dream at night, I dream all day; I dream for a living." Jiminy Cricket reminds us, "When you heart is in your dreams, no request is too extreme." And Walt Disney, who named Jiminy Cricket and brought him to life in movies, shares this advice: "If you can dream it you can do it. Remember this whole thing was started by a mouse."

To dream properly you have to put aside all those pesky worries. Say, for example, that you want to embark on a new career that has great potential to bring you tremendous joy and satisfaction. You start thinking about being a sport's writer, how wonderful it would be to cover football, baseball, golf, etc. The idea that someone would pay you to be in such an exciting environment sounds, well, too good to be true.

Just as you're dreaming away, you get this overwhelming feeling of dread. You say to yourself, "I have to be crazy to think like this. I'll have to go to school, be on a reduced income until I can land a position, people will think I've lost my marbles to give up my engineering job with its healthy income and stock options. I've taken myself so far in this field. People respect the work I do. What in the world am I thinking?" By ruminating about all the reasons why not, all the obstacles and sacrifices, by caring too much what other people think, you have single-handedly changed a dream into a nightmare. Great job!

Try this instead. Set aside some time to relax. Turn off the phone. Find a spot where no one will disturb you. Get really comfortable. Close your eyes and picture yourself as a sportswriter, or whatever passionate pursuit gets you into an enjoyable, exciting dream zone. If rotten, worrisome thoughts enter your head, passively let them go by telling yourself that you'll think about these later. But for now you are going to focus on the dream.

Sample all the terrific possibilities that this dream has to offer. Spend 10 to 15 minutes in your reverie. Repeat this exercise often. You'll be surprised what you learn by allowing the dream to unfold without the "garbage." Pay attention to the words of Paula Vaull Starr: "Reach high, for stars lie hidden in your soul. Dream deep, for every dream precedes the goal." Suzanne Zoglio, author of *Create a Life That Tickles Your Soul*, recommends, "Decorate the rooms of your mind as you would decorate a favorite retreat… with things that calm your spirit and fire your imagination… Dream until you get light-headed."

CONFRONT YOUR FEARS, BE WILLING TO TAKE RISKS

Following your passion can take mountains of courage. When your vision has taken form and your level of excitement is brimming, schedule some time to consider the changes and obstacles that may come when you pursue your passion. Make this activity short and focused, being careful and determined not to start ruminating.

You can be in control if you set firm boundaries on the time allotted and use distraction strategies to maintain control over disruptive thinking. Should the rumination about the negatives begin, put your brain in time-out as you would a child who's misbehaving. Distraction techniques, such as the Self-Control Triad detailed in Chapter 7, are examples of time-out for the errant human brain. Remember, you get to choose what goes on between your ears!

Rate the potential changes and obstacles on two scales. First, on a 1-10 scale, with 10 being the worst on the "Awful Scale," how adversely would it affect you if such and such a change took place or if you had to deal with such and such an obstacle? Second, on a 1-10 scale, with 10 being the greatest probability on the "Probability

Scale," how likely is it that this change will occur or how likely is it that this obstacle will stand in your way? Be objective! If you have trouble being objective, ask a mentor or wise friend for his or her opinion.

If a change or an obstacle is high on both scales, consider if it is a deal breaker or just a problem to be solved. Before you relegate it to the deal breaker category, try using disputing skills to rope these into reality (discussed in Chapter 7). It often helps to break your concerns into behavioral steps rather than be overwhelmed by the sheer magnitude of your undertaking. Explore creative solutions. Consult with people who have already accomplished what you want to do. Ask to be mentored if possible. Give your dream a real chance.

Some people give up because it's habitual – they've learned to take the path of least resistance again and again. It's pretty darn easy to become brilliant at avoiding risk-taking. Imagine you're advising a friend who wants to follow a new and exciting course of action. How would you counter his or her objections and misgivings?

According to Suzanne Zoglio, "Beyond the familiar... just past fear... that's where life expands... when you take a risk, learn something new, or move into places you haven't been before, your life is never the same. Moving through the fear gives you confidence, and experiencing the joy offers a promise. You know you can and you know it's worth it."

If you've developed a behavior pattern in which you're frozen by fear, pay attention to an approach called "systematic desensitization," or exposure learning (Chapter 7), to overcome the avoidance trap. By not allowing fear to deter you from your quest of passion and purpose, you'll afford yourself a special chance for growth and fulfillment. Following your passion means being willing to take the necessary risks. For your own sake, make it your mission to be brave and proactive! Take Helen Keller's sage advice: "One can never consent to creep when one feels the impulse to soar."

IDENTIFY YOUR PURPOSE AND VALUES

What is meaningful to you? What are your values? What would bring you fulfillment and self-respect and, at the same time, imbue you with wonder and excitement?

Do you experience great satisfaction from helping others or creating a masterpiece or inventing something? What do you want to be remembered for?

A major component of passion is purpose, explained all those years ago by the Roman poet, Virgil, born in 70 B.C. "Your profession is not what brings home your paycheck. Your profession is what you were put on earth to do. With such passion and such intensity that it becomes a spiritual calling."

Oprah Winfrey contemplates, "The work of your life is to discover your purpose and get on with the business of living it out. The only courage you need is the courage to follow your passion." Marian Wright Edelman, founder of the Children's Defense Fund in 1973, which supports the causes of poor, minority and handicapped children, reflects on purpose in her life: "I'm doing what I think I was put on earth to do. And I'm really grateful to have something that I'm passionate about and that I think is profoundly important." A magnificent, powerful combination: the alignment of purpose, values and passion.

To follow your purpose, you must believe in both that purpose and yourself. Pablo Picasso was encouraged to be a believer: "My mother said to me, 'If you become a soldier, you'll be a general, if you become a monk, you'll end up as Pope.' Instead, I became a painter and wound up as Picasso." Purpose comes in so many forms and honestly is quite a personal journey. Your purpose must be discovered and nurtured by you. As Tom Thiss suggests, "Having a purpose is the difference between making a living and making a life."

And how do you discover your purpose? Howard Thurman recommends, "Don't ask what the world needs. Rather ask – what makes you come alive? Then go and do it! Because what the world needs is people who come alive." Marcia Weider suggests, "You can come to understand your purpose in life by slowing down and feeling your heart's desires." What could you do or be a part of doing that would be fervently celebrated in the deepest part of you – today and for many days to come? Answer that one and you will have defined your purpose.

LEARN MORE ABOUT FINDING FLOW

In his book, *Flow: The Psychology of Optimal Experience* (1990), Mihaly Csikszentmihalyi, a former chairman of the Department of Psychology at the University of Chicago and current professor at Drucker School of Management, has identified and researched a state he calls "flow," a state which has many of the elements of passion and enthusiasm. The concept of flow, according to Csikszentmihalyi, involves a subjective state which commonly occurs in people when they experience a certain type of internal order.

This internal order develops when one is engrossed in a challenging activity and believes that he or she has the ability to work through it effectively. The primary goal is to master and enjoy the activity simultaneously. There is total focus and engagement in the endeavor; time slows down, and the person achieves a complete clarity of goals.

The feelings experienced are so positive that the person wants to do the activity again and again. Flow is about the way people feel when what they are doing is working so well or when they are enjoying themselves so much that they lose themselves in the activity. Csikszentmihalyi posits three requirements for a state of flow to occur: there must be clear-cut goals; there must be fast, accurate feedback on the progress toward the goals; and the level of challenge must be commensurate with the person's skill level. Flow can occur in many activities such as athletics, work or creative endeavors. It's about being in the moment, being engaged, ebullient and productive.

In an interview with Elizabeth Debold in 2002, titled "Flow with Soul," Csikszentmihalyi relates interesting findings that positioned him on the path to understanding flow. He asked people in a variety of activities, including chess, basketball, rock climbing and music, to explain how they were feeling and what was going on for them when the activity in which they were engaged was moving along quite well. His prediction had been that there would be great diversity in their descriptions. But alas, such was not the case. The focus in most of the interviews was on the quality of what was transpiring for them.

People talked about being completely focused and involved; they knew what needed to be accomplished each step of the way. They reported that there was continuous, rapid and exact feedback on their performance and that they were being challenged but not overpowered by the demands of the task. Their usual worries were gone during this period.

Since these interviews in the early 1970's, ten thousand people in many places and cultures worldwide, engaged in a variety of activities, have reported the same phenomena. Their experiences are fundamentally the same. Fascinating indeed! For anyone interested in more detailed information on this subject, Dr. Csikszentmihalyi has authored a number of other books, including: *Creativity: Flow and the Psychology of Discovery and Invention* (1997) and *Good Business: Leadership, Flow and the Making of Meaning* (2004). Some of these titles are also available in audio formats.

ADOPT AN OPTIMISTIC ATTITUDE

An optimistic attitude is essential in the cultivation of passion. Helen Keller fervently believes that, "No pessimist ever discovered the secret of the stars, or sailed to an uncharted land, or opened a new doorway for the human spirit." The major elements of optimism to remember and embrace are:

- Believe you are a force in your future
- Believe that you deserve to be successful and live passionately
- Look far and wide for opportunities
- Be undaunted by obstacles, setbacks and failures; use them to your advantage
- Accept things that are out of your control
- Focus on what is going well and what has worked for you
- Appreciate all the good things in your life
- Believe you are capable of many great things. Thomas Alva Edison, perhaps the most prolific inventor of all time declares, "If we did all the things we were capable of doing, we would literally astound ourselves." James T. McKay tells us, "No matter what the level of your ability, you have more potential than you can ever develop in a lifetime."
- Believe that your journey is unique and ongoing. keep in mind the advice of Mihaly Csikszentmihalyi: "A joyful life is an individual creation that cannot be copied from a recipe." And from Walt Whitman: "All life is an experiment." Use the tools to define your creation. Experiment, experiment, experiment!

TAKE RESPONSIBILITY FOR YOUR PASSION AND ENTHUSIASM

Passion is a gift and a responsibility. Passion and persistence are mutually supportive strengths; that is, when one is pursuing passion, the likelihood of being persistent is greater. When one is decidedly persistent, passion has a better chance of being discovered and maintained. Thus, all the nuts and bolts that go with persistence pertain here.

- Develop reasonable expectations about how the world works. Things take time, patience and planning. Following a passionate path may not occur in the time frame you would like. Oh well!
- Do what needs to be done; don't wait for others to get the ball rolling. Remember what Reggie Leach points out: "Success is not the result of spontaneous combustion. You must set yourself on fire." Gordon Parks suggests that, "Enthusiasm is the electricity of life. How do you get it? You act enthusiastic until you make it a habit."
- Do an assessment of your cognitive and behavioral strengths and weaknesses. Identify specific thoughts, beliefs and behaviors that compete with your dreams and goals, as well as those that strengthen and support the desired outcomes.
- Formulate a plan for making the necessary cognitive and behavioral changes (see Chapter 7).
- Define the specific steps you'll take to reach your goal. As the Swedish Proverb goes, "God gives every bird a worm, but He does not throw it in the nest." You have to spell out how you're going to get to where you want to go, including back-up plans if things stall.
- Reflect often on your choices, level of excitement and fulfillment. Things change and so do you. Change is not a problem, but ignorance of change and its ramifications can stall your little red wagon. Change is not something to fear. It is something that can re-energize you if you see it for its possibilities. So beware of internal and external changes that may affect your ongoing pursuit of a life filled with enthusiasm.

DON'T ALLOW ANYONE'S EXPECTATIONS OF YOU TO INTERFERE

I'm referring here to unreasonable expectations you may have for yourself as well as the unhelpful expectations others have of you. Expectations imbedded in perfectionism need to given the heave-ho. I stress the importance of identifying perfectionism because I've witnessed the emotional destruction that this belief system can exact.

Believing that only one outcome – the perfect one – is acceptable is a body and brain drain that's incompatible with the emotional and creative freedom of passionate living. Think about it for a moment. If something has to be done to a tee, there's not much room for exploration and discovery. As Debbie Ford suggests, "Our society nurtures the illusion that all the rewards go to the people who are perfect. But many of us are finding out that trying to be perfect is costly."

Costly, debilitating and not much fun! Keep in mind that the perfectionist is worried about all the details of the outcome. That's a powerful way to put the fire out. Perfectionists often bristle when given criticism, which, even when constructive, may be taken as a personal affront. This circumstance can marginalize growth and be a real action stopper. Charles A. Cerami has an opinion I share: "Most great men and women are not perfectly rounded in their personalities but are instead people whose driving enthusiasm is so great it makes their faults seem insignificant."

Besides being a slave to our own ridiculous self-expectations, we often are held hostage by the way others see us and wish us to behave. Keep in mind that when it comes to your exuberance and your little red wagon, other people may be clueless, or may not care or may even have contravening ideas that serve their own selfish purposes. The bottom line is, figure out what expectations are conducive to paving the path of your heart, and then go for it. Be assertive with others when they are over the boundary lines of your personal rights and responsibilities.

SHARE, MODEL ENTHUSIASM; SPEND TIME WITH ENTHUSIASTIC PEOPLE

Enthusiasm has abundant social value as a connector and a motivator. You can share it with others by modeling it and by creating circumstances that encourage others to see its possibilities and reap its benefits. You can be on the receiving end by choosing to be with people who are getting a kick out of life. Edward Bulwer-Lytton posits that, "Nothing is so contagious as enthusiasm; it moves stones, it charms brutes. Enthusiasm is the genius of sincerity, and truth accomplishes no victories without it."

It's a wonderful goal to model and share with your children. Margaret Ramsey MacDonald recommends that, "Whatever you do, put romance and enthusiasm into the life of your children." Enthusiasm and passion bolster children with grit – the wherewithal to keep going when things go awry. Henry Ford explains that,

"Enthusiasts are fighters. They have fortitude. They have staying abilities. Enthusiasm is at the bottom of all progress! With it there is accomplishment. Without it there are only alibis." And F. Scott Fitzgerald, the Irish American novelist, contends that, "Vitality shows in not only the ability to persist, but the ability to start over."

If you want to promote cooperation and teamwork, enthusiasm is a smart way to go. Paul J. Meyer posits that, "Enthusiasm is the way you trigger other people's emotions so they instinctively help and support you." Franklin Field believes, "The simplest man fired with enthusiasm is more persuasive than the most eloquent man without it." Charles Schwab discloses, "I consider my ability to arouse enthusiasm among men the greatest asset I possess."

READ, RESEARCH, SHADOW OTHERS, FIND A MENTOR

You can find passionate people wherever you are and in whatever endeavors energize you. William Shakespeare says, "Passion I see is catching." Just as with the other strengths, the more time you spend with folks of the passion persuasion, the more likely you are to get caught up in it. Personally, I have found mentoring and being mentored promote learning, growth and a high level of excitement.

Shadowing involves spending time just watching someone being active in an undertaking of potential interest to you. This is a technique often recommended in career counseling. It can be helpful in the first stages of deciding if some avenue is for you, as well as in later stages when you want your enthusiasm to be reinforced.

USE THE BREAKOUT PRINCIPLE WHEN YOU GET STUCK

A fascinating book by Herbert Benson, M.D. and William Proctor, *The Breakout Principle,* offers intriguing possibilities and information for the pursuer of passion and peak experiences. Briefly summarized, "The Breakout Principle" refers to a powerful mind-body phenomenon that occurs when one is experiencing a hard mental or physical struggle and "backs off" from the activity.

This "backing off" often triggers an improvement in the ability to have a peak experience. Benson and Proctor suggest that this powerful biological switch can produce "greater mental acuity, enhanced creativity, increased job productivity, maximal athletic performance and spiritual development."

Benson found that the "backing off" or "letting go" that often precedes the breakout may cause the release of nitric oxide throughout the body. Nitric oxide counters the negative effects of the stress hormone, norepinephrine, severing prior mental patterns, even those that occur during high levels of stress and emotional trauma. By so doing, the way is opened up for peak experiences of many kinds.

NOW WHAT DO I DO?

This is an adventure of possibilities… all the wonderful possibilities that come with embracing enthusiasm with your whole heart. Your mission is to develop the belief that you can do what needs to be done, commit to a course of action and promise yourself that giving up is not an option. The reminder of this chapter contains many strategies to help you achieve enthusiastic beliefs and behaviors, including:

- The Chart on Enthusiasm is an assessment tool to help you identify the beliefs and behaviors that need to be changed
- The Treasury of Motivators features several components that offer alternatives to tired old ways of thinking and believing: Quotations to Dispute Faulty Thinking, prose, movie synopses and motivational quotes
- Techniques and tools that are applicable to developing enthusiasm and passion (presented in Chapter 7)
- Recommendations on additional resources

It is attitude adjustment time… you can do it!

CHART ON ENTHUSIASM – BELIEFS AND BEHAVIORS

Use the following chart to determine the beliefs and behaviors that you need to change in order to fire up your enthusiasm. Those in the left column promote enthusiasm, while those in the right column deplete it. Make a list of all right column beliefs and behaviors that describe your repertoire, putting them in the order of those to be addressed first, second and so on.

How do you choose the order? There are a couple of ways. One is to start with the belief or behavior that you think will change with the most ease and when that one is under control, target the next one on that scale and so on. Or you can start with the belief or behavior you think will make the most difference and when that one is under control continue with the next one on this scale, and so on. Either way gets you on the path. Your choice, your little red wagon, your life! Once you've identified what needs to be changed, review your options for modifying these using the tools presented in Chapter 7.

BELIEFS

Beliefs That Foster Enthusiasm

1. I believe that exploring possibilities and dreaming about what excites me are proactive and productive ways to expand my life.

2. Change is exhilarating and replete with opportunities.

3. Engaging in exciting, fulfilling activities will have a positive impact on my future.

4. Mistakes, obstacles and failures are part of the path of passion and purpose and are not to be feared.

5. Living passionately is my right and my responsibility.

6. Passion and persistence are compatible. Goals take time, effort and patience.

7. Trying to be perfect competes with passion and enthusiasm.

Beliefs That Hinder Enthusiasm

1. I consider possibilities and dreaming to be a waste of my time and energy.

2. Change is upsetting and often means I have to give up things I don't want to give up.

3. Being practical means doing what is expedient, not necessarily what is exciting.

4. I should avoid following my passion because it is risky business. Taking chances means I can get hurt.

5. Passionate living is a frivolous approach to life.

6. Passion and persistence don't go together.

7. Doing things perfectly is more important to me than doing what is exciting.

| 8. I believe it is important to take risks. | 8. Safety is more important to me than excitement. |

BEHAVIORS

Behaviors That Foster Enthusiasm	*Behaviors That Hinder Enthusiasm*
1. I dream, dream, dream and formulate a vision.	1. I am practical. I don't waste time on dreaming.
2. I commit to a course of action and develop a plan with goals and steps to increase my passion.	2. Whatever I do, I don't take proactive steps to become excited.
3. I identify thoughts, beliefs, expectations and behaviors that compete with my passion. I utilize strategies to change the problem responses.	3. I allow defeatist thoughts and behaviors to control my life.
4. I try new experiences of all kinds.	4. I stick with the same 'ole same 'ole.
5. I spend time with enthusiastic people and people who can mentor me.	5. I don't make it a point to be with or be mentored by passionate people.
6. I have an internal dialogue or mantra with which I promote my dedication to a life of passion.	6. I stick with my familiar thoughts, worries and fears.
7. I manage fear proactively and commit to taking risks – with a plan for doing so.	7. I allow fear to take the fun and purpose out of life.

THE TREASURY OF MOTIVATORS

The Treasury of Motivators offers a wealth of enthusiasm-generating words and thoughts. These can be helpful in maintaining your motivation and resolve on the journey to your chosen destinations. Choose the treasures that are meaningful and inspirational for you. You may also enjoy your own treasure hunt for pieces that are personally energizing and encouraging. Incorporate these into your everyday internal world. Some you can commit to memory; others can be placed in spots where you'll be reminded of what you want to believe and say to yourself. Focus on them often. Focus on out with the garbage, and in with your own special pep talk!

QUOTATIONS ON ENTHUSIASM THAT DISPUTE FAULTY THINKING

The following statements are harmful beliefs, expectations and thoughts that people repeat to themselves over and over again, often with strong conviction. The irrationality and toxicity of these debilitating cognitions are hardly ever questioned. These cognitions compete with the strength of enthusiasm. You need to learn to talk back to them in meaningful and potent ways.

The goal is to reduce the frequency, intensity and duration of each of them by distraction methods and to neutralize them by disputing or arguing with their content. Disputing can be done by utilizing pertinent, meaningful quotes provided for you in this chapter or by developing your own reality-based, effective retorts. Note that you may have cognitions in your repertoire that are not contained in this list of Harmful Beliefs.

Take a personal inventory of these in a separate notebook, then choose powerful quotes or other responses to question and contradict these cognitions. Remember, practice, practice, practice, so you're ready when they come for real! Besides increasing your readiness, practicing also decreases the potency of any noxious self-statements, aiding in your quest to be more courageous. Distraction and disputing techniques are discussed in Chapter 7.

Harmful:
"There is no time for enthusiasm and passion. I have obligations and problems to solve."

Instead:
"The worst bankruptcy in the world is the person who has lost his enthusiasm."
H. W. Arnold

"If you aren't fired with enthusiasm, you will be fired with enthusiasm."
Vince Lombardi

"Desire creates power."
Raymond Hollingwell

"Life is too short to be little. Man is never so manly as when he feels deeply, acts boldly, and expresses himself with frankness and fervor."
Benjamin Disraeli

"A strong passion for any object will ensure its success, for the desire of the end will point out the means."
Henry Hazlett

Harmful:
"I don't want to get my hopes up. So I choose safe goals to avoid disappointment and despair."

Instead:
"Get excited about your dream. This excitement is like a forest fire — you can smell it, taste it, and see it from a mile away."
Denis Waitley

"If you care enough for a result, you will most certainly achieve it."
William James

"Enthusiasm is the glory and hope of the world."
Bronson Alcott

"The world belongs to the enthusiast who keeps cool."
William McFee

"There is real magic in enthusiasm. It spells the difference between mediocrity and accomplishment."
Norman Vincent Peale

Harmful:
"I am afraid of what others will think of me if I do what really energizes and excites me."

Instead:

"Great spirits have always encountered violent opposition from mediocre minds."
Albert Einstein

"Do it no matter what. If you believe in it, it is something very honorable. If someone around you or your family does not understand it, then that is their problem. But if you do have a passion, an honest passion... just do it."
Mario Andretti

"Enthusiasm is the way you trigger other people's emotions so they instinctively help and support you."
Paul J. Meyer

"No man who is enthusiastic about his work has anything to fear from life."
Samuel Goldwyn

Harmful:

"It would probably be a waste of my time and energy to follow my passion and dreams."

Instead:

"When work, commitment, and pleasure become one and you reach that deep well where passion lives, nothing is impossible."
Author Unknown

"A rock pile ceases to be a rock pile the moment a single man contemplates it, bearing within him the image of a cathedral."
Antoine De Saint-Exupery

"If you want to build a ship, don't herd people together to collect wood and don't assign them tasks and work, but rather teach them to long for the endless immensity of the sea."
Antoine De Saint-Exupery

"A bird doesn't sing because it has an answer, it sings because it has a song."
Maya Angelou

"Imagination is the beginning of creation. You imagine what you desire; you will what you imagine, at last you create what you will."
George Bernard Shaw

ENTHUSIASM IN PROSE, MOVIES AND QUOTES

Prose, movies and motivational sayings often touch people in ways that are meaningful and inspirational. In my clinical practice I found that utilizing thematic works that resonate with individuals is an effective and enjoyable way to keep their little red wagons moving forward – even in the most discouraging times and circumstances. The Treasury of Motivators for enthusiasm contains prose, a movie synopsis and motivational quotes that might appeal to you on your quest to free yourself from the ravages of indifference. After you've read them, choose the ones that have meaning for you, or go on your own search for a work that fits the theme of enthusiasm. Read these often; think about the theme every day. When you have a chance, watch the movie. When you are discouraged, disenchanted or afraid to be enthusiastic, use your Treasury of Motivators to bolster your spirits and faith in yourself.

There is Vitality...

Martha Graham, the American dancer, choreographer and pioneer of modern dance, spoke to Agnes de Mille about vitality. According to Ms. De Mille in her 1991 biography, *Martha, the Life and Work of Martha Graham,* "The greatest thing she ever said to me was in 1943... I was bewildered and worried that my entire scale of values was untrustworthy. I confessed that I had a burning desire to be excellent, but no faith that I could be. Martha said to me quietly:

> There is a vitality, a life force, an energy, a quickening that is translated through you into action, and because there is only one of you in all of time, this expression is unique. And if you block it, it will never exist through any other medium and it will be lost. The world will not have it. It is not your business to determine how good it is nor how valuable nor how it compares with other expressions. It is your business to keep it yours clearly and directly, to keep the channel open. You do not even have to believe in yourself or your work. You have to keep yourself open and aware to the urges that motivate you. Keep the channel open. ...No artist is pleased. [There is] no satisfaction whatever at any time. There is

only a queer divine dissatisfaction, a blessed unrest that keeps us marching and makes us more alive than others.

Enthusiasm in the Movies

I'd be willing to wager that most people can name something, at least one thing, that gets their enthusiasm juices flowing and serves as the answer to the question, "if you could do or be just one thing in your life, what would it be?" In fact, I bet a lot of people who pay attention to their passions could name more than one. Concert pianist? Possibly. Ironman triathelete? Why not? Master chef? Let's get cookin'! Major league ballplayer? If you can dream it, you can do it!

Of course, some dreams are a little more challenging than others. But for my money, your passion, your enthusiasm for what you really want in life is a strength you'll need to possess if you want any chance of turning your dreams into reality. It's a strength that Ray Kinsella had, and you know what happened to Ray. You know, that is, if you're familiar with the inspirational 1989 movie, *Field of Dreams*, starring Kevin Costner, Amy Madigan, James Earl Jones, Ray Liotta and Burt Lancaster. If you need a refresher course on the strength of enthusiasm, you can't do much better than this classic film.

There are baseball players in it, but it's more than a baseball story. There's an Iowa farmer, a Pulitzer Prize-winning author and a small town doctor in it too, but it's not about what they do, either. What the movie is about – and what it ultimately holds for you and me – is a fantastic story about people who are finally able to fulfill their dreams by allowing themselves to follow their passions.

As the film opens, Ray Kinsella (Kevin Costner) is a 36-year-old husband and father who does the "one crazy thing in his life:" he buys a farm near his wife's Iowa hometown and begins harvesting corn for a living. But farming is light years away from Ray's roots in Brooklyn, New York – where he was an avid Dodger fan simply because his father, John, was totally dedicated to the New York Yankees.

You see, John had been a minor league ballplayer whose dream of playing in the big leagues went unfulfilled, so Ray became his surrogate and was force-fed the game from an early age. Not that Ray didn't like baseball, he did... it was his father he didn't like, and he stated as much when he left home abruptly at the age of 17.

"I could never respect anyone whose hero was a criminal," Ray exclaimed to his father, referring to John's favorite player "Shoeless" Joe Jackson who, as a member of Chicago White Sox, was accused of accepting bribes to throw the 1919 World Series – and was subsequently banned from baseball forever. Eventually, Ray came to regret how he treated his father, but he never had the chance to say "I'm sorry" or to "have a catch" with his Dad. He returned home only to attend his father's funeral many years later.

Anyway, back on the farm and working in his corn field, Ray hears a voice, whispering, *"If you build it, he will come."* He hears it again, and again. In fact, he's the only one who can hear it, and he thinks he's going nuts. Days go by and he can't stop thinking, "build what?" and "who will come?" Late one night, while looking out the window, Ray sees a vision of a baseball field where his corn is growing, complete with night lights, seating, fences, grass, the whole works. Ray believes that the voice is telling him to build a ball field so that Shoeless Joe Jackson can play baseball again.

Of course, if Ray didn't plow under half his corn to build a baseball diamond, the story would end here. Using all their savings, Ray and his family do another crazy thing – all under the bewildered stares of the town folk who've come to watch a cornfield become a ball field.

Months pass, winter comes and goes, but nothing happens with, or on, the field. Finally one spring day, a solitary figure in a baseball uniform appears, and Ray goes out to introduce himself. It's the young Shoeless Joe Jackson (Ray Liotta), looking like he did in 1919. As Shoeless Joe fields some popups and takes a few swings at Ray's pitching, dreams start to become real. "God I miss this game," says Shoeless Joe. "I'd have played for food money. Hell, I'd have played for nothing."

Now things are taking shape. Shoeless Joe's passion for the game is paying off, giving him and dozens of other long-departed major leaguers a chance to "live" their dream of once again being on a baseball field. But what about Ray? Where's his dream, especially since the existence of this baseball field is causing him significant financial hardship? Well, he's not yet done with the voices or the people whose passions will intersect his. "Ease his pain," the voice says to Ray one evening. "Who?" says Ray, frustrated. "What pain?"

Cut to the next night when, at a town meeting, residents are voting to censor school books they believe are "immoral" – including those of Terrence Mann, an author revered by both Ray and Anni. That night, Ray and Anni have the same dream and revelation: Ray must go to Boston to see Terrence Mann – and "ease his pain." Mr. Mann (James Earl Jones) is a Pulitzer Prize-winner novelist, social critic and renaissance man whose passion for life has come and gone. He's also a baseball fanatic whose dream was to meet Jackie Robinson and play ball on Ebbitts Field in Brooklyn. Ray must convince Terrence to attend a Boston Red Sox game with him at Fenway Park. Why? Ray has no idea; he just knows something important will be revealed.

Sure enough, at Fenway Park, Ray hears the voice again: "Go the Distance," and he sees a message on the center field screen: "Archibald 'Moonlight' Graham, Chisolm, Minnesota." Terrence tells him, "I wish I had your passion, Ray, misguided though it might be. I used to feel that way about things, but…" Just as Ray is about to set out for Minnesota, Terrence admits to seeing, and hearing, the same revelations, and he believes that he too must make the journey.

Archie "Moonlight" Graham (played by Burt Lancaster)… the final piece of the puzzle. Fifty years ago he had been a minor league ballplayer but never made it in the bigs; instead, "Moonlight" left the game to become "Doc" in his hometown of Chisolm. But Doc Graham, dead for almost 18 years, had held onto a wish; he wished he could have stepped up to the plate just one time in the major leagues. Could Ray Kinsella and Terrence Mann make that wish come true?

Driving back to Iowa with no clue of what awaits them, Ray and Terrence pick up a young, boyish-looking hitchhiker hoping to find a town in the Midwest where he can play baseball. "Hi," he says. "I'm Archie Graham." When they reach Ray's farm, the Field begins to deliver on everyone's Dream. The youthful Archie Graham meets Shoeless Joe Jackson and gets his coveted one time at bat against a major league pitcher. Shoeless Joe and dozens of other greats of the game relive their passion for "when it was a game." Terrence Mann is invited to join the players – out in the corn – so he can write about "Shoeless Joe Jackson comes to Iowa" and, hopefully, meet his hero, Jackie Robinson. Only Ray seems confused. "What's in it for me!" he cries.

Shoeless Joe looks at Ray and simply says, *If you build it, he will come* and then slowly turns his head toward the last remaining ballplayer on the field, the catcher next to home plate. With a jolt, Ray suddenly realizes that the ballplayer is his father as a young man, way before Ray was born, handsome, vibrant, still with hope for the future, still with enthusiasm for life. As the movie concludes, Ray finally makes good on the "game of catch" that he had refused his dad so many years ago.

Yes, *Field of Dreams* may be a fantasy, but its message is anything but. Shoeless Joe, Terrence Mann, Archie Graham, John Kinsella, Ray Kinsella… in their own way they were all passionate and enthusiastic about one thing in particular, and that was baseball. It could have been anything. In the end, they lived their dreams because they allowed themselves to follow that passion.

MOTIVATIONAL QUOTES THAT BUILD ENTHUSIASM

There are several subject categories that are relevant to the strength of enthusiasm or the lack thereof. Wise quotations about a specific subject can serve to teach you proactive beliefs, expectations and thoughts to replace the reactive garbage that blocks your forward progress. For example, if dreams don't play a prominent role in your life, find a quote or quotes that promote the importance of dreaming. Repeat it to yourself often, replacing any internal dialogue that diminishes the importance of dreaming.

On Enthusiasm
"The worst sin… is… to be indifferent."
George Bernard Shaw

"Zeal is a volcano, the peak of which the grass of indecisiveness does not grow."
Kahlil Gibran

"None are as old as those who have outlived their enthusiasm."
Henry David Thoreau

"Vitality! That's the pursuit of life, isn't it?"
Katharine Hepburn

"Exuberance is beauty."
William Blake

On Excuses

"An excuse is worse and more terrible than a lie; for an excuse is a lie guarded."
Alexander Pope

"He that is good for making excuses is seldom good for anything else."
Benjamin Franklin

"I attribute my success to this – I never gave or took any excuse."
Florence Nightengale

"There are two kinds of people in the world; those who make excuses and those who get results. An excuse person will find any excuse for why a job was not done and a results person will find any reason why it can be done."
Alan Cohen

"Don't look for excuses to lose. Look for excuses to win."
Chi Chi Rodriguez

On Dreams

"To accomplish great things, we must not only act but also dream, not only plan, but also believe."
Anatole France

"The future belongs to those who believe in the beauty of their dreams."
Eleanor Roosevelt

"None of us will ever accomplish anything excellent or commanding except when he listens to this whisper which is heard by him alone."
Ralph Waldo Emerson

"Your imagination is your preview of coming attractions."
Albert Einstein

"Nothing happens unless first a dream."
Carl Sandburg

On Opportunities

"Have you really lived ten thousand or more days, or have you lived one day ten thousand or more times?"
Wayne Dyer

"So you see! There's no end to the things you might know, depending how far beyond Zebra you go."
Dr. Seuss

"Life is a series of surprises."
Ralph Waldo Emerson

"When we think positively and imagine what we want, we risk disappointment; when we don't we ensure it."
Lana Limbert

"The strongest and sweetest songs yet remain to be sung."
Walt Whitman

On Risks

"Is life not a hundred times to short to bore ourselves?"
Friedrich Nietzsche

"You can't find peace by avoiding life."
Michael Cunningham in "The Hours"

"You must push yourself beyond all your limits all the time."
Carlos Castaneda

"Life is too short to be little. Man is never so manly as when he feels deeply, acts boldly, and expresses himself with frankness and with fervor."
Benjamin Disraeli

EFFECTIVE, PRACTICAL TECHNIQUES FOR BUILDING ENTHUSIASM

In order to change the beliefs and behaviors that you identified as problematic in the

Chart on Enthusiasm, the following information and techniques will assist you:

✓ Principles of Behavior Change
✓ The Stress Response
✓ Abdominal Breathing
✓ Imagery Relaxation
✓ Progressive Muscle Relaxation (PMR)
✓ The Relaxation Response
✓ Systematic Desensitization
✓ Assertiveness
✓ Disputing
✓ Distraction

These techniques are discussed in detail in Chapter 7.

ADDITIONAL RESOURCES: RECOMMENDED READINGS

Recommended Readings:

Benson, H. and Proctor, W. (2003) *The Breakout Principle*

Canfield, J. (2005) *The Success Principles*

Cassidy, G. (2000) *Discover Your Passion: An Intuitive Search to Find Purpose In Life*

Chang, R (2000) *The Passion Plan: A Step by Step Guide to Discovering, Developing, and Living Your Passion*

Csikzentmihalyi, M. (1990) *Flow: The Psychology of Optimal Experience*

Jamison, K.R. (2004) *Exuberance: The Passion for Life*

Scott, S. (1998) *Steps to Impossible Dreams*

Zoglio, S. (2000) *Create a Life that Tickles Your Soul: Finding Peace, Passion and Purpose*

ENTHUSIASM ENDNOTES

Pg. 127   Chang, R. (2000) *The Passion Plan.* New York: Jossey-Bass

Pg. 128   Peterson, C. and Seligman, M. (2004) *Character Strengths.* Oxford: Oxford University Press, p. 274.

Pgs. 128, 136-138   Csikszentmihalyi, M. (1990) *Flow: The Psychology of Optimal Experience.* New York: Harper & Row Publishers, Inc.

Pg. 129   Duskoch, P. "The Winning Edge." *Psychology Today,* Nov/Dec 2005

Pgs. 134-135   Zoglio, S. (2000) *Create a Life That Tickles Your Soul.* Doylestown, PA: Tower Hill Press, pgs. 35 and 90.

Pg. 137   Debold, E. "Flow With Soul." *What is Enlightenment?* www.wie.org/j21/csiksz.asp

Pgs. 141-142   Benson, H. and Proctor, W. (2003) *The Breakout Principle.* New York: Scribner.

Chapter Five

LIVING IN THE PRESENT
Give Yourself This Gift

"May you live all the days of your life."

Jonathon Swift

It's a hectic and crazy world in which we live! Time sometimes rules over us like a malevolent dictator. We watch the clock, we try to beat the clock and, of course, we often lose to the clock. We live by calendars, appointment books and palm pilots. Life seems sometimes more about putting out fires than anything else. We often reside in an environment of rigid expectations and "shoulds," dictated by others and by ourselves. In our inner world, we shift from past pain to present distress to future trepidation.

The notion of focusing on the moment may sound like a preposterous idea in this hurried existence. The way things are arranged, we're generally not encouraged to behold and smell the proverbial roses. In fact, even if we did, many of us would be clueless as to how to go about such a foreign endeavor.

The idea of being so connected to the here and now probably sounds a little over the top to some people, but bear with me. I'd like to make my case for why living in the present can be so enlightening, gratifying and downright healthy for body and mind! Learning to live in the moment is a source of power and energy in the successful and enjoyable navigation of your little red wagon.

THE REWARDS OF LIVING IN THE PRESENT

Consider this important question posed by Thomas Crum, author of *Journey to the Center* and *The Magic of Conflict*: "What would it be like if you lived each day, each breath as a work of art in progress? Imagine that you are a masterpiece unfolding every second of every day, a work of art taking form with every breath." How do you suppose that shift in perception, purpose and focus would change your life?

A change of focus to the moment offers an array of gifts, because the present is such a special place to be. The present is where our power lies. It's where robust and satisfying relationships are nourished and where better communication and active listening take place. The present is where happiness can be found and where laughter, play, fun and excitement flourish. It's where we find out who we are, what we think and what we want. It's where creativity takes place and performance excellence manifests.

The present is where adversities and challenges faced head on teach strength and mastery. It's where we discover that we can be subjected to pain and suffering and endure, even thrive. It's where persistence and intelligent decision-making become the norm. It's where problems are solved, where learning takes place, and where memory is enhanced. It's where we can have sensory experiences of a thousand kinds. It's where we have the power to promote physical and mental well-being, even when the body and mind have been plagued by illness. And it's where we engender hope and aspire to fulfill dreams for the future.

Self-Empowerment
Living in the present avails us the opportunity to be powerful and successful on our own behalf, to embrace the possibilities, to become wise, insightful and connected in relationships.

We exercise our own power by being present. Louise L. Hay tells us, "The point of power is always in the present moment." Leo Tolstoy, one of Russia's greatest authors, advises, "Remember then: there is only one time that is important – now! It is the most important time because it's the only time when we have power."

Being in the moment deepens our connections in relationships and in life. Thich Nhat Hanh, the Vietnamese Zen Buddhist monk, points out, "Life can be found only in the present moment. The past is gone, the future is not yet here, and if we do not go back to ourselves in the present moment, we cannot be in touch with life." He also tells us, "The most precious gift we can offer others is our presence. When mindfulness embraces those we love, they will bloom like flowers."

Living in the present offers us the chance to absorb more of our world, to listen more fully and genuinely to others, and to be more actively involved in the lives of those we care about. Shaun Kerry, M.D., the social psychiatrist, tells us that, "Mindful people make good husbands and wives and parents. They get along well with others and have a sense of empathy and conscience. They tend to be responsible, yet still understand the importance of play."

Present living fosters growth and makes change our ally instead of our foe. L. Trinidad Hunt points out, "Life is made up of millions of moments, but we live only one of these moments at a time. As we begin to change the moment, we begin to change our lives."

Jack Kornfield, the psychologist and former Buddhist monk, believes, "To live is to let go and die with each passing moment, and to be reborn in each new one." Anatole France, the French author, suggests, "All changes, even the most longed for, have melancholy; for what we leave behind us is a part of ourselves; we must die to one life before we can enter another."

We learn more about what is wise and prudent in life when in the moment. Jon Kabat-Zinn, an expert in the area of mindfulness training and stress reduction, believes that, "Stillness, insight and wisdom arise only when we can settle into being complete in this moment, without having to seek or hold on to or reject anything." Charles Schultz shares his wisdom with us: "In the book of life's questions, the answers are not in the back."

Think for a moment about the sage advice of Winnie the Pooh: "Sometimes, if you stand on the bottom rail of a bridge and lean over to watch the river slipping slowly away beneath you, you will suddenly know everything there is to be known," and, "Rivers know this: there is no hurry. We shall get there some day."

We learn about possibilities that were overlooked in a non-present, mindless mode. Eden Phillpotts, the English novelist and poet, surmises that, "The universe is full of magical things patiently waiting for our wits to grow sharper." Kahlil Gibran suggests, "And forget not that the earth delights to feel your bare feet and the winds long to play with your hair."

Michael Jones, pianist and author of *Artful Leadership: Awakening the Commons of the Imagination*, tells us, "These possibilities come not only from searching for something new, but also from unlearning or forgetting what had gone before. In that moment of emptiness the mind is open to a new possibility."

Mental and Physical Wellness

Being in the moment presents each of us with healthy ways to bolster physical and mental well-being. In the present state of mind, we are not worrying about the future and are not angry or depressed by visions of the past. Worry, anger and depression engage the body's alarm system, and should this occur excessively, it can have seriously adverse effects on physical and psychological functioning.

Buddha maintains, "The secret of health for both body and mind is not to mourn for the past, not to worry about the future, not to anticipate troubles, but to live in the present moment wisely and earnestly." Abraham Maslow, the American psychologist, believes, "I can feel guilty about the past, apprehensive about the future, but only in the present can I act. The ability to be in the moment is a major component of mental wellness."

Research in mind-body medicine has illustrated the positive effects of living in the present. "Mind-body medicine," according to the National Center for Complementary and Alternative Medicine, "focuses on the interaction among the brain, mind, body, and behavior and the powerful ways emotional, mental, social, spiritual, and behavioral factors can directly affect health."

At centers in the United States and other countries, people are learning to utilize present focus, especially in the form of mindfulness meditation, as an adjunct to their medical regimen. Mindfulness-Based Stress Reduction (MBSR) a combination of Mindfulness, Behavior Therapy and Cognitive Therapy, has shown consistent and reliable reductions in medical and psychological symptoms for many diagnoses. Mind-body medicine is a wonderful and powerful complement to traditional Western medicine.

According to data compiled at the Stress Clinic at the University of Massachusetts Medical School, 16,000 people with medical and psychological conditions have enrolled in MBSR programs since 1979. And the very good news is that the research shows that most participants have experienced long-lasting improvements in medical and psychological symptoms, along with positive changes in attitudes, behaviors and perceptions.

Immune function, chronic pain and breast cancer are only some of the medical problems in which MBSR has been an impressive adjunct. Mood, anxiety, eating disorders and Borderline Personality Disorder have also responded positively to a treatment regimen that includes this approach.

According to Jim Hopper, Ph.D., a psychologist on staff at Harvard Medical School, mindfulness can slow the pace of thoughts, increase the spaciousness of present awareness, reduce the intensity of unhelpful habitual responses and aid in the cultivation of positive experiences and emotions.

Athletic Performance

Athletic performance is greatly improved by being in the moment. For example, success in golf is made more likely by focusing only on the shot you're preparing to hit. Thinking about past or future shots is decidedly counter-productive. Many professional golfers hire sports psychologists to train them in the fine art of focusing solely on the current challenge. Tom Watson, a prominent and accomplished professional golfer, believes, "Confidence in golf means being able to concentrate on the problem at hand with no outside interference."

Bob Toski, author of the classic manual, *How to Feel a Real Golf Swing: Mind-Body Techniques from Two of Golf's Greatest Teachers,* explains, "When I joined the Tour I studied the best players to see what they did that I didn't do. I came to the conclusion that the successful players had the three C's: Confidence, Composure, Concentration."

Michael Jordan, considered by many people to be the greatest basketball player of all time, discloses, "When I step onto the court, I don't have to think about anything. If I have a problem off the court, I find that after I play, my mind is clearer and I can come up with a better solution. It's like therapy. It relaxes me and allows me to solve problems."

John Brodie, former quarterback for the San Francisco Forty-Niners, asserts that, "The player's effectiveness is directly related to his ability to be right there, doing that thing, in the moment. He can't be worrying about the past or the future or some extraneous event. He must be able to respond in the here and now."

Creativity

Being in the here and now and nurturing the play instinct create an environment in which creativity can blossom. Stephen Nachmanovitch, author of *Free Play: Improvisation in Life and Art,* suggests that, "Creative work is play. It is free speculation using materials of one's chosen form," and "The most potent muse of all is our own inner child."

Carl Jung, the Swiss psychiatrist and founder of analytical psychology, relates to us that, "The creation of something new is not accomplished by the intellect but by the play instinct acting from inner necessity. The creative mind plays with the objects it loves." Pablo Picasso maintains, "All children are artists. The problem is how to remain an artist once one grows up." Consider this: who is more in the moment than a child at play?

Ellen Langer, psychologist and author of *On Becoming an Artist: Reinventing Yourself through Mindful Creativity,* believes that mindfulness is an effortless, simple process that consists of drawing novel distinctions, that is, noticing new things. The more we notice, the more we become aware of how things change depending on the context and perspective from which they are viewed."

Rollo May, the American psychologist, suggests, "Creativity arises out of the tension between spontaneity and limitations, the latter (like the river banks) forcing the spontaneity into the various forms which are essential to the work of art or poem." Georges-Louis Lederc Buffon, the French naturalist, is of the opinion that, "The human mind cannot create anything. It produces until after having been fertilized by experience and meditation, its acquisitions are the gems of its production."

Michael Jones, author of *Life and Artful Leadership: Awakening the Commons of the Imagination,* shares his experience as a pianist: "As I played, another dimension of sound welled up unexpectedly from inside the piano and burned through my fingers… There was no more pianist and no more piano. In this undefended moment of free flight, something changed in my body and God slipped in. As soon as my mind noticed, God slipped back out again."

According to Mihaly Csiksentmihalyi in *Creativity: The Flow and Psychology of Discovery,* "Creativity is a central source of meaning in our lives… Most of the

things that are interesting, important, and human are the results of creativity…
[and] when we are involved in it, we feel that we are living more fully than during
the rest of life."

John W. Gardner, recipient of the Presidential Medal of Freedom and the founder
of Common Cause, suggests this about creativity: "When Alexander the Great
visited Diogenes and asked whether he could do anything for the famed teacher,
Diogenes replied: 'Only stand out of my light.' Perhaps someday we shall know
how to heighten creativity. Until then, one of the best things we can do for creative
men and women is to stand out of their light."

Happiness
Happiness is made possible by being in the moment. Nathaniel Hawthorne, the
19th century American author, believes, "Happiness is a butterfly which when
pursued, is always just beyond your grasp, but which if you will sit down quietly,
may alight upon you." Margaret Bonnano tells us, "It is only possible to live happily
ever after on a day to day basis."

Denis Waitley posits that, "Happiness cannot be traveled to, owned, earned, worn
or consumed. Happiness is the spiritual experience of living every minute with love,
grace and gratitude." Greg Anderson suggests, "Only one thing has to change for us
to know happiness in our lives: where we focus our attention." J. Donald Walters
points out, "Happiness is not a brilliant climax to years of grim struggle and anxiety.
It is a long succession of little decisions simply to be happy in the moment."

Albert Camus, the French author and philosopher, proclaims, "But what is happiness
except the simple harmony between a man and the life he leads." And Mahatma
Gandhi, the spiritual leader of India, contends, "Happiness is when what you
think, what you say and what you do are in harmony." Leo Buscaglia, professor
and author of *The Joy of the Moment* believes, "What we call the secret of happiness
is no more a secret than our willingness to choose life."

Leo Tolstoy recommends, "If you want to be happy, be." If you don't want to be
happy take the advice of Charles Schultz's character, Charlie Brown: "This is 'my
depressed stance.' When you're depressed, it makes a lot of difference how you
stand. The worst thing you can do is straighten up and hold your head high because

then you'll start to feel better. If you're going to get any joy out of being depressed, you've got to stand like this."

Haim Ginott, the child psychologist and author of *Between Parent and Child*, tells us, "Happiness... is not a destination; it is a manner of traveling. Happiness is not an end in itself. It is a by-product of working, playing, loving and living." Diane Sawyer believes, "The joy is in the journey and not arriving at the destination." William Morris posits that, "The true secret of happiness lies in taking a genuine interest in all the details of daily life and elevating them to an art."

In his book, *Finding Flow: The Psychology of Engagement with Everyday Life,* Mihaly Csikszentmihalyi posits, "To live means to experience – through doing, feeling, thinking. Experience takes place in time, so time is the ultimate scarce resource we have. Over the years, the content of experience will determine the quality of life. Therefore, one of the most essential decisions any of us can make is about how one's time is allocated or invested."

William Blake captures the essence when he says, "He who binds himself a joy does the winged life destroy; but he who kisses the joy as it flies lives in eternity's sunrise."

Resilience
Living in the present, being mindful, helps us weather the storms of life. Michael Jones, author of *Creating an Imaginative Life,* believes, "When the wind strips us bare, the present moment is often the safest place to be." No matter what has rocked your world, being able to center yourself in the here and now offers you a path to greater stability.

Mindfulness enhances emotional resilience by fostering progressive movement out of a pattern of avoidant behavior. One can step out of the cycle and with each step forward become stronger. Being mindful and centered in the present helps reduce the overwhelming feelings of helplessness that are so often a result of experiencing distressing life events.

Jack Kornfield, co-author of *Seeking the Heart of Wisdom*, points out that, "When we come into the present, we begin to feel the life around us again, but we also encounter whatever we have been avoiding. We must have the courage to face whatever is present – our pain, our desires, our grief, our loss, our secret hopes, our love – everything that moves us deeply."

Henri Nouwen, the Dutch Catholic priest and writer, tells us, "When we become aware that we do not have to escape our pains, but that we can mobilize them into a common search for life, those very pains are transformed from expressions of despair into signs of hope." John Updike, author and Pulitzer Prize winner, suggests we remember, "We do survive every moment, after all, except the last one." Jon Kabat-Zinn advises "You can't stop the waves, but you can learn to surf."

THE CHALLENGE OF LIVING IN THE PRESENT

Living in the present is a choice. That's right, we get to choose where our attention is directed – the past, the present, or the future, and we get to decide exactly what we listen to on those channels. We have all the wiring we need to direct the focus of our attention. It's like spending money; there's only so much, and it's important to decide wisely where it goes. Some people are better at money management than others, but it's a skill that can be learned. And the same holds true for the management of your attention – it can be learned.

Let's talk about the past, the present and the future. My theory is that when deciding where one's attention ought to go, a 10-80-10 split is a healthy guideline: 10 percent for the past, 80 percent for the present and 10 percent for the future. What you choose to focus on within those domains also has important ramifications. For example, when thinking about the past, you can choose to focus on negative meanderings that depress you or on uplifting memories that bring inspiration and warmth. Personally, I consider this a no-brainer!

The Past

The negative images and thoughts of the past primarily take the form of guilt, shame, regret, resentment and nostalgia. Your thoughts get stuck in the "if only" mode: if only I hadn't done that; if only he hadn't done that to me; if only I could still be in that place and time. Nostalgia is not always negative, but is better in small amounts. Some nostalgic folks spend so much time remembering the past (often with a halo effect, I might add) that it remains their reality when it's long, long gone.

Ten percent is a reasonable and healthy amount of time to relegate to the past. Now mind you, the negative feelings mentioned above are unhealthy and a colossal waste of your precious time and energy, and frankly, garbage. A wise use of this 10 percent is twofold: first to determine from the events that produced these feelings the lessons that will deter you from repeating your missteps.

The second and much larger share of the 10 percent is comprised of positive memories, images and feelings, such as the color of a beautiful sunset, your first romantic kiss, your baby's smile at four months of age, or for the Boston baseball fan, the 2004 World Series in which the Red Sox finally broke the "Curse of the Bambino." And don't forget those accomplishments that were so special to you when you brought them to fruition.

Throw out the garbage and focus on the gifts, making the time dedicated to the past to be limited, productive and well spent. Press the delete button on the "if onlys." If you do this, imagine how much time and energy you'll have freed up for yourself.

The Future
The future is a 10 percent solution, too. Attention to the future generally involves worry, fear, doubt, longing, and dreams. As A.J. Cronin so aptly put it, "Worry never robs tomorrow of its sorrow; it only saps today of its strength." The worry, fear and doubt expenditure is the garbage part. It makes sense to identify relevant factors in formulating strategies to achieve goals. This won't take a lot of time and energy once you've eliminated the torturing trio: worry, doubt and fear.

Then there's the longing, waiting part, which is also a waste of time and thus garbage. This involves thoughts and emotions dedicated to the belief that some milestone has to be reached or some situation has to materialize in order for you to really be in your stride. It is a terrific thing to dream; however this is more about being held hostage. You tell yourself that you need to have such and such happen in order to enjoy your life. It's as if you're holding your breath.

Bette Howland confesses to having been caught in this perverse belief system: "For a long time it seemed to me that real life was about to begin, but there was always some obstacle in the way. Something had to be got through first, some unfinished business; time still to be served, a debt to be paid. Then life would begin. At last it dawned on me that these obstacles were my life."

Dr. Seuss observes, "Waiting for the fish to bite or waiting for wind to fly a kite. Or waiting around for Friday night or waiting perhaps for Uncle Jake or a pot to boil or a better break or a string of pearls or a pair of pants or a wig with curls or another chance. Everyone is just waiting." Or you're waiting to turn sixteen or graduate from college or retire and you're damn sure that is when happiness or whatever you seek will permanently be yours.

HA! Think this way and you become a hostage to a very faulty belief system. There's a great line from *The Music Man:* "Pile up too many tomorrows and you'll find that you collected nothing but a bunch of empty yesterdays." Dr. Seuss poses a very apt question: "How did it get so late so soon? It's night before it's afternoon. December is here before it's June. My goodness how the time has flewn. How did it get so late so soon?"

The answer is, of course, that the questioner was living for tomorrow instead of for today – that's how it got so late so soon!

The future garbage is defined by the "what ifs:" what if bad things happen, what if I fail, what if the future is the only place where I can find happiness? Instead of the wastefulness of this garbage, the much larger portion of future attention, the fun and energizing part, is best allotted to dreams and possibilities. Imagine in your world deleting the "what ifs." How much time and energy would that free up? Now, you're getting it; get rid of the garbage, enjoy the dream, and it's a whole new ballgame!

Ronald Bissell, surgeon and author, captures the importance of the moment in defining and creating the future when he says, "Each moment is a crystal in formation. It is the seed of your future and as such gives power to what may seem like a lost second but in reality is a chrysalis waiting to be opened. It is energy waiting to be born and the gift you give to your future. Each moment is a capsule of love just eager to be seen amid the chaos of an ever noisy world."

The Present

The present is an 80 percent solution. This means spending the lion's share of your non-sleep time truly awake, genuinely in the moment. Being in the moment does not include the "shoulds," and other unreasonable expectations of yourself; these are garbage. The shoulds tell us that having fun, relaxing, living in the present waste precious time that is better spent attending to obligations, responsibilities and actions that will lead to something desired.

In terms of expectations, we often lose our way by deciding how we are supposed to behave, setting up standards for ourselves that make no sense and only frustrate us. Remember: "Expectation minus reality = frustration." Delete the "shoulds" and review expectations, proactively determining which ones are appropriate, reasonable and reality-based. Press the save button on those.

In my clinical and coaching practice, I've seen many clients desperately seeking answers, including what to believe, what decisions to make, what actions to take, and what will bring meaning to their lives. The approach the client has taken, thus far, is to obsess, fret and worry over the same tired territory, second guessing steps taken and steps to take. I brilliantly and subtly point out to the client that this approach doesn't appear to be working all that well.

I ask the client what the definition of insanity is. Some know and others wait for the punch line. The answer, according to Benjamin Franklin, among others, is, "doing the same thing over and over and expecting a different result." The answers apparently are not in the region of the brain being consulted by the client. The solution I propose is to take a very different tact: collect more information by engaging in new experiences and tuning into them in ways not done before. The client simply does not have enough data!

Having an open, interactive relationship with the world on a moment to moment basis offers voluminous information. You will be amazed at how much less taxing and how much more enjoyable and enlightening the journey will be with this approach. Remember, the present gets 80% of your attention! As Ralph Waldo Emerson questions, "What would be the use of immortality to a person who cannot use well a half hour?"

So you ask, "what is living in the moment really, and how does one go about bringing it into full bloom?" It's a state of mind in which you are paying close attention to what is occurring on many levels experientially. You're paying attention to where you are, what you're doing and what you're feeling. You're actively involved. You accept what's happening without making judgments or trying to change the elements. You accept yourself in this situation. You flow with what is happening. You're not distracted by past or future garbage. The moment may be serious, playful, reflective, humorous, loving, sad and on and on. When this is happening, you are practicing mindfulness.

MINDFULNESS

Mindfulness is a comprehensive, research-based approach that elucidates methods to bring about living in the present; it provides powerful tools in the pursuit of your goals and dreams. Mindfulness embraces such core principles as acceptance of what's happening, non-judgmental awareness and detachment from emotional experiences. This may sound incompatible with the more action-oriented approaches in other chapters but, in fact, practicing mindfulness will complement rather than compete with those strengths and skills.

According to Jon Kabat-Zinn, Ph.D., in his book, *Wherever You Go, There You Are:*

> Mindfuness is a simple concept. Its power lies in its practice and its application. Mindfulness means paying attention in a particular way: on purpose, in the present moment and non-judgmentally. This kind of attention nurtures greater awareness, clarity, and acceptance of the present-moment reality. It wakes us up to the fact that our lives unfold only in moments. If we are not fully present for many of those moments, we may not only miss what is most valuable in our lives but also fail to realize the richness and the depth of our possibilities for growth and transformation.

Professor Kabat-Zinn directs the Center for Mindfulness in Medicine, Health Care and Society at the University of Massachusetts Medical Center in Worcester, Massachusetts. His research is indicating the multiplicity of mental and physical health benefits of embracing mindfulness. It has a positive impact on the brain, the immune system and the rumination so prevalent in depression. He points out that the prefrontal cortex of the brain increases in activity with present focus. This region of the brain is associated with a happier state of mind, and activating this region can be learned.

Mindfulness has its origin in Buddhism; it's a form of Insight Meditation. Thich Nhat Hahn, the Buddhist Monk, tells of a conversation between the Buddha and a philosopher that sheds light on this concept:

> When the Buddha was asked about what he and his followers practice, he answered, "We walk, we eat, we wash ourselves, we sit down."
>
> The philosopher asked, "What is so special about that? Everyone walks, eats, washes, sits down."
>
> "Sir," the Buddha said, "When we walk we are aware that we are walking, when we eat, we are aware that we are eating. When others walk, eat, wash or sit down, they are generally not aware of what they are doing."

In *Seeking the Heart of Wisdom* (1987), Joseph Goldstein and Jack Kornfield tell another story about the Buddha and the meaning of mindfulness:

> It is said that soon after his enlightenment, the Buddha passed a man on the road who was struck by the extraordinary radiance and peacefulness of his presence. The man stopped and asked, "My friend, what are you? Are you a celestial being or a god?"
>
> "No," said the Buddha.
>
> "Well then, are you some kind of magician or wizard?" Again the Buddha answered, "No."
>
> "Are you a man?"
>
> "No."
>
> "Well, my friend, what are you?"
>
> "I am awake."

The name Buddha means "One who is awake." Being awake brings us truth about our experiences.

Henepola Gunaratana, the Sri Lankan Buddhist monk, enumerates some of the main characteristics of mindfulness in his book, *Mindfulness in Plain English*. When practicing mindfulness, one:

- Observes without judging or criticizing
- Observes with disinterest, i.e., does not try to avoid negative mental states or become possessed with good mental states
- Has "bare attention" in which you're not entangled by mental phenomena such as concepts and opinions
- Observes in the here and now
- Is not concerned with self. For example, pain is noted as a sensation not as connected to the individual. The pronoun "I" is not used.
- Observes changes as they occur, noting the effect on one's own feelings and the effects on other people
- Takes part and observes simultaneously
- Has an accurate appraisal of what is occurring

Is mindfulness a panacea? Is it comprehensive in addressing all aspects of human functioning? What relationship does it have to psychological methods? Jack Kornfield, psychologist and former Buddhist monk, gives us his perspective on these questions: "For most people meditation practice doesn't 'do it all.' At best, it's one important piece of a complex path of opening and awakening. I used to believe that meditation led to the higher, more universal truths, and that psychology, personality, and our own 'little dramas' were a separate, lower realm. I wish it worked that way, but experience and the non dual nature of reality don't bear it out. If we are to end suffering and find freedom, we can't keep these two levels of our lives separate."

The discovery process involves different choices for different people. It's likely that your strengths and shortcomings are not the same as mine. Each of us has to choose what we want to change and what methods are motivating and promising. Most often the success of living the life we want is made more probable by the use of a number of methods.

DEVELOPING IN THE MOMENT LIVING

Beliefs to Adopt

As in the development of all the core strengths, it's helpful to start with your beliefs regarding the strength of present living and the behaviors and cognitions that produce and maintain it.

Norman Cousins, journalist, professor and author of a collection of best-selling books on illness and healing, posits, "The greatest force in the human body is the natural drive of the body to heal itself – but that force is not independent of the belief system, which can translate expectations into psychological change. Nothing is more wondrous about the fifteen billion neurons in the human brain than their ability to convert thoughts, hopes, ideas, and attitudes into chemical substances. Everything begins, therefore, with belief."

Ask yourself where you stand on the following:

- It is only in the present moment that you can discern what is really happening.
- The moment is to be appreciated and accepted, not judged.
- I have a choice about where my attention is directed. I do not have to be a slave to the past, present or future garbage. The power belongs to me.
- It is important for me to have compassion for myself and others.
- I do not have to believe what my thoughts tell me and I don't have to react to them.
- The present is my best chance for happiness.
- The present is where my power lies.
- Focusing on the moment, relaxing, enjoying myself are healthy, worthwhile endeavors.

Thoughts from Jon Kabat-Zinn:
- Being mindful is simple observation in order to be more aware of the events taking place inside and outside you.
- Kabat-Zinn uses the metaphor of the ocean and its waves; you observe, you do not attempt to alter what happens to the waves.
- Relax, breathe, be tuned in to what is occurring without being connected to it.
- Be mindful of what really matters to you.
- When facing adversity, observe the lessons in what is going on; appreciate the instruction you are receiving in the commonplace.
- Being mindful involves practicing acceptance. "Acceptance, of course, does not mean passivity or resignation. On the contrary, by fully accepting what each moment offers, you open yourself to experiencing life much more completely and make it more likely that you will be able to respond effectively to any

situation that presents itself. Acceptance offers a way to navigate life's ups and downs – what Zorba the Greek called 'the full catastrophe' – with grace, a sense of humor, and perhaps some understanding of the big picture, what I like to think of as wisdom." (p.2, www.ramsjb.com/talamasca/avatar/mindfulness.html).

- Everyday activities such as riding to work or fixing dinner present excellent chances to practice mindfulness.
- "...Imagine you are going into your special chamber where nothing else matters except you and the stillness." (p. 2, http://beststeps.com. Interview with Richard Streitfeld).
- Believe in your body even when you are ill.

Recommendations from Harvey Rich, M.D., author of In the Moment, for celebrating each day:

- Identify and acknowledge moments as they occur; see their uniqueness.
- Give the moment a title or name so that you become aware of it and embrace it.
- Consciously experience moments with others – this gives more importance to whatever the moment is about.
- "In celebration, we open ourselves and bring ourselves forth most fully into a thoughtful and sensory awareness of the moment. When our minds are open fully to the senses, to memory and to wonder, to pain and joy, and to those who share the moment with us, our conscious interaction with the moment loosens the barriers to the unconscious, allowing us to experience the moment in a deeper way" (p.21).
- In a moment see all the amazing enigmas and the mystery of this world.

Breathing from Thich Nhat Hanh

Author of *Peace is Every Step*. Breathing is a very important component of mindfulness. Thich Nhat Hanh, a Vietnamese Buddhist monk, explains the following:

There are a number of breathing techniques you can use to make life more enjoyable. The first exercise is very simple. As you breathe in, say to yourself, "Breathing in, I know that I am breathing in." And as you breathe out, say "Breathing out, I know that I am breathing out." Just that. You recognize your in-breath as an in-breath and your out-breath as an out-breath. You don't even need to recite the whole sentence; you can use just two words, In and Out.

This technique can help you keep your mind on your breath. As you practice, your breath will become peaceful and gentle and your mind and body will also become peaceful and gentle. This is not a difficult exercise. In just a few minutes you can realize the fruit of meditation.

Breathing in and out is very important and it is enjoyable, as breathing is the link between our body and our mind. Sometimes our mind is thinking of one thing and our body is doing another, and mind and body are not unified.

By concentrating on our breathing, In and Out, we bring body and mind back together, and become whole again. Conscious breathing is an important bridge. Just breathing and smiling can make us very happy, because when we breathe consciously we recover ourselves completely and encounter life in the present moment.

AN EXERCISE IN BEING IN THE MOMENT

Below I describe an individual moment. Imagine that you're the person in the moment. Follow the guided imagery and focus exclusively as if it is your present moment. If past, present or future thoughts unrelated to the moment come to mind, passively let them go and return to the images. Here goes:

A Serene Moment

You're standing by your baby's crib watching her sleep in her room, which is dark except for the Winnie-the-Pooh night light. Her stomach is moving up and down as she breathes deeply and slowly. Her soft hair is in ringlets around her chubby face. Her skin seems to sparkle. You become aware as you gaze at her that your heart is so full of love you think you might just burst. Her feet move slightly and a faint smile crosses her lips. You hear her whimper and burp at the same time, and you can't help but chuckle in delight. The room is warm and you notice that your hands are clasping the rails of the crib. Time has disappeared.

NOW WHAT DO I DO?

This is an adventure of possibilities... all the wonderful possibilities that come with living in the present. Your mission is to develop the belief that you can do what needs to be done, commit to an informed course of action and promise yourself that giving up is not an option. You can do it! The tools to help you:

- The Chart on Living in the Present is an assessment tool to help you identify the beliefs and behaviors that need to be changed and those that are your strong points
- The Treasury of Motivators features several components that offer alternatives to tired old ways of thinking and believing including: Quotations to Dispute Faulty Thinking, poems, movie synopses and motivational quotes by subject
- Techniques and tools applicable to developing in the present living (presented in Chapter 7)
- Recommendations on additional resources

CHART OF LIVING IN THE PRESENT – BELIEFS AND BEHAVIORS
BELIEFS

Beliefs That Foster Living in the Present	*Beliefs That Hinder Living in the Present*
1. If I have hurt someone, I should make amends, forgive myself and let it go.	1. I deserve to feel guilty for a long time if I have cause harm to someone else.
2. Mistakes are a normal part of life; I refuse to let regrets about mistakes dominate my current world.	2. When I make a mistake, it is appropriate for me to feel shame for a long time.
3. Resentment is unhealthy and unproductive; it interferes in present living.	3. I resent how some people have treated me in the past; I feel entitled to hold on to these feelings. They help me keep my guard up.
4. The past should play only a limited role in my present life.	4. The past was so wonderful. Nothing can top it. My happiest moments are spent reminiscing.

5. Worry about the future will not make things better, but will only compromise the joys and power of the present.

5. I'm afraid if I don't worry about what could go wrong in the future, I won't be prepared to handle it.

6. The present is my best chance for happiness.

6. The future is my best chance for happiness. I can't wait until I'm age 16, 21, married, etc.

7. The present is where my power lies.

7. The present makes me feel so helpless with the problems I am facing. Things are not the way I want them to be; focusing on the present is stressful.

8. Focusing on the moment, relaxing, enjoying myself are healthy, worthwhile endeavors.

8. Being in the moment is a waste of precious time. I should be accomplishing things instead of loafing.

BEHAVIORS

Behaviors That Foster Present Focus

1. I am aware of what I'm doing, thinking, feeling, where I am. I'm awake and aware of my sensory responses.

Behaviors That Hinder Present Focus

1. I allow distractions to take my focus from the here and now.

2. I name moments.

2. I allow one moment to run into the next, as if unimportant.

3. I accept what is happening without judgment.

3. I scrutinize and have an opinion about each happening. I look for the negatives in each situation.

4. I trust my experiences.

4. I question all aspects of what is happening. I assume the worst.

5. I take in and recognize new information about my life by being in the present.	5. I keep looking for answers in my head.
6. I recognize how special each moment is.	6. I let moments go by without attending to their uniqueness.
7. I use cognitive techniques to manage distractions and unwanted intrusions.	7. I allow "what ifs" and "shoulds" and other garbage thoughts to overwhelm me.
8. I use relaxation techniques and stress management skills to create an internal environment that frees me to be in the moment.	8. I wing it. I don't waste time on skills that would allow me to focus on the present.

THE TREASURY OF MOTIVATORS

The Treasury of Motivators offers you a wealth of present focus words and thoughts. These will be helpful in maintaining your motivation and resolve on the journey to your chosen destinations. Choose the treasures that are meaningful and inspirational for you.

You may also enjoy your own treasure hunt for pieces that are personally energizing and encouraging. Incorporate these into your everyday internal world. Some you can commit to memory; others can be placed in spots where you'll be reminded of what you want to believe and say to yourself. Focus on them often. Focus on out with the garbage, and in with your own special pep talk!

QUOTATIONS ON PRESENT LIVING THAT DISPUTE FAULTY THINKING

The following statements are harmful beliefs, expectations and thoughts that people repeat to themselves over and over again, often with strong conviction. The irrationality and toxicity of these debilitating cognitions are hardly ever questioned. These cognitions compete with the strength of living in the present. You need to learn to talk back to them in meaningful and potent ways.

The goal is to reduce the frequency, intensity and duration of each of them by distraction methods and to neutralize them by disputing or arguing with their content. Disputing can be done by utilizing pertinent, meaningful quotes provided for you in this chapter or by developing your own reality-based, effective retorts. Note that you may have cognitions in your repertoire that are not contained in this list of Harmful Beliefs.

Take a personal inventory of these in a separate notebook, then choose powerful quotes or other responses to question and contradict these cognitions. Remember practice, practice, practice, so you're ready when they come for real! Besides increasing your readiness, practicing also decreases the potency of any noxious self-statements, aiding in your quest to be more in the present. Distraction and disputing techniques are discussed in Chapter 7.

Harmful:
"The guilt I feel from the mistakes I have made and the people I have hurt overwhelms me. I deserve to feel awful about these things for a long time."

Instead:
"One of the most basic issues we face in our lives is the feeling of failure or guilt. I come from a minority group, a family where F stood for feedback or flow and not for failure. F's on a test meant a failed test and not a failure as a human being. F's helped me find my place in the universe because the family attitude was, 'It was meant to be.' And now we would see what good would come of this event."
Bernie Siegel, M.D.

"There is no saint without a past and no sinner without a future."
Shri Haidakan Babaj

"The past is a guidepost not a hitching post."
L. Thomas Holdcraft

"Whatever your past has been you have a spotless future."
Melanie Gustafson

Harmful:
"I resent how some people have treated me in the past; I just don't want to let go of these feelings."

Instead:
"Events in the past can be roughly divided into those which probably didn't happen and those which do not matter."
William Ralph Inge

"To carry a grudge is like being stung to death by one bee."
William H. Walton

"Hanging on to resentment is letting someone you despise live rent-free in your head."
Ann Landers

"Holding on to anger is like grasping a hot coal with the intent of throwing it at someone else; you are the one who gets burned."
Buddha

"Resentment is like drinking poison and waiting for the other person to die."
Malachy McCourt

Harmful:
"The past was so wonderful. Those were the days… I wish I could go back. Nothing can top my past experiences."

Instead:
"It's but little good you'll be doing watering last year's crops."
George Eliot

"The past should be a springboard not a hammock."
Irving Bell

"One problem with gazing too frequently into the past is that we may turn around to find the future has run out on us."
Michael Cibenko

"Don't cry because it's over. Smile because it happened."
Dr. Seuss

"Never let yesterday use up today."
Richard H. Nelson

Harmful:
"The future is my best chance for happiness. I intend to put most of energy and thoughts into securing the future."

Instead:
"Life is what happens to us while we are making other plans."
Thomas La Mance

"The trick is to make sure you don't die while waiting for prosperity to come."
Lee Iacocca

"The best thing about the future is that it comes only one day at a time."
Abraham Lincoln

"A preoccupation with the future not only prevents us from seeing the present as it is but often prompts us to rearrange the past."
Eric Hoffer

"Real generosity toward the future lies in giving all to the present."
Albert Camus

Harmful:
"I can't wait until _____ (fill in the blank – 'I'm a teenager, I'm 21, I get my college degree, I get my first good job, I get married, I get rich, the kids are grown so I can do my thing, I retire, etc.'). This is when I will finally be happy and life will be the way I want it to be."

Instead:
"As if you could kill time without injuring eternity."
Henry David Thoreau

"Life moves pretty fast. If you don't look around once in a while you could miss it."
Ferris Bueller in Ferris Bueller's Day Off

"Waiting for the fish to bite, or waiting for wind to fly a kite. Or waiting around for Friday night or waiting perhaps for their uncle Jake or a pot to boil or a better break or a string of pearls or a pair of pants or a wig with curls or another chance. Everyone is just waiting."
Dr. Seuss

"We are here and it is now. Further than that knowledge is moonshine."
H.L. Mencken

"Most of us spend our lives as if we had another one in the bank."
Ben Irwin

Harmful:
"Having fun, relaxing, enjoying myself, being in the moment are a waste of precious time. I should be accomplishing things instead of loafing."

Instead:
"If you never did, you should. These things are fun and fun is good."
Dr. Seuss

"Man is born to live, not to prepare to live."
Boris Pasternak

"We don't stop playing because we grow old: we grow old because we stop playing."
George Bernard Shaw

"Only he is rich who owns the day."
Ralph Waldo Emerson

"We should consider every day lost on which we have not danced at least once. And we should call every truth false which was not accompanied by at least one laugh."
Friedrich Nietzsche

PRESENT LIVING IN POEMS, SONGS, MOVIES

Poems, songs and movies often touch people in ways that are motivating and inspiring. In my clinical and life coaching practice, I've found that utilizing thematic works that resonate with an individual can be an effective and enjoyable way to keep his or her little red wagon moving forward – even in the most discouraging times and circumstances.

The Treasury of Motivators for the present contains poems, songs and movie synopses that might be appealing in your quest to live in the moment. After you have read them, choose the ones that have meaning for you, or go on your own search for a work that fits the theme of living in the present.

Read the pieces you have chosen often; think about the theme every day. When you have had a chance, watch the movies. Listen to the songs, sing them to yourself. When you are discouraged, disenchanted or afraid, use you Treasury of Motivators to bolster your spirits and faith in yourself.

Poem From Alcoholics Anonymous
Author Unknown

> Today is mine
> It is unique
> Nobody in the world has one exactly like it
> It holds the sum of all my past experiences
> And all my future potential
> I can fill it with joyous moments
> Or ruin it with fruitless worry
> If painful recollections of the past come into my mind,
> Or frightening thoughts of the future,
> I can put them away
> They cannot spoil me for today

Listen to the Exhortation of the Day
By Kalidasa (Indian Sanskrit Poet, 5th Century A.D.)

Look to this day!
For it is Life, the very Life of Life.
In its brief course lies all the
Verities and Realities of your Existence.
The Bliss of Growth,
The Glory of Action,
The Splendor of Beauty;
For Yesterday is but a Dream,
And Tomorrow is only a vision;
But Today well lived makes
Every Yesterday a Dream of Happiness,
And every Tomorrow a Vision of Hope.
Look well therefore to this Day!
Such is the Salutation of the Dawn!

Present Tense
By Jason Lehman

Available online at:
http://www.matrixmonet.us/journal/archives/121-Present-Tense.html
(Can also be found in Dear Abby's Keepers)

This sad poem talks of the person who, no matter what season it is, longs for another season, and no matter what age he or she is, longs to be another age. The last two lines punctuate the folly of this path, "My life was over, but I never got what I wanted."

Cats in the Cradle
By Harry Chapin

Available online at:
http://www.lyricsdepot.com/harry-chapin/cats-in-the-cradle.html

This haunting song captures the story of a father who was never present for his son the child and the teenager. He was always too busy, too occupied to respond to this child's desire to spend time with him. And sadly, when he is old and has time for his son, his son has no time for him. The father laments, "And as I hung up the phone it occurred to me that he'd grown up just like me, yeah, my boy was just like me."

Today
Words and music by Randy Sparks
Recorded by the New Christy Minstrels

Available online at: www.asiaa.sinica.edu.tw/~syliu/html/today.ly.html

This song of enchantment with the present proclaims repeatedly, "Today while the blossoms still cling to the vine I'll taste your strawberries, I'll drink your sweet wine, a million tomorrows shall all pass away ere I forget all the joy that is mine today."

Present Living in the Movies – #1
Carpe Diem. When the poet Horace urged his fellow Romans to "seize the day" in 20 B.C., little did he know that 2000 years later a fictional young man by the name of Ferris Bueller would provide the contemporary definition of exactly what he meant. Yes, living in the present is raised to an art form in *Ferris Bueller's Day Off,* a wonderful 1986 film featuring Matthew Broderick in the title role. And while it's clear that Ferris is an unabashed conniver whose skills at deception and diversion are top notch, he's also the modern-day poster boy for knowing how to squeeze the most out of every moment on this particular day. In this, he has something to teach us all.

As the movie begins, Ferris is launching his patented "I'm so sick" charade so he can skip his ninth day of school that semester. Why? Because the temperature is going to be in the 70's, the sky is a vibrant blue peppered with a few whispery clouds and, as Ferris blithely proclaims, "How could I possibly be expected to go to school on a day like this?" (Which proves to be a legitimate question given the uninspiring teachers we meet later in the film.) As Ferris so aptly states, "Life moves pretty fast… if you don't stop and look around, you might miss it!"

The reality is that Ferris has a plan for that day, one that involves much more than simply ditching school, and it involves his best friend Cameron and girl friend Sloane. Cameron is a card-carrying hypochondriac who's wound tighter than a steel drum and whose life is governed by fear and negativity. Ferris is intent on showing Cameron how much fun life can be if he'd just, well, stop and look around once in a while.

After coercing Cameron into "borrowing" his father's vintage 1961 Ferrari sports coupe, they fabricate an excuse to have Sloane released from school and speed off toward downtown Chicago. "What are we doing to do today?" asks Sloane. "The question isn't what are we going to do today," replies Ferris. "The question is, what *aren't* we going to do today."

As we're about to see, Ferris isn't one to exaggerate. They begin with a visual tour of the Chicago skyline from atop the Sears Tower, the world's tallest building at the time and an apt metaphor for the endless possibilities the day holds. They make their way to the Chicago Mercantile Exchange for a glimpse at a typical day in the lives of floor traders. They enjoy lunch at one of Chicago's swankiest restaurants as Ferris successfully passes himself off as Abe Froman, the "sausage king of Chicago." Even a potential confrontation with his father upon leaving the restaurant doesn't faze Ferris. "The meek get pinched, and the bold survive... surrender never!" he proclaims emphatically.

They attend a Chicago Cubs baseball game, where Ferris gleefully informs Cameron, "If we played by the rules, right now we'd be in gym!" They visit the Chicago Museum of Contemporary Art and become immersed in the priceless beauty of masterpieces by Picasso, Van Gogh, Monet and other artists. But when Ferris asks, "Well, what have you seen today?", Cameron responds incredulously, "Nothing good." In a final attempt to buoy his friend's spirits, Ferris climbs aboard a float at the city's German-American parade and proceeds to lip-synch the lyrics to *Danke Schoen* and *Twist N' Shout* – dedicating the songs to his best friend Cameron. "All I wanted to do is give him a good day," he says.

On the drive home, Cameron's mood further deteriorates upon realizing that the additional mileage on the Ferrari's odometer means only one thing – another violent confrontation with his father. He becomes catatonic, staring straight ahead, unable to speak. Ferris and Sloane believe he's having a total breakdown. Hours go by with no change in Cameron's physical or mental state. Suddenly he launches himself into the pool and huddles at the bottom. Ferris and Sloane dive in and bring him to the surface, only to realize that Cameron's "suicide" is just an act. But what *isn't* an act is the epiphany he is experiencing.

"I've been meditating," explains Cameron, "watching myself from the inside, realizing it's ridiculous, being afraid, worrying about everything… I'm tired of it! *This has been the best day of my life!* I've gotta take a stand. I put up with everything, never saying anything. Well, I've gotta take a stand against my father and defend my life as it unfolds!!" Then with newfound confidence and courage, Cameron says, "I'll take the heat, I want it. When Morris (his father) comes home, he and I will have a little chat… it's cool," he assures as a wry smile crosses his face.

"I've said it before and I'll say it again," proclaims Ferris Bueller at the film's conclusion, "life moves pretty fast. If you don't stop and look around once in a while, you could miss it." Ferris doesn't miss what's important in his life, and after sharing an eventful and meaningful day together, Cameron now sees the light as well… *Carpe diem.*

Present Living in the Movies – #2
"I'm afraid you have a rare, incurable disease," says the doctor. *"You have only six months to live."* For you and me, hearing these words would be devastating, as it is for Joe Banks. But unbeknownst to Joe, he is about to enter a personal twilight zone where news of a terminal illness is exactly what he needs to hear to save his life. The lessons he subsequently learns about the art of "living" would serve us all very well.

Joseph Banks, played by actor Tom Hanks, is the main character in the 1990 film, *Joe Versus the Volcano.* And while the title might suggest something other than a movie masterpiece, it is masterful in its portrayal of a young man whose life is resurrected when he learns what it means to live in the moment.

When we're introduced to Joe, he is – in a figurative but eerily real sense – already dead. Having left a heroic but dangerous firefighting career, Joe is barely functioning in a boring, dead-end administrative job. A badgering boss, a lifeless fluorescent-lit cinder block office, a cast of zombie-like colleagues just going through the motions all combine to make Joe's already hypochondriacal life that much more sickly. Having failed to determine the cause of his constant headaches despite myriad trips to the doctor, Joe's newest physician uncovers the source of his problem – *a brain cloud*; extremely rare, incurable, terminal in six months. While shocked and confused by this bizarre diagnosis, Joe is also relieved to finally learn what he believes is the truth.

Now back at work, energized by the reality of his mortality and with newfound purpose, Joe does a "180." He lashes out at his boss, quits his job, empties his desk, and invites a co-worker (Meg Ryan) to join him for dinner that evening. Joe is finally doing the things he has always wanted to do... what a difference a diagnosis makes!

The next evening, an eccentric businessman ("Mr. Graynamore," played by Lloyd Bridges) visits Joe at his apartment and, armed with knowledge of Joe's bravery as a fireman as well as his "terminal" medical condition, makes a proposition. A remote, South Pacific island ("Waponi Woo") is the only source of a rare material that's critical to his semiconductor business, and he needs uninterrupted access to it. However, the native inhabitants are threatening to cut off that access unless he produces a human willing to jump into the island's resident volcano (the Big Woo) in a sacrificial act designed to appease their god. Joe Banks is the perfect candidate for the job.

Joe accepts without hesitation. And why not... he has nothing to lose! Equipped with several no-limit credit cards and escorted by a wise and worldly limo driver, Joe prepares for his voyage by outfitting himself in the best designer clothing and travel accessories, eating at the finest restaurant, staying at the most luxurious hotel in New York City, and undergoing a physical transformation that's nothing less than amazing. Finally, Joe is beginning to live – and it's all because he's going to die! (Hmmm... what a concept!)

After a first-class flight to Los Angeles, Joe sets sail for Waponi Woo on a ship owned by Mr. Graynamore and captained by his daughter, Patricia. Initially abusive and distant, Patricia soon warms up to Joe, and he to her, once they begin to understand why they've been thrown together on this strange voyage. A horrific typhoon catapults them even closer together when Joe saves Patricia from the sinking ship and tends to her unconscious body aboard a makeshift raft crafted out of four watertight steamer trunks.

For what seems an endless number of days and nights adrift, Joe takes care of Patricia, keeping her alive and protected from the searing sun. And while the situation is dire and the outlook is bleak, Joe begins to realize what's happening to him aboard this floating "life preserver." Each day he amuses himself with the few items he managed to salvage from the shipwreck. Each night he marvels at the sight of a gazillion shimmering stars whose brilliance against the unlit sky is simply beyond his imagination.

One night a gigantic, full moon, lit up like a Christmas ornament, beckons Joe from the edge of the horizon, dwarfing him as he screams out in a heatstroke-induced euphoria. Has Joe found God? Or the meaning of life? Whatever it is, Joe is living his life in unchartered territory, with no past to recall, and no future to behold… only today, keeping himself and Patricia alive.

As Patricia regains consciousness, the craft approaches their island destination – and Joe, who still believes he will eventually succumb to his "brain cloud," absolves to make good on his promise. Only problem is, Joe is in love with Patricia, and she with him, and she cannot stand the thought of living without him. In a ceremony presided over by the island chieftain, Joe and Patricia become husband and wife and prepare to jump into the rumbling volcano together, hand in hand. The moment they do, the volcano lets loose with a powerful gas explosion that propels them both out to sea, where they conveniently splash down next to the steamer trunks still floating offshore.

Only then does Patricia learn of Joe's condition, and only then does Joe learn that the doctor who diagnosed his "brain cloud" was actually in the employ of Patricia's conniving father. Joe Banks learns that he doesn't have a rare, terminal disease after all, but as the film comes to a close, it's clear he has learned something else: he has life, he has someone he loves, and he has today. What more could one ask for??

MOTIVATIONAL QUOTES THAT PROMOTE PRESENT LIVING

On the Present

"Time is a companion that goes with us on a journey. It reminds us to cherish each moment, because it will never come again. What we leave behind is not as important as how we have lived."
Captain Jean-Luc-Picard in Star Trek: Generations

"We do not remember days, we remember moments."
Cesare Pavase

"Only that day dawns to which we are awake."
Henry David Thoreau

"How we spend our days, is of course, how we spend our lives."
Annie Dillard

"Life is not lost by dying; life is lost minute by minute, day by dragging day, in all the thousand small uncaring ways."
Stephen Vincent Benet

"The butterfly counts not months, but moments, and has time enough."
Rabindranath Tagore

"All of man's problems stem from his inability to sit quietly with himself."
Pascal

On Control by Others

"To free us from the expectations of others, to give us back to ourselves—there lies the great, singular power of self-respect."
Joan Didion

"There is only one success – to spend you life in your own way, and not to give other absurd, maddening claim upon it."
Christopher Morley

"No bird soars too high if he soars with his own wings."
William Blake

"Within your house dwells the treasure of joy; so why do you go begging from door to door?"
Sufi Saying

"There is good tired and there is bad tired. Ironically enough, bad tired can be the kind of day when you've won, but you chased other people's dreams, you fought other people's battles, you struggled through other people's agendas, and when you hit the hay at night, victorious, you twist and turn because somehow it wasn't your day, it wasn't your life. Ironically enough, good tired can be a day that you lost everything, but fought your battles, chased your dreams, lived your day, and when you hit the hay at night you sleep the sleep of the just. You rest easy, and you say 'take me away!'"
Harry Chapin

On Guilt, Shame
"Guilt is the very nerve of sorrow."
Horace Bushnell

"There is no saint without a past and no sinner without a future."
Shri Haidakan Babaj

"Things that are done, it is needless to speak about, things that are past, it is needless to blame."
Confucius

"Waste not tears on old griefs."
Euripedes

"When guilt rears its ugly head, confront it, discuss it and let it go. It is time to ask what we can do right, not what we did wrong. Forgive yourself and move on. Have the courage to reach out for help."
Bernie Siegel, M.D., in Love, Medicine and Miracles

"Shame is the lie someone told you about yourself."
Anais Nin

On Self-Pity

"Self-pity is our worst enemy and if we yield to it, we can never do anything wise in this world."
Helen Keller

"Self-pity is easily the most destructive of the non-pharmaceutical narcotics; it is addictive, gives momentary pleasure and separates the victim from reality."
John W. Gardner

"Self-pity in its earliest stages is as snug as a feather mattress. Only when it hardens does it become uncomfortable."
Maya Angelou

"There are few human emotions as warm, comforting and enveloping as self-pity. And nothing more corrosive and destructive. There is only one answer; turn away from it and move on."
Dr. Megan Reik

"Expecting the world to treat you fairly because you are good is like expecting the bull not to charge you because you are a vegetarian."
Dennis Wholey

EFFECTIVE, PRACTICAL TECHNIQUES FOR BUILDING PRESENT LIVING

In order to change the beliefs and behaviors that you identified as problematic in the Chart on Living in the Present, you'll need to learn some specific concepts and techniques. These include:

- ✓ Principles of Behavior Change
- ✓ The Stress Response
- ✓ Abdominal Breathing
- ✓ Imagery Relaxation

- ✓ Progressive Muscle Relaxation (PMR)
- ✓ The Relaxation Response
- ✓ Systematic Desensitization
- ✓ Assertiveness
- ✓ Disputing
- ✓ Distraction

These techniques are discussed in detail in Chapter 7.

ADDITIONAL RESOURCES: RECOMMENDED READINGS AND WEBSITES

Recommended Readings:

Benson, H. (2000) *The Relaxation Response* [latest edition]

Benson, H. (1984) *Beyond the Relaxation Response*

Csikzentmihalyi, M. (1990) *Flow: The Psychology of Optimal Experience;* (1991) *Flow;* (1997) *Finding Flow*

Guarantana, H. (1993) *Mindfulness in Plain English*

Goldstein, J. and Kornfield, J. (1987) *Seeking the Heart of Wisdom*

Kabat-Zinn, J. (1990) *Full Catastrophe Living: Using the Wisdom of Your Body and Mind to Face Stress and Illness;* (1994) *Wherever You Go, There You Are: Mindfulness Meditation in Everyday Life*

Langer, E. (1997) *The Power of Mindful Learning*

Levine, M. (2000) *The Positive Psychology of Buddhism and Yoga*
Salzberg, S. and Goldstein, J. (2001) *Insight Meditation: A Step by Step Course on How to Meditate*

Audio/Visual:

Kabat-Zinn, J. *Mindfulness Meditation.* Compact Disc.

Linehan, M. (2003) *This One Moment: Skills for Everyday Mindfulness.* 55 minute VHS.

Weil, A. and Kabat-Zinn, J.(2004) *Meditation for Optimal Health: How to Use Mindfulness and Breathing to Heal Your Body and Refresh Your Mind.* Compact Disc.

Websites:

Mindfulness-Based Stress Reduction
Center for Mindfulness in Medicine, Healthcare and Society
http://www.umassmed.edu/cfm/index.aspx

Duke Center for Integrative Medicine/Mind Body Stress Reduction (MBSR)
Program; http://www.dukehealth.org

Kabat-Zinn, J. Mindfulness Meditation
http://www.selfgrowth.com/experts/jon_kabat_zinn.html
http://lioncel.tripod.com/jonkabatzinn.html

Mindfulness Literature Review, University of Chicago
http://stonepathcenter.org/links.php

LIVING IN THE PRESENT ENDNOTES

Pg. 159   Kerry, S. World Prosperity Ltd. 1999 – 2002 http://www.school-
                 reform.net/mindfulness.htm

Pgs. 160-161   Center for Mindfulness in Medicine, Healthcare and Society
                 http://www.umassmed.edu/cfm/index.aspx

Pg. 161   Hopper, J. and Schmidt, "Mindfulness: An Inner Resource for
                 Recovery from Childhood Abuse." http://www.jimhopper.com/
                 mindfulness/#whatis

Pgs. 162-163   Csiksentmihalyi, M. (1996) *Creativity: The Flow and Psychology
                 of Discovery.* New York: Harper Collins Publishers

Pg. 164   Csiksentmihalyi, M. (1998) *Finding Flow: The Psychology of
                 Engagement With Everyday Life.* Basic Books

Pgs. 164-165,   Goldstein, J. and Kornfield, J. (1987) *Seeking the Heart of Wisdom.*
170   Boston: Shambihala Publications, Inc.

Pg. 169   Kabat-Zinn, J. (1994) *Wherever You Go There You Are: Mindfulness
                 Meditation In Everyday Life.* New York: Hyperion Books

Pg. 171   Gunaratana, H. (2002) *Mindfulness in Plain English.* Somerville,
                 MA: Wisdom Publications

Pgs. 172-173 Kabat-Zinn, J. (1994) *Wherever You Go There You Are: Mindfulness Meditation in Everyday Life.* New York: Hyperion Books
(1993) "Mindfulness Meditation". http://talamasca.org/avatar/mindfulness.html
(1990) *Full Catastrophe Living: Using the Wisdom of Your Body and Mind to Face Stress and Illness.* Delta
http://beststeps.com
http://livinginthepresent.com

Pg. 173 Rich, H. (2002) *In the Moment.* New York: Harper Collins Books

Pgs. 170, 173-174 Hanh, T. N. *Peace is Every Step.* USA: Bantam Books

Chapter Six

RESILIENCE
Bounce Back From Serious Adversity

"Mishaps are like knives that either serve us or cut us as we grasp them by the blade or the handle."

James Russell Lowell

Resilience is a superlative strength of power and mastery; in fact, it's a melding of the other five strengths discussed in the preceding chapters. The synergy of these core strengths can provide you with mighty tools to prevail, even thrive, when you've been subjected to whatever disturbances life sends along. And life often sends along some pretty tough stuff that can be overwhelming, grueling and sometimes downright tragic.

Turning troubles into growth, bouncing back from tragedy, trauma and stinging failure, believing that life's major difficulties are surmountable and that the future holds the promise of renewal and opportunity are the distinguishing marks of resilience. As a resilient individual, you'll have the wherewithal to fight back and win when the going gets tough. By facing the black clouds you'll have the opportunity to become a more confident and accomplished person. The first step toward managing serious adversity in healthy ways is to understand and accept three important realities:

REALITY #1

Bad things happen to everyone. Really bad things happen to many people. Loved ones die. Serious physical and mental illness plagues us or someone close to us. Natural disasters such as fires, floods, tornadoes and hurricanes bring horror into many lives. Some of us are terrorized by people who hate us.

Some of us lose jobs, have serious marital problems or raise children who manifest heartbreaking difficulties. Many of us fail to achieve important goals at one time or another, often repeatedly. Some of us are abused as children or adults. Some of us grow up in poverty or live our adult lives in poverty. Some of us know the hell of war or captivity. Most of us experience times when numerous changes and difficulties besiege us all at once, what I call the "pile on effect." And on and on they go. These realities cross all cultures and walks of life.

REALITY #2

We often have little or no control over the occurrence of traumatic events and serious problems.

REALITY #3

We have a choice about how we perceive, react to and utilize these situations. Some people are overwhelmed by very stressful events to the point of being out of commission entirely, while others react to such occurrences with a diminished ability to cope and enjoy life. Then there are individuals with a skill set that enables them to return to pre-difficulty functioning, or even more amazingly, to a state of greater strength, wisdom, commitment and connection to life.

Understanding and accepting these realities is an important step on the path to becoming resilient. People who are resilient, who handle trouble deftly, are not lucky – they're skilled. They have beliefs and behaviors that are adaptable and proactive. Those without the skills are often at the mercy of life's travails and are susceptible to responses of anguish and despair that can last a very long time. Fortunately for them, these skills can be learned.

I have often heard questions like, "why can't life be easy," or "why me?" The straight answer is that life has easy times, challenging times and ultra challenging times for you, me and everybody. Period. Dr. Seuss explains, "I'm sorry to say, but sadly it's true, that bang-ups and hang-ups can happen to you." Elbert Hubbard, the American philosopher and writer, makes an accurate point in observing that, "Life is just one damned thing after another." Oh, well! As I tell my clients, "I don't make the rules. I simply try to figure out what they are and pass that information on to you."

You may look at others and wonder why life is so easy for them. The old "grass is greener" way of thinking. You may conclude that the relative ease of their lives is because they have money, good looks, perfect body size and the like. As a psychologist, I have worked with a wide variety of folks, some rich, some poor, some beautiful, some not so beautiful, some thin and some not so thin. It's clear to me that these are not the factors that prevent bad things from happening, nor do they ensure a hardy way of responding when unwanted events occur. And, of course, we're often unaware of the pain and suffering of others. Their lives may be quite different from what they appear to be.

If you accept these beliefs, you will be less likely to react in shock and awe when unwanted disturbances turn your world upside down. You will be in a better position to formulate an effective behavioral and cognitive approach for these times – a plan that helps you resume the forward movement of your little red wagon. Hooray!!

THE AMERICAN PSYCHOLOGICAL ASSOCIATION

In response to the terrorist attacks of September 11, 2001, the American Psychological Association developed materials to guide people in their quest to become resilient. At the end of this chapter I have provided information about locating these resources. The following points have been adapted from the APA-copyrighted document, "The Road to Resilience" available at http://www.apahelpcenter.org/featuredtopics/feature.php?id=6:

- Resilience is the process of adapting well in the face of adversity, trauma, tragedy, threats or even significant sources of stress – such as family and relationship problems, serious health problems or workplace and financial stressors.
- Research has shown that resilience is ordinary, not extraordinary.
- Resilient people do experience difficulty and distress. Emotional pain and sadness are common in people who have suffered major adversity or trauma in their lives. In fact, the road to resilience is likely to involve strong negative emotions.
- Resilience is an ongoing process that requires time, effort and steps.
- Developing resilience is a personal journey. People do not react in the same way to traumatic and stressful life events. Strategies that work for one person may not work for another. Effective approaches may vary from culture to culture.

RESILIENCE: THE ULTIMATE GIFT OF THE OTHER STRENGTHS

The behaviors and beliefs that go into building optimism, courage, persistence, present living and enthusiasm are the very same ones that help fortify the individual who's rebounding from, and even flourishing in, the heart of darkness. Dr. Seuss, in a pep talk on negotiating our journey through life, with all its challenges and obstacles, tells us that we must go on even when we incur stormy weather, face insurgents and travel great distances. He implores us to meet difficulties with "care and great tact and remember that Life's a Great Balancing Act." And when we do, he assures us, our odds of success are astounding!

THE ROLE OF OPTIMISM

When your world is disrupted and shaken by adverse events, it can be extremely difficult to believe that the future will be better. But that's just what the resilient person has learned to do. To be resilient, you must be an optimist who is confident that there's hope and renewal in the days to come and that this period of being under a very dark cloud is not personal, permanent or pervasive.

The optimist understands that bad things happen to everyone, and just because an unwanted event occurs, it does not mean that it was self-inflicted or engineered by a vindictive, vicious force. The optimist believes that there is a statute of limitations on the length of suffering – that the effects of the negative events won't last forever, and that the storm need not cause a downpour over other aspects of one's life.

Resilience is about combating and even becoming immune to despair. An optimistic attitude provides some of the tools for such a worthy endeavor. George Eliot, author of *Silas Marner,* notes that, "There is no despair so absolute as that which comes with the first moments of our first great sorrow, when we have not yet known what it is to have suffered and be healed, to have despaired and have recovered hope... But what we call despair is often only the painful eagerness of unfed hope."

Walter Anderson believes that, "True hope dwells on the possible, even when life seems to be a plot written by someone who wants to see how much adversity we can overcome." Helen Keller, an optimist through and through, proclaims that, "Hope sees the invisible, feels the intangible and achieves the impossible." And Lucille Ball, the much revered comedienne, declares, "One of the things I learned the hard way was that it doesn't pay to get discouraged. Keeping busy and making optimism a way of life can restore your faith in yourself."

Abraham Lincoln reminds us of something important: "It is said an eastern monarch once charged his wise men to invent a sentence, to be ever in view, and which should be true in all times and situations. They presented him with the words, 'And this, too, shall pass away.' How much it expresses! How chastening in the hour of pride! How consoling in the depths of affliction!"

Dr. Seuss's first children's book was rejected by 43 publishers, but he didn't let that or much of anything else derail his goals and dreams. He proclaims: "I have heard there are troubles of more than one kind. Some come from ahead and some come from behind. But I've bought a big bat. I'm all ready you see. Now my troubles are going to have trouble with me."

Anne Frank, the Jewish teenager in war-torn Germany, kept a deeply moving diary about her daily life hiding from the Nazis, showing us what optimism and resilience are all about. Her book, *The Diary of a Young Girl,* was published posthumously and is one of the most widely read non-fiction books of all time. She reveals her thoughts on the perilous life she was leading and her future plans:

> I have often been downcast, but never in despair. I regard our hiding as a dangerous adventure, romantic and interesting at the same time. In my diary I treat all the privations as amusing. I have made up my mind to lead a very different life from other girls and, later on, different from ordinary housewives. My start has been so very full of interest and that is why I have to laugh at the humorous side of the most dangerous moments.

An Example: Helen Keller
Helen Keller, a remarkable woman whose optimism allowed her to live a life of purpose and fulfillment in spite of very challenging handicaps, was born on June 27, 1880. At the age of 19 months she contracted "brain fever," which is probably what would be diagnosed today as scarlet fever. She suffered a complete loss of her hearing and sight. She lived in a dark, silent, angry internal world until, at the age of seven, Anne Sullivan became her teacher.

After many attempts to communicate, Miss Sullivan ("The Miracle Worker") broke through the barriers of blindness and deafness by splashing water on Helen's hands, while simultaneously formulating in her hand the word for water in sign language. Anne Sullivan became a beloved friend, confidante and guiding force in Helen's life.

Against tremendous odds, Helen Keller achieved great accomplishments as an author, speaker and activist. She modeled courage, persistence and optimism in ways that impressed millions of people. She traveled throughout the world, campaigning for civil rights, women's rights, voting rights and world peace. She was a devoted advocate for the blind and handicapped. By viewing her limitations as opportunities to make the world a better place, Helen Keller was a shining example of resilience, optimism and commitment.

She is an inspiration in telling us, "We could never learn to be brave and patient, if there were only joy in this world;" that "character cannot be developed in ease and quiet. Only through experience of trial and suffering can the soul be strengthened, ambition inspired and success achieved;" that "self-pity is our worst enemy and if we yield to it, we can never do anything good in this world;" that "no pessimist ever discovered the secret of the stars or sailed to an uncharted land, or opened a new doorway for the human spirit."

THE ROLE OF COURAGE

To be resilient you need a cartful of courage. Many of us, when confronted with serious difficulty, temporarily lose confidence in our perception of how the world works and how much power we have in that world. Helpless, defeated and frightened, even if only temporarily, we need courage to get back up and face what scares us, face what has caused the disruption and its fallout. It's a time that often requires bold decisions and firm commitment to taking risks, a time to embrace the gifts we do have, a time to resume the pursuit of dreams in order to regain equilibrium.

Courage is related to resilience in a number of ways. According to Catherine Britton, "Courage is reclaiming your life after a devastating event robs you of your confidence and self-esteem. It is facing tomorrow with a firm resolve to reach deep within yourself to find another strength, another talent. It is taking yourself to another level of your own existence where you are once again whole, productive, special."

Paul E. Pfuetze, the author of *Self, Society, Existence,* posits that, "... the alternative to despair is courage. And human life can be viewed as a continuous struggle between these two options. Courage is the capacity to affirm one's life in spite of the elements which threaten it. The fact that courage usually predominates over despair in itself tells us something important about life. It tells you that the forces that affirm life are stronger than those that negate it."

Dorothy Thompson, the prominent journalist and political commentator who was the inspiration for Katharine Hepburn's character in the film *Woman of the Year* believes that, "Courage, it would seem, is nothing less than the power to overcome danger, misfortune, fear, injustice, while continuing to affirm inwardly that life with all its sorrows is good; that everything is meaningful even if in a sense beyond our understanding and that there's always tomorrow."

An Example: James Anthony Piersall
And what does this brand of courage look like? In 1952, James Anthony Piersall, known in the sports world as Jim Piersall, was just 22 years old and playing center field for the Boston Red Sox when he had a complete mental breakdown on the ball field for all the world to see.

Diagnosed with Bipolar Disorder, he entered treatment, seven months of which he can hardly recollect. According to *Library Journal,* Piersall's story is one of triumph due to the medical care he received, his wife's devotion, the support of Red Sox fans, his teammates, the manager and "above all his own splendid courage." His comeback to baseball and life – the restoration of his mental health and confidence – was nothing short of amazing.

Fear Strikes Out: The Jim Piersall Story, is his poignant autobiography that was made into a movie of the same name. Anthony Perkins starred as the baseball great who confronted his serious psychological and emotional challenges head on. Piersall returned to baseball in the 1953 season, remaining in the Red Sox lineup until 1958. He was named to the American League All-Star team in 1954 and 1956, and he won the Gold Glove Award in 1958 and again in 1961 as a Cleveland Indian.

His professional career in baseball continued until 1968. And what was his attitude toward his illness? He said in his book, "Probably the best thing that ever happened to me was going nuts. Whoever heard of Jimmy Piersall until that happened?"

THE ROLE OF PERSISTENCE

To rise from the depths of difficulty, it takes time, patience, endurance and tenacity. Persistence reinforces resilience through certain beliefs that strengthen a person's steadfastness in the tough times. In subscribing to the importance of persistence, one understands the road is often plagued by detours and that progress takes time. One further eschews the victim mentality, sees mistakes and failures as room to grow, and views change as an integral part of life that is to be embraced rather than avoided. The persistent individual refuses to be unduly influenced by the discouraging feedback of others.

Being committed to a persistent stance and a resilient outcome means knowing, as C. B. Newcomb says, "Disappointment should always be taken as a stimulant and never viewed as a discouragement." And B.C. Forbes, the author and journalist who founded *Forbes* magazine contends, "History has demonstrated that the most notable winners usually encountered heartbreaking obstacles before they triumphed. They won because they refused to become discouraged by their defeats."

From Harriet Beecher Stowe, the author of *Uncle Tom's Cabin:* "When you get into a tight place and everything goes against you, till it seems as though you could not hold on a minute longer, never give in, for that is just the place and time that the tide will turn." Benjamin Franklin asserts that, "Energy and persistence conquer all things." Persistence is about planning, acting and being determined to get where you want to go regardless of the intervening twists of fate.

The American Psychological Association suggests that the resilient individual has developed the capacity to make realistic plans and is able to take the steps to carry them out. This individual has confidence in his strengths and has the capacity to solve problems. He or she is able to manage strong feelings and impulses and be flexible – when one approach is not working, energy is directed to another path of possibility.

An Example: Marie Sklodowska Curie
Marie Sklodowska Curie, better known as Madame Curie, was born in 1867 in Warsaw, Poland, and was the personification of persistence in tragic circumstances.

The struggles and personally devastating events she endured did not dissuade her from her brilliant work. Her discovery of polonium and radium led to the science of radioactivity, changing the understanding of matter and energy and spearheading a new era in medical research and treatment.

Tragedy entered her life on more than one occasion. Her sister and mother died when she was very young. About these losses she wrote later, "Never let one be beaten down by persons or events." Tragedy struck again in the spring of 1906 when her husband, Pierre Curie, who worked by her side in the research of radium, died in a terrible accident in which he was struck down by a horse and wagon. She was 38 years old and the mother of two daughters.

The day after the funeral, Marie returned to work. She explained, "Crushed by the blow, I did not feel able to face the future. I could not forget, however, what my husband used to say, that even deprived of him, I ought to continue my work." The French government offered to support her and her children, but Marie was resolved to do that on her own.

And though she suffered from periods of depression in which she was incapacitated, she would find the determination to return to her work. She believed that, "Life is not easy for any of us. But what of that? We must have perseverance and confidence in ourselves." Her remarkable contributions to the world were made possible by her steadfast tenacity and buoyancy.

THE ROLE OF LIVING IN THE PRESENT

When major disruptions occur in life, people often play over and over the thoughts and images connected to the untoward events. These thoughts and images can serve to maintain the painful, frightened feelings that were evoked by the difficulty. Or these folks may imagine what terrible things might happen in the future because of their compromised state and significant losses. These thoughts and images also can maintain the painful, frightened feelings.

Specific, horrifying reruns from the past and/or "Bela Lugosi" movies of the future have invaded the person's present world and put the brain in lock-down mode. These incessant ruminations about the past and the frightening visions of the future can literally make a body sick!

I'm not advocating that you deny the distressing event ever took place or attempt to relegate it to a position of non-importance in your life or pretend it will not affect the future in any way. That would be crazy and unhealthy, not to mention virtually impossible. But the other extreme – to focus most or all of your energy, attention and emotion on the horror and its fallout – is also unhealthy. This approach excludes moments of many other kinds, moments that can be uplifting, reenergizing and healing.

Living in the present and being mindful can be powerful potions in the healing process and important components of resilience. Kahlil Gibran, the Lebanese poet, artist and author of *The Prophet* and *Broken Wings* recommends, "Love the moment. Flowers grow out of dark moments. Therefore, each moment is vital. It affects the whole. Life is a succession of such moments and to live each is to succeed."

James Gordon Gilkey, once a teacher and chaplain at Amherst College, explains:

> Most of us think of ourselves as standing wearily and helplessly at the center of a circle bristling with tasks, burdens, annoyances and responsibilities which are rushing in upon us. At every moment we have a dozen problems to solve, a dozen strains to endure. We see ourselves as overdriven, overburdened, overtired. This is a common mental picture and it is totally false. No one of us, however crowded his life, has such an existence. What is the true picture of your life? Imagine that there is an hour glass on your desk. Connecting the bowl at the top with the bowl at the bottom is a tube so thin that only one grain of sand can pass through it at a time. That is the true picture of your life, even on a super busy day. The crowded hours come to you always one moment at a time. That is the only way they can come. The day may bring many tasks, many problems, strains, but invariably they come in single file. You want to gain emotional poise? Remember the hourglass, the grains of sand dropping one by one.

Lance Armstrong, the retired professional cyclist and winner of the Tour de France a record seven years in a row, met the challenge of an even more grueling battle when he was diagnosed with testicular cancer that had metastasized to his lungs and brain.

He now contends, "I take nothing for granted, I have now only good days or great days." Helen Keller says, "Turn your face to the sunshine and all the shadows fall behind," and, "Not the senses I have but what I do with them is my kingdom."

Emily Dickinson, the acclaimed 19th century poet, declares, "To live is so startling it leaves little time for anything else." A Chinese Proverb suggests, "When you have only two pennies left in the world, buy a loaf of bread with one, and a lily with the other." And Gilda Radner, the actress and comedienne of Saturday Night Live fame, who lost her battle with ovarian cancer, describes her journey: "I wanted a perfect ending. Now I've learned the hard way, that some poems don't rhyme and some stories don't have a clear beginning, middle and end. Life is about not knowing, having to change, taking the moment and making the best of it, without knowing what's going to happen next."

An Example: Trisha Meili

Trisha Meili, known as the "Central Park Jogger," was the victim of a gruesome crime in which she was brutally attacked and raped on April 19, 1989. At the time she was 28 years old and working as an investment banker. She was cut and beaten viciously; the pipe that smashed her head caused serious brain damage. Her coma lasted 12 days and her physicians believed that if by some miracle she survived, her brain functioning would be severely compromised. For some time, she was unable to walk or dress herself.

This amazing woman is a heartwarming model of profound resilience. She tells her story, *I Am the Central Park Jogger: A Story of Hope and Possibility,* as one of healing, support, love and enlightenment. She has become a guiding light for many who are challenged by serious, overwhelming problems. She offers hope and the ever-presence of possibilities in her lectures and writings and is particularly dedicated to brain-injured and rape victims.

In November, 2005, she spoke at the American Psychological Association's (APA) Annual Convention. Her moving message to the APA membership was about her journey in reclaiming her life and becoming whole emotionally, physically and spiritually. She spoke of how she sought support from others and found the power of the present moment. She confided to the group her belief that, "I felt like a survivor, rather than a victim." She noted that she decided it was important to grow beyond what was once considered possible. She has accepted herself as she is now.

THE ROLE OF ENTHUSIASM

How do enthusiasm and passion serve you in the tough times? If you infuse your life with vitality and possess the ability to become deeply involved in personally exciting and rewarding endeavors, you will have provided yourself with robust reinforcements that can help stem any emotional tide that threatens you.

With enthusiasm, your learning repertoire will include compelling thoughts, images and activities that are a strong and fixed part of your world. These potent tools can calm you during the disruption and its aftermath. Having positive activities will help you disengage the triggers that evoke feelings of powerlessness. And in time, it's possible that your enthusiasm and passion will be part of a successful approach to reclaim a positive focus in both your internal and external worlds.

Enthusiasm adds balance and positive energy to life. Many people tend to put most or all their marbles in one basket. But life has a way of dumping over that whole basket – and then what? If you develop enthusiasm and competence in your life, then you can mitigate some of the unwanted effects of problems that threaten to paralyze you. It's an opportunity to remember good feelings, if only for short periods. Perhaps you've been laid off from a job you love and your funds are very low; obsessing and worrying won't pay the bills or mend your heart. Going back to that yoga class you so enjoy or playing your special music may put a new face on the moment or set of moments, engendering a welcome feeling reminiscent of better times.

It may even open a door to a new, more adaptive perspective on your situation. Dr Seuss taps into his passion in this way: "I like nonsense, it wakes up the brain cells. Fantasy is a necessary ingredient in living. It's a way of looking at life through the wrong end of a telescope which is what I do to laugh at life's realities." Allan Cox declares, "Enthusiasm reflects confidence, spreads good cheer, raises morale, inspires associates, arouses loyalty and laughs at adversity."

Elbert Hubbard notes that, "Enthusiasm is the great hill climber." F. Scott Fitzgerald, the American novelist and short story writer, believes that, "Vitality shows not only in the ability to persist, but in the ability to start over." Henry Ford, who revolutionized the automobile industry, claims that, "Enthusiasts are fighters. They have fortitude.

They have staying abilities. Enthusiasm is at the bottom of all progress. With it there is accomplishment. Without it there are only alibis."

Walt Disney was a very resilient guy. A nervous breakdown, many financial catastrophes and a long, arduous road to his dreams could not deter him from his journey toward Mickey Mouse and Disneyland. He recalls, "He [Mickey Mouse] popped out of my head onto a drawing pad... on a train ride from Manhattan to Hollywood at a time when business fortunes of my brother Roy and myself were at lowest ebb, and disaster seemed right around the corner."

Disney further notes, "When we opened Disneyland, a lot of people got the impression that it was a get-rich-quick thing, but they didn't realize that behind Disneyland was the great organization that I built here at the studio, and they all got into it and we were doing it because we loved to do it." He concludes that, "All the adversity I've had in my life, all my troubles and obstacles, have strengthened me... You may not realize it when it happens, but a good kick in the teeth may be the best thing in the world for you."

An Example: Neil Young
Neil Perceival Kenneth Robert Ragland Young, nicknamed "Don Grungio", is an eminently accomplished rock and folk guitarist, singer and songwriter, known to most of us as simply Neil Young. His creative genius and superb musical talent have inspired and entertained audiences and listeners for several decades.

His first encounter with fame came in 1966 as a founder, guitarist and vocalist for the band "Buffalo Springfield." Later, after performing solo for a time, he joined the wildly successful group, "Crosby, Stills, Nash and Young," with whom he found even greater success.

He was also was a member of the band "Crazy Horse," and he has produced and performed in a number of concert films. Among his most famous recordings are *Keep on Rockin' in the Free World, Heart of Gold, Old Man,* and *Alabama.* He was inducted into the Rock and Roll Hall of Fame in 1997. He penned the song *Ohio* after the shootings at Kent State in 1970.

But with all this success, Neil Young's life has been riddled with heartbreak and serious illness. As a child he suffered from polio and was diagnosed with epilepsy in his twenty's. His two sons have cerebral palsy.

One morning in March, 2005, when he was preparing to record his song, *The Painter,* Neil Young experienced explosive head pain, shaking on his left side and distorted vision, symptoms so intense they required immediate medical attention. He was presented with very bad news indeed – the presence of a brain aneurysm that necessitated surgery. Instead of horror and self-pity, he did something quite amazing. For the few days prior to surgery, he wrote eight songs for his album, *Prairie Wind.*

Young explained to Lisa Birnbach, in her interview for *Parade Magazine,* that even though the aneurysm makes him different from the way he was before its onset, he needs to go on. He believes that all the adversities he has encountered are just part of life, and life is hard. He maintains that, "Things happen, and you've got to be able to bounce back." Another belief for which he is well known: "It's better to burn out than fade away."

DEVELOPING RESILIENCE

There are three excellent resources I recommend for the reader who wants to learn more about developing the strength of resilience:

Recommendations From the American Psychological Association (APA)

In response to the public's interest in the topic of resilience, the APA has prepared a public education initiative on resilience that includes the co-production of a documentary with the Discovery Health Channel, a national cable network that is part of the Discovery Network.

The documentary uses real-life stories to highlight the steps to building one's capacity to rebound from adversity, grow beyond difficult experiences and enjoy life despite difficult times.

In addition to the documentary, APA has developed a brochure on resilience that is available to the public through APA's consumer website (apahelpcenter.org), or by calling 1-800-964-2000. An online version of "The Road to Resilience" can be viewed at APAHELPCENTER.ORG.

The following suggestions for developing resilience are adapted from "The Road to Resilience:"

- Make connections with friends, family, people in the community. Carve out time to be connected to their support and encouragement.
- Avoid blowing the situation out of proportion.
- Move toward goals; do something regularly; focus on a task that has a good probability of success.
- Focus and work on an optimistic attitude.
- Take care of yourself – pay attention to your needs and feelings. Participate in activities you find enjoyable and relaxing. Get enough rest, eat healthy, exercise.
- Learn from your past. Ask yourself:
  - ✓ What events in the past have been stressful for me?
  - ✓ How do these events affect me?
  - ✓ In the past, to whom did I reach out with positive results?
  - ✓ What helps me be more hopeful about the future?
- Consider the situation in a broader context.
- Let yourself experience strong emotions; understand that you may need to have times when you let go the thoughts and emotions associated with the difficult situation so that you can keep functioning.
- Take action to deal with problems and meet the demands of daily living.
- Visualize what you want instead of worrying about your fear.
- Validate your fear, share it with others; create a safe environment.

The Power of Resilience (2004)
by Robert R. Brooks, Ph.D. and Sam Goldstein, Ph.D.

In their research, Brooks and Goldstein have found that resilient people manifest assumptions and cognitions that lead to effective behaviors and skills. They refer to this as a mindset that is characterized by self-control and the understanding of others. Among the suggestions the authors make are:

- Engage in purposeful activities.
- Be competent in a number of areas to allow yourself choices if one path is blocked.

- Practice empathy; see the world as others see it.
- Learn to deal with mistakes.
- Learn to deal with success.
- Learn to communicate with others and listen to them in a proactive fashion.
- Connect with others .

The Resilience Factor: 7 Essential Skills for Overcoming Life's Inevitable Obstacles (2002), by Karen Reivich, Ph.D. and Andrew Shatte, Ph.D.

Reivich and Shatte examine seven skills that promote resilience:

- Listen to your thoughts, identifying what you say to yourself when you're experiencing adversity; understand how your thoughts affect your feelings and behaviors.
- Know the eight mistakes in thinking that can detour you from a resilient approach: mind reading, jumping to conclusions, tunnel vision, magnifying and minimizing, personalizing, externalizing, overgeneralizing, and emotional reasoning; learn effective ways to thwart these traps.
- Be aware of and dispute beliefs regarding how others should behave and how the world should work when these deeply held beliefs get in the way of what you desire in life.
- Change thinking styles that lead to misinterpretations of the causes of a problem, leading to a wrong solution.
- Learn not to overwhelm yourself with "what ifs" – which turn a problem into a catastrophe.
- Learn what to do when you're beset by stress and emotion.
- Develop skills that change disabling thoughts into more resilient thoughts.

NOW WHAT DO I DO?

This is an adventure of possibilities… all the wonderful possibilities that come with being resilient on your own behalf. Your mission is to develop the belief that you can do what needs to be done, commit to an informed course of action and promise yourself that giving up is not an option. The tools to help you:

- The Chart on Resilience is an assessment tool to help you identify the beliefs and behaviors that need to be changed.

- The Treasury of Motivators features several components that offer alternatives to tired old ways of thinking and believing including: Quotations to Dispute Faulty Thinking, poems, movie synopses and motivational quotes.
- Techniques and tools that are applicable to developing resilience (presented in Chapter 7).
- Recommendations on additional resources.

It's time for an attitude adjustment… you can do it!!

CHART ON RESILIENCE – BELIEFS AND BEHAVIORS

Use the following chart to determine the beliefs and behaviors that you need to change in order to enhance your resilience. Those in the left column promote resilience, while those in the right column deplete it. Make a list of all right column beliefs and behaviors that describe you, putting them in the order of those to be addressed first, second and so on.

How do you choose the order? There are a couple of ways. One is to start with the least threatening situation, and when that situation is under your control, target the next least threatening and then the next. Another approach is to work on the thoughts and behaviors most likely to make a difference for you. Either way gets you on the path. Your choice, your little red wagon, your life! Once you've identified what needs to be changed, review your options for modifying these using the tools presented in Chapter 7.

BELIEFS

Beliefs That Foster Resilience
1. Crises and difficulties often hold hidden opportunities

2. When something bad happens, it will take time and effort to get things back to where I want them.

Beliefs That Hinder Resilience
1. Nothing good can come from adversity and difficulties.

2. When bad things occur, I want them to return to normal right away; the longer it takes, the more overwhelmed I become.

3. I can't control everything that affects the people I care about.

3. I should be able to control what goes on. When I'm not in control, it's very unsettling.

4. Handling tough breaks in life can make me stronger and more confident.

4. I'm not capable of being strong in tough times. Facing difficulties depletes my confidence and energy.

5. I believe that change, even many changes at one time, can be manageable and can avail me opportunities.

5. I'm scared of change and I especially can't handle many changes at the same time.

6. When something bad happens, I don't allow myself to think about it incessantly. Obsessing won't diminish the negative and will probably compromise my ability to cope.

6. The outcome of a tough situation may be worse if I stop thinking about it over and over.

7. When I have serious problems, I still believe the future will be positive and promising.

7. I lose hope in the future when I am experiencing serious difficulties.

8. I believe that I'm not helpless, even when dire circumstances occur. I can't control everything, but I can control some things.

8. I feel victimized and helpless when crises, tragedies or troubles occur in my life. I wonder, "why me?"

9. I believe that doing things I find enjoyable and fulfilling can help me feel better and more confident when my life has been turned upside down.

9. I don't think doing things I used to be enthused about will improve my circumstances and mood.

10. I believe it's important when besieged by difficulties to be mindful of what is happening now and to count my blessings.

10. In the middle of problems, my mind should be on what happened or what's going to happen.

11. In terrible situations I must face my fears or they will take over my life.

11. I'm not strong enough to handle my fears in tough times.

BEHAVIORS

Behaviors That Foster Resilience

1. I have a vision of my goals and dreams and return to my vision as soon as I can when difficulties interfere with my life.

Behaviors That Hinder Resilience

1. When difficulties arise I put all my energy into "the problem" in an obsessive way.

2. I try to find any humor in a difficult situation. I remember humorous times from the past and try to find uplifting subjects to think about and positive places to be.

2. I am serious all the time. It would be inappropriate to laugh now when I am having problems.

3. I take time to think about my strengths and accomplishments.

3. I spend all my time thinking about how weak and out of control I feel. I forget that I have strengths.

4. I utilize stress management techniques on a regular basis. I make the strategies that keep me healthy a priority.

4. I forget about stress management Instead, I stick to a steady diet of worrying and catastrophizing to fill up my time.

5. I spend time with people who are loving, encouraging and upbeat. I limit my time with pessimistic people.

5. I either hang around people who like to talk about how bad things are, or I isolate myself from human contact.

6. I evaluate the situation and its effects objectively. I determine what I can and can't control. I focus my time and energy on what I can control.

6. I spend every waking moment being upset about those things over which I have little or no control. I do not have a plan for taking control of what is possible.

7. I take time to consider possible opportunities, hidden or otherwise, of which I can take advantage.

7. I don't have time for anything, so I just keep recycling my thoughts and actions.

8. I develop a number of areas in which I am capable, interested and fulfilled so that I have balance and choices in my life. I spend time doing these before, during and after the onslaught of trouble.

8. I put all my eggs in one basket and hope for the best!

9. I get a reasonable perspective on the problem; I take into account how past learning and future variables may improve the eventual outcome.

9. I decide that the interruption is the worst thing that could happen to anyone and that past learning and and future possibilities cannot offset the magnitude of what's happened.

10. I assess those factors that evoke stress, anxiety and other negative reactions and then find ways to manage these better.

10. An assessment might make me more anxious, so I don't attempt it.

11. I get help when it's warranted; I am aware of the signs of clinical depression and anxiety. I understand that there are times when it is too overwhelming to face my problems alone.

11. I tough it out no matter what, even when my world is spinning out of control. I don't want to let anyone know how badly I'm handling things. Getting professional help will only verify that I am not handling things well at all.

THE TREASURY OF MOTIVATORS

The Treasury of Motivators offers a wealth of resilience-generating words and thoughts. These can be helpful in maintaining your motivation and resolve on the journey to your chosen destinations. Choose the treasures that are meaningful and inspirational for you. You may also enjoy your own treasure hunt for pieces that are personally energizing and encouraging. Incorporate these into your everyday internal world.

Some you can commit to memory; others can be placed in spots where you'll be reminded of what you want to believe and say to yourself. Focus on them often. Focus on "out with the garbage," and "in with your own special pep talk."

QUOTATIONS ON RESILIENCE TO DISPUTE FAULTY THINKING

The following statements are harmful beliefs, expectations and thoughts that people repeat to themselves over and over again, often with strong conviction. The irrationality and toxicity of these debilitating cognitions are hardly ever questioned. These cognitions compete with one's ability to be resilient in the face of serious challenges and events. You need to learn to talk back to them in significant and potent ways.

The goal is to reduce the frequency, intensity and duration of each by distraction methods and to neutralize them by disputing or arguing with their content. Disputing can be done by utilizing pertinent, meaningful quotes provided for you in this chapter or by developing your own reality-based, effective responses. You may have cognitions in your repertoire that are not contained in the following list of Harmful Beliefs and these need to be identified as well.

Take a personal inventory of these in a separate notebook, then choose quotes or other responses to question and contradict these cognitions. Remember – practice, practice, practice, so you're ready when they come for real! Besides increasing your readiness, practicing also decreases the potency of any noxious self-statements, helping you in your quest to be more resilient.

Harmful:

"I dread bad news; I know I will feel helpless and be unable to cope. If I fall, I won't be able to get back up."

Instead:

"The turning point in the process of growing up is when you discover the core of strength within you that survives all hurt."
Max Lerner

"In the depth of winter, I finally learned that within me lay an invincible summer."
Albert Camus

"The real glory is being knocked to your knees and then coming back. That's real glory. That's the essence of it."
Vince Lombardi

"It is a shameful thing for the soul to faint while the body perseveres."
Marcus Aurelius Antoninus

Harmful:
"When bad things happen I think, "why me?" I don't believe that I should have so many problems. It's not fair."

Instead:
"If my doctor told me I had only six minutes to live, I wouldn't brood, I'd type a little faster."
Isaac Asimov

"To have become a deeper man is the privilege of those who have suffered."
Oscar Wilde

"You play the hand you're dealt. I think the game's worthwhile... I am a lucky man."
Christopher Reeve

"In times like these, it is helpful to remember that there have always been times like these."
Paul Harvey

"It's foolish to tear one's hair in grief, as though sorrow would be made less by baldness."
Cicero

Harmful:
"Nothing good comes out of failure, difficulty or tragedy."

Instead:
"Every adversity, every failure, every heartache carries with it the seed of an equal or greater benefit."
Napoleon Hill

"What doesn't kill me makes me stronger."
Albert Camus

"When the Japanese mend broken objects, they aggrandize the damage by filling the cracks with gold. They believe that when something's suffered damage and has a history it becomes more beautiful."
Barbara Bloom

"Damaged people are dangerous. They know how to survive."
Josephine Hart

"The reward of suffering is experience."
Aeschylus

Harmful:
"If something goes wrong, I have to depend on others to get me through; I'm not strong enough to handle problems."

Instead:
"He knows not his own strength who hath not met adversity."
Samuel Johnson

"Too many parents make life hard for their children by trying, too zealously, to make it easy for them."
Goethe

"I owe much to my friends; but, all things considered, it strikes me that I owe even more to my enemies. The real person springs life under a sting even better than under a caress."
Andre Gide

"Not I, not anyone else can travel that road for you. You must travel it for yourself."
Walt Whitman

"Rule of survival: Pack your own parachute."
Ti Hakala

Harmful:

"Why should I have to keep adapting to the world? My life should be smooth and stress free."

Instead:

"What a man needs is not a tensionless state but rather the striving and struggling for some goal worthy of him. What he needs is not the discharge of tension at any cost, but the call of a potential meaning waiting to be fulfilled by him."
Victor Frankl

"The spirit, the will to win, and the will to excel are the things that endure. These qualities are so much more important than the events that occur."
Vince Lombardi

"You can't run away from trouble. There's no place that far."
Uncle Remus

"It is not the strongest of the species that survive, nor the most intelligent, but the most responsive to change."
Charles Darwin

"The weather-cock on the church spire, though made of iron, would soon be broken by the storm-wind if it did not understand the noble art of turning to every wind."
Heinrich Heine

Harmful:

"When things are difficult or tragic, that is all I can think about over and over. It affects my whole life."

Instead:

"That was tough… Thing to do now is try and forget it… I guess I don't quite mean that. It's not a thing you can forget. Maybe not even a thing you want to forget… Life's like that sometimes… Now and then for no good reason a man can figure out, life will just haul off and knock him flat, slam him agin the ground so hard it seems like all his insides is busted. But it's not all like that. A lot of it is mighty fine,

and you can't afford to waste the good part frettin about the bad. That makes it all bad... Sure, I know – saying it's one thing and feelin' it's another. But I'll tell you a trick that's sometimes a big help. When you start lookin' around for something good to take the place of the bad, as a general rule you can find it."
From the movie Old Yeller

"The heart's affections are divided like the branches of the cedar tree; if the tree loses one strong branch, it will suffer but it does not die; it will pour all its vitality into the next branch so that it will grow and fill the empty place."
Kahlil Gibran

"Little minds attain and are subdued by misfortunes; but great minds rise above them."
Washington Irving

Harmful:
"When things are really difficult, I lose hope that better days are ahead."

Instead:
"Evils in the journey of life are like hills which alarm travelers on their road. Both appear great at a distance, but when we approach them we find they are far less insurmountable than we had conceived."
Charles Caleb Colton

"No man is beaten until his hope is annihilated, his confidence gone. As long as a man faces life hopefully, confidently, triumphantly, he is not a failure; he is not beaten until he turns his back on life."
Orison Swett Marden

"Believe it is possible to solve your problem. Tremendous things happen to the believer. So believe the answer will come. It will."
Norman Vincent Peale

Harmful:
"When terrible things happen, I feel like throwing in the towel."

Instead:
"It's a little like wrestling a gorilla. You don't quit when you're tired, you quit when the gorilla is tired."
Robert Strauss

"I ask not for a lighter burden, but for broader shoulders."
Jewish Proverb

"You don't drown by falling in the water; you drown by staying there."
Edwin Louis Cole

"I've never been poor, only broke. Being poor is a frame of mind. Being broke is only a temporary situation."
Mike Todd

"It is better to light a candle than to curse the darkness."
Confucius

Harmful:
"It makes no sense that surviving failure or serious difficulties will help me be more successful in achieving my goals and dreams."

Instead:
"Watch out for emergencies. They are your big chance."
Fritz Reiner

"Success is how high you bounce when you hit bottom."
General George Patton

"I believe the greater the handicap, the greater the triumph."
John H. Johnson

"If we study the lives of great men and women carefully and unemotionally we find that, invariably, greatness was developed, tested and revealed through darker periods of their lives. One of the largest tributaries of the RIVER OF GREATNESS is always the STREAM OF ADVERSITY."
Cavett Robert

"Out of difficulties grow miracles."
Jean De La Bruvere

"A successful man is one who can build a firm foundation with the bricks that others throw at him."
David Brinkley

Harmful:
"There is no way that difficulties, traumas and setbacks are going to make me a happier person."

Instead:
"Happiness requires problems."
H. L. Hollingworth

"To strive with difficulties, and to conquer them, is the highest human felicity."
Samuel Johnson

"Even a happy life cannot be without a measure of darkness, and the word happy would lose its meaning if it were not balanced by sadness. It is far better to take things as they come along with patience and equanimity."
Carl Jung

"Suffering, I was beginning to think, was essential to a good life, and as inextricable from such life as bliss. It's a great enhancer. It might last a minute, or a month, but eventually it subsides, and when it does, something else takes its place, and maybe that thing is a greater space for happiness. Each time I encountered suffering, I believe that I grew, and further defined my capacities – not just my physical ones, but my interior ones as well, for contentment, friendship, or any other human experience."
Lance Armstrong

"He who sings frightens away his ills."
Miguel de Cervantes

"It is a great act to laugh at your misfortune."
Danish Proverb

RESILIENCE IN POEMS AND MOVIES

Poems and movies often touch people in ways that are motivating and inspiring. In my clinical practice I found that utilizing thematic works that resonate with an individual can be an effective and enjoyable way to keep his or her little red wagon moving along – even in the most discouraging times and circumstances.

The Treasury of Motivators for Resilience contains poems and a movie synopsis that might appeal to you. After you've read them, choose the ones that have meaning for you, or go on your own search for a work that fits the theme of resilience. Read the poems and movie synopsis often; think about the theme every day. When you have a chance, watch the movie. When you're discouraged, disenchanted or afraid, use your Treasury Motivators to bolster your spirits and faith in yourself.

Still I Rise
By Maya Angelou
http://www.poemhunter.com/poem/still-i-rise/

After a While
By Veronica Shoffstall
http://www.storybin.com/wisdom/wisdom101.shtml

Hope is the Thing with Feathers
By Emily Dickinson
http://academic.brooklyn.cuny.edu/english/melani/cs6/hope.html

The Rainy Day
By Henry Wadsworth Longfellow
http://www.quotations.about.com/cs/poemlyrics/a/The_Rainy_Day.htm

Resilience in the Movies
I've stated my belief that building resilience calls for a heaping helping of the other five strengths: optimism, enthusiasm, courage, persistence and living in the present. Think of it as getting six for the price of five!

And if you'd like to see a terrific example of resilience in a movie, you need look no further than a 2004 Academy Award-nominated film featuring three of Hollywood's most popular actors, along with one unknown, but no less inspiring, player. When Tobey Maguire, Jeff Bridges and Chris Cooper join up with a four-legged newcomer to star in the movie *Seabiscuit,* the result is one of filmdom's most compelling arguments for the power of resilience.

Set in Depression-era America and expertly adapted from Laura Hillenbrand's true-life novel of the same name, the film begins by introducing us to three disparate individuals whose lives are about to become inextricably entwined. Charles Howard (Jeff Bridges) is a wealthy entrepreneur who's making his mark in the automobile business. Tom Smith (Chris Cooper) is a cowboy in the old-west mold and a skilled "horse whisperer." And Johnny "Red" Pollard (Tobey Maguire) is the son of Irish immigrants who displays early on a special gift for riding and handling horses.

When the U. S. stock market crashes in 1929, our heroes are swept up in a maelstrom of desperation, fear and misery called the Great Depression. And as if this cataclysmic event isn't enough, deeply personal events impact them as well. Charles Howard loses his only child, a son, in an automobile accident, and with the ensuing emotional upheaval, his marriage soon dissolves. Tom Smith cannot find work and must ride the rails throughout the west in search of employment. And Red Pollard's parents – fearing they'll be unable to provide a decent life for their son – reluctantly leave him with a race promoter so he can build a life around his special abilities. Unfortunately, Red's initial lack of success on the track forces him into the boxing ring to earn money, and constant pummeling by his more skillful opponents turns him into an angry, belligerent young man.

Soon, fate intercedes and brings our characters together in Tijuana, a popular destination that provides access to alcohol, gambling and other diversions not available in the U.S. Here, Charles immerses himself in horse racing as he attempts to sooth his pain. Red Pollard hopes to prove his skill as a jockey and rekindle his love of horse racing. And Tom Smith seeks out the one thing he knows and loves the most: horses.

It's here where Tom encounters Seabiscuit, a wild, undersized colt who appears incapable of being handled. When he first makes eye contact with the rambunctious animal, Tom says "the horse looked right through me." But despite a lineage dating back to the legendary Man-O-War, Seabiscuit is deemed too small to be a winner and is used instead as a training foil – taught to lose to bigger opponents while being abused by trainers and whipped by jockeys.

At Tom Smith's recommendation, Charles Howard purchases Seabiscuit and enlists Tom to be the colt's trainer. Needing a rider, Tom turns to a young man who's also been on the receiving end of abuse by the other jockeys, but on the giving end of care, compassion and understanding for Seabiscuit: Red Pollard.

Several months of training transform Seabiscuit into just what the doctor ordered for a weary America laid low by the Depression: an underdog who becomes a winner. "We're winning because we gave Seabiscuit another chance," exclaims Charles Howard. "I think a lot of people out there know what I'm talking about!" At one point, Seabiscuit wins six consecutive races – one shy of the all-time record! Seabiscuit becomes America's motivational champion, the favorite of everyone coast to coast. But there's more to overcome in this story of resilience.

While training for the ultimate test – a winner-take-all, head-to-head contest between Seabiscuit and the vaunted War Admiral – Red Pollard is thrown from a friend's horse and dragged hundreds of yards, shattering both legs. Doctors who operate on Red say he'll never ride again; he'll be lucky to walk. But rather than cancel the race, Red turns to his friend George "The Iceman" Woolf (wonderfully portrayed by real-life jockey Gary Stevens) to ride in his place. In an inspiring, triumphant scene, George rides Seabiscuit to a stunning, run-away victory over War Admiral. Seabiscuit is on top of the world; but as Red Pollard knows, that world can be shattered.

In his very next event, Seabiscuit ruptures a ligament coming out of the starting gate. The vet informs Charles Howard that the horse will never race again and offers to put him down. But Howard declines and instead returns to his farm where Seabiscuit and Red are reunited.

Their bond now stronger than ever, Red and Seabiscuit are inseparable as together they endure the painstaking therapy that leads to healing, both emotionally and physically. Within 10 months, Seabiscuit is walking, then trotting, and finally – incredibly – galloping full speed in an emotionally charged scene that speaks volumes about the resilient spirit. And Red Pollard is not about to be a spectator any longer either. Outfitted with a crude leg brace, Red insists on riding Seabiscuit in his next competitive race, and Charles Howard agrees.

As they're lining up at the starting gate, Red notices George Woolf on a horse several stalls away. As they break from the gate, with Red in obvious pain, the two jockeys maneuver their horses side by side so that Seabiscuit can look his equine competition in the eye. With urging from his friend The Iceman, Red lets Seabiscuit explode into his next gear. Then in one of the most emotional closing scenes ever filmed, Seabiscuit surges through the field, deftly weaving in, out and in between the other horses, toward the finish line and ultimate victory.

"Everybody thought we found this broken down horse and fixed him," says Red in the closing scene as he and Seabiscuit triumphantly approach the finish line and the end of the film. "But he fixed us... every one of us. And we fixed each other, too." The story of Seabiscuit illustrates how ordinary men can overcome devastating personal hardships and do extraordinary things if they possess optimism, enthusiasm, courage, persistence, the ability to live for the day... and the resilient spirit of one extraordinary, "broken down" horse.

MOTIVATIONAL QUOTES THAT BUILD RESILIENCE

On Resilience

"It is not every calamity that is a curse, and early adversity is often a blessing. Surmounted difficulties not only teach, but hearten us in our future struggles."
James Sharp

"You cannot prevent the birds of sorrow from flying over your head, but you can prevent them from building nests in your hair."
Chinese Proverb

"He knows not his own strength who hath not met adversity."
Samuel Johnson

"The greater the obstacle, the more glory in overcoming it."
Moliere

"If you live in the river you should make friends with the crocodile."
Indian Proverb

"Oh, my friend, it's not what they take away from you that counts. It's what you do with what you have left."
Hubert Humphrey

"To hope and to act, these are our duties in misfortune."
Boris Pasternak

"When we become aware that we do not have to escape our pains, but that we can mobilize them into a common search for life, those very pains are transformed from expressions of despair into signs of hope."
Henri Nouwen

"The art of living lies less in eliminating your troubles than in growing with them."
Bernard M. Baruch

"Character cannot be developed in ease and quiet. Only through experience of trial and suffering can the soul be strengthened, vision cleared, ambition inspired, and success achieved."
Helen Keller

"What doesn't kill me makes me stronger."
Albert Camus

EFFECTIVE, PRACTICAL TECHNIQUES AND INFORMATION THAT BUILD RESILIENCE

In order to change the beliefs and behaviors that you identified as problematic in the Chart on Resilience, you'll need to learn some specific concepts and techniques. These include:

- ✓ Principles of Behavior Change
- ✓ The Stress Response
- ✓ Abdominal Breathing

✓ Imagery Relaxation
✓ Progressive Muscle Relaxation (PMR)
✓ The Relaxation Response
✓ Systematic Desensitization
✓ Assertiveness
✓ Disputing
✓ Distraction

These techniques are discussed in detail in Chapter 7.

ADDITIONAL RESOURCES: RECOMMENDED READINGS, WEBSITES AND STATE ASSOCIATIONS

Recommended Readings:

Brooks,R. and Goldstein, S. *Raising Resilient Children: Fostering Strength, Hope, and Optimism in Your Child (2001)*

Seligman, M. *The Optimistic Child: Proven Program to Safeguard Children from Depression and Build Lifelong Resilience (1995)*

Websites for Grief, Stress and Trauma:

American Academy of Experts in Traumatic Stress: http://www.aaets.org/

Post Traumatic Stress Disorder Screening: http://www.adaa.org/Public/Selftest_ptsd.htm

Trauma: www.trauma-pages.com/vanderk.html

American Psychological Association: http://helpingapa.org/daily/traumaticstress.html

Griefnet: http://www.griefnet.org/

The Compassionate Friends: http://www.compassionatefriends.org

To Contact State Psychological Associations for referrals for professional help, go to www.apa.org

Permissions

The author gratefully acknowledges permission to reprint material from "The Road to Resilience." Copyright © 2004 American Psychological Association. Adapted with permission. www.apahelpcenter.org/featuredtopics/feature.php?id=6&ch=2

RESILIENCE ENDNOTES

Pgs. 197, American Psychological Association (APA) "The Road to Resilience,"
202, 205, APA Help Center. www.apahelpcenter.org.
208-209

Located in Washington, D.C., APA is the largest scientific and professional organization in the United States and is the world's largest association of psychologists.
APA's membership includes more than 155,000 researchers, educators, clinicians,
consultants and students. APA works to advance psychology as a science and
profession and as a means of promoting health and human welfare.

Pg. 208 Birnbach, L. "I just keep going." *Parade* magazine, Feb. 19, 2006,
12-14.

Pgs. 209-210 Brooks, R. and Goldstein, S. (2004) *The Power of Resilience.* New
York: McGraw-Hill Books

Pg. 210 Reivich, K. and Shatte, A. (2002) *The Resilience Factor: 7 Essential Skills
for Overcoming Life's Inevitable Obstacles.* New York: Broadway Books

Chapter Seven

TOOLS & TECHNIQUES FOR BUILDING YOUR CORE STRENGTHS

In order to change the beliefs and behaviors identified as problematic in the charts you prepared for the six core strengths, you'll need to learn some specific concepts and techniques. These include:

- ✓ Principles of Behavior Change
- ✓ The Stress Response
- ✓ Abdominal Breathing
- ✓ Imagery Relaxation
- ✓ Progressive Muscle Relaxation (PMR)
- ✓ The Relaxation Response
- ✓ Systematic Desensitization
- ✓ Assertiveness
- ✓ Disputing
- ✓ Distraction

PRINCIPLES OF BEHAVIOR CHANGE

The past 50 years have seen a significant amount of research that substantiates the strategies that make behavior change possible. And yes, you can implement these changes yourself! Changing behavior is challenging – as we all know – but it's certainly doable for the person who makes a firm decision and commits the time and energy needed.

There are several principles within the psychology of behavior change that are relevant for our purposes. First, in programming achievement, you need to evaluate approach behaviors and avoidance behaviors, both of which play a significant role in effecting change.

Approach behaviors or habits are those behaviors we do over and over, some of which are healthy, positive behaviors and others which are unhealthy, negative behaviors. A habit of getting to work on time serves you well, while a habit of drinking too much alcohol does not.

Avoidance behaviors are either fear-based or aversion-based. Fear-based behavior involves the avoidance of situations, people, tasks or objects due to fear, anxiety or discomfort, while aversion-based behavior involves avoidance of situations, people, tasks or objects because you just don't like whatever you're avoiding. Determining if a behavior is approach or avoidance is the first step in choosing the appropriate strategies to bring about desired outcomes.

A second important principle is that approach and avoidance behaviors occur on three levels. You'll be gathering information regarding the relevant factors on all three levels; then, depending on the information you compile, you will choose interventions for the levels that are relevant. These three levels of behavior – external, internal psychological and internal physiological – interact; that is, each often affects one or both of the other levels. Think of a loop with each of these levels preceding or following the other.

THE THREE LEVELS OF BEHAVIOR

1. External behavior: refers to behavior that is observable and measurable; examples are eating, walking, avoiding your mother-in-law.
2. Internal psychological: includes thoughts, feelings, beliefs, expectations, images, etc.
3. Internal physiological: encompasses all unobservable (without technology) physical phenomena such as pain, hunger, heart rate, blood pressure, etc.

In order to implement the changes you want, you will be evaluating approach and avoidance behaviors on these three levels and then deciding which changes are to occur for each. The factors that affect behavior are those situations that act as cues for behavior (precede) and those situations that follow the behavior, which either increase or decrease the chances of it recurring.

Antecedents (cues, triggers) preceding the behavior

Example: food advertisements on television influencing eating behavior

Behavior – the target unit defined in measurable terms

Eating behavior – any event in which you put food in your mouth and swallow; decide what measurements are appropriate for the specific behavior

Consequences – those events that follow a behavior which affect its probability of occurring in the future:

1. Reinforcements increase the probability
2. Punishments decrease the probability

Antecedents, behaviors and consequences can be quantified:

1. Frequency: number of occurrences per hour, day, week, month, etc. Example: I ate five times on Monday and two times on Tuesday.
2. Intensity: strength of the behavior on a 1 to 10 scale, 10 being the most intense. Example: you may avoid something that scares you with strong behaviors of an eight – your heart was racing and you ran very fast to get away.
3. Duration: length of time one behavior lasts.

THE STRESS RESPONSE

"It's not stress that kills us, it is our reaction to it."

Hans Selye

One very important step in taking control of your little red wagon is the management and mastery of the stress response. The stress response, also known as the "fight or flight response," has been a major part of our make-up since the caveman days. It serves the vital role of compelling us to fight fiercely or flee quickly when a dangerous situation puts us in jeopardy.

When a person perceives that a circumstance is perilous, that message is swiftly conveyed to the hypothalamus, a non-thinking part of the brain that activates the sympathetic nervous system (SNS). Many changes occur in the body when the

SNS is engaged. Blood pressure and heart rate increase, breathing moves from the diaphragm to the chest and blood flow shifts to the large muscles and to the brain, away from the stomach and the extremities, restricting digestion and causing the hands and feet to become cold. Muscles tighten in readiness to run or fight. Pupils dilate, the mouth becomes dry and erections become inhibited. The immune system and tissue repair are restricted.

This is nature's way of ensuring the survival of the species. By redirecting and heightening the body's activity, blood flow and energy, the person in crisis has the resources to run fast or fight hard, increasing the likelihood of staying alive. The changes that occur put the body into a very uncomfortable and demanding state. Should this huge drain become chronic, serious physiological and psychological problems often manifest.

Just as nature equipped us with a nervous system to survive calamity, it also equipped us with a nervous system to maintain a state of calm: it's called the parasympathetic nervous system (PNS). The characteristics or actions of the PNS are largely the opposite of the SNS, and for all intents and purposes, when one is engaged, the other is disengaged. Thus, the goal of stress management is to harness the methods that promote a state of calm and that inhibit the stress response. The following strategies have been widely researched and shown to be effective:

External
What you do to manage the world outside you can go a long way in reducing your susceptibility to the stress response:

- ✓ Assertiveness
- ✓ Reducing, eliminating or learning to react differently to stressors
- ✓ Improving communication
- ✓ Eliminating self–defeating behaviors
- ✓ Having clear goals
- ✓ Managing time in positive ways

Internal Psychological
Keep in mind that the message sent to the hypothalamus may be about an actual threat or about a perceived, benign threat. You are served well by the stress response

when you are actually in danger. You are not served well when you trick yourself. So the following strategies help you make the distinction:

- ✓ Cognitive Restructuring
- ✓ Distraction
- ✓ Disputing
- ✓ Having Rational Beliefs vs. Irrational Beliefs
- ✓ Appropriate Expectations

Internal Physiological

There are calming techniques that tell the brain you are not in trouble. These can be used to disengage the response or, on an ongoing basis, to prevent it from being elicited:

- ✓ Breathing
- ✓ Imagery Relaxation
- ✓ The Relaxation Response
- ✓ Progressive Muscle Relaxation
- ✓ Insight Meditation
- ✓ Biofeedback
- ✓ Hypnosis

ABDOMINAL (OR DIAPHRAGMATIC) BREATHING

"For breath is life, and if you breathe well you will live long on earth."

Sanskrit Proverb

It's hard to emphasize enough the importance of breathing in your quest to manage the stress response and take control of your life. It's your choice: deep abdominal breathing or shallow chest breathing. The diaphragm, which is under the lungs and just above the abdomen, is the most efficient breathing muscle and is connected to the relaxed nervous system, the parasympathetic nervous system (PNS). Abdominal breathing is deep and slow, promoting mental concentration, decreased body tension and anxiety, and a greater supply of oxygen to the brain.

Chest breathing is shallow and rapid and the numerous muscles in the chest are in a state of tension. This type of breathing is connected to the stress nervous system, the sympathetic nervous system (SNS), with all its symptoms, including increased heart rate and blood pressure, decreased mental acuity and concentration and elevated anxiety levels. Some chest breathers are prone to hyperventilation, which is a very uncomfortable state.

There are three very important things I have learned over the years about breathing. First, most people don't have a clue about their breathing patterns; second, breathing abdominally makes a huge difference in stress levels and an overall sense of personal control; and third, breathing abdominally is easy to learn and maintain. What good news!

Step 1
Find a comfortable, quiet place, preferably lying on a bed, recliner or on a blanket on the floor. Choose a spot where you won't be disturbed for at least the next 10 minutes.

Step 2
Close your eyes. Put your right hand over your chest and your left hand over your abdomen in the area of your belly button. Keep these hands in place for the duration of the exercise. This is how you'll be able to tell where you're breathing.

Step 3
Take several deep breaths paying attention to which hand is moving. If your right hand is moving you are chest breathing; if your left hand is moving, you are abdominally breathing. You may find that both hands are moving. The goal is to have only the left hand moving when you inhale.

Step 4
Imagine you have a red balloon in your abdomen underneath your belly button, and that there's a tube extending from your chest to the opening of the balloon where the tube is attached. Inhale through your nose sending the air straight down the tube (no movement in the chest) and to the balloon, blowing it up like a child's party balloon. Pause for three seconds, and then exhale, sending the air back up the tube and out your nose or mouth, whichever is more comfortable.

Step 5

Wait three seconds before inhaling again. Inhale through the nose and direct the air to inflate the red balloon. Keep the balloon inflated for three seconds and then exhale slowly, waiting three seconds before the next breath. Be aware of your hand positions and where the breathing movement is occurring on the inhale.

Repeat this pattern for 10 minutes. Do this twice a day.

Step 6

After you've practiced this for several days and are confident that you're breathing abdominally during the exercise, check your breathing in a variety of circumstances and locations to see if you're chest or belly breathing. For example, check yourself when you're reading, walking, cooking dinner or working. If your breathing is shallow, imagine the red balloon and shift the breathing to your abdomen. Your goal is to generalize your abdominal breathing so it becomes a habit that can serve you most, if not all, of the time. Continue to check this frequently.

Step 7

The image of the red balloon that you've practiced and used in general is a learned image that can help you when you're feeling stressed or anxious. Whether you're in the middle of a stress situation or anticipating some stressful circumstance, just imagine the red balloon and do as much of the abdominal breathing exercise as you can wherever you are.

Step 8

Continue practicing the 10-minute breathing exercise every day, or at least several times a week. Practicing often reduces the stress response in general and keeps you focused on maintaining abdominal breathing.

IMAGERY RELAXATION

"There is no need to go to India or anywhere else to find peace. You will find that deep place of silence right in your room, your garden or even your bathtub."

Elisabeth Kubler-Ross

Guided Imagery is a wonderful way to learn to relax. There are many relaxation audiotapes and compact discs available that may appeal to you. The following imagery script is one I have recorded and provided to my clients. You might want to record this script for yourself, or ask someone else to do it. If you choose someone else, it should be a person whose voice is relaxing and positive for you.

The script should be read at a very slow pace, pausing for five seconds between sentences. Some people enjoy soothing background music. Using this recording each day can help reduce your general stress level over a 12 to 24-hour period. For stressful situations that come up throughout the day, focus on one of the images from the tape to compete with the effects of the stressor. Choose one image each day so you're ready when trouble comes.

Guidelines

There are some guidelines that will help this be very effective. Find a quiet place where you will not be disturbed. Get comfortable. Lying on a couch, bed or recliner works well. Scan your muscles to identify areas that are tense. Try to let tense muscles relax. Turn on the tape, close your eyes and follow the words being spoken. If you get distracted, passively come back to the voice on the tape.

In this script, I am using the warmth of the sun and a beach with sand. If, for any reason, the sun and beach do not appeal to you, you can make substitutions. Instead of the sun, find something that suggests warmth, such as a fire in a fireplace or the heat from a campfire. Instead of the beach you could be anywhere that is relaxing and enjoyable for you. Here goes...

The Script

You're on a beautiful, deserted beach. You're lying comfortably on a soft blanket. You don't have a care in the world. The sun is shining and the sky is a stunning, clear blue. You smell the refreshing salt air. The temperature is just right. You gently close your eyes, enjoying the feeling of the sun spreading its warmth over your body.

You feel the warmth on your face and the muscles begin to relax. Your forehead is becoming loose and limp. Your eyelids are heavy, warm and heavy, very warm and heavy, almost too heavy to lift. You feel the sun on your nose and on your cheeks and mouth. A feeling of comfort and peace comes over you. Take a few moments to enjoy the feeling of relaxation.

Now you feel the warmth of the sun on your neck, on the front and on the sides. You are aware that all the stored-up tension is rising out of your body. You can see it leaving your body. You feel your neck muscles relaxing, relaxing, relaxing. Take a few moments to enjoy the warmth, relaxation and peace you are feeling.

You feel the sun on your chest and abdomen. Each of the muscles in your chest is becoming loose and limp and very deeply relaxed. You notice that your stomach muscles are letting go, letting go, letting go. And as your abdominal and chest muscles relax, you watch your breathing become slow and deep, slow and deep. Take a moment to relax and watch the rhythm of your breathing.

You feel the sun on your left arm, on the shoulder, on the upper arm, the lower arm and on your hand. Your left arm is becoming warm and heavy, warm and heavy, so warm and heavy, too heavy to lift. Take a few moments to enjoy the relaxation.

You feel the sun on your right arm, on the shoulder, on the upper arm, the lower arm and on your hand. Your right arm is becoming warm and heavy, warm and heavy, so warm and heavy, too heavy to lift. Take a few moments to enjoy the feeling of relaxation.

You feel the warmth of the sun on your left leg, the upper leg, the lower leg and on your foot. Your left leg is becoming warm and heavy, warm and heavy, too heavy to lift. Take a few moments to enjoy the deep relaxation.

You feel the warmth of the sun on your right leg, the upper leg, the lower leg and on your foot. Your right leg is becoming warm and heavy, warm and heavy, too heavy to lift. Take a few moments to enjoy the feeling of relaxation and comfort.

Then in your mind you gently roll over. The sun's warmth spreads over the back of your neck (pause), down your back (pause) and the back of your legs. Take a few moments to enjoy the feeling of deep relaxation and peace.

Your body is profoundly relaxed. You are aware that your breathing is deep and slow. Remain still for several moments basking in the glow of the sun and the feeling of peace and comfort. I am going to count down from 10 to one, and with each number you will become more deeply, deeply relaxed. (Pause for three seconds after each number.) Ten, Nine, Eight, Seven, Six, Five, Four, Three, Two, One.

You are in a beautiful meadow, walking on grass that feels like a soft, soft carpet. Everything around you is beautiful. To your right is a babbling brook with the sun shining on the water like shimmering diamonds. On the left are three waterfalls reflecting the sun. There are brightly colored flowers all around and a hill in the distance. A feeling of relaxation sweeps over you and you feel so content and peaceful.

Straight ahead is a mountain with a snow cap. You are walking slowly enjoying the beauty around you. The waterfalls are gently foaming and there are majestic orange leaves on the trees. The ripples of the brook have a calming effect. You hear the rustling of the leaves. As you walk slowly, you become more and more relaxed. Take several moments to enjoy your walk in the meadow.

You are watching a feather blowing in the breeze, blowing from side to side. As you watch that feather blow from side to side to side, you are becoming very deeply, deeply relaxed. Take a few moments to watch the feather as it blows in the breeze.

You are feeling very good about yourself. You are feeling worthwhile, comfortable and peaceful. I am going to count to three and when you open your eyes, you will be refreshed and relaxed. (Pause for three seconds between each number) One, two, three.

Recommended Readings

Fanning, P. (1988) *Visualization for Change*

Davis, M. and Eshelman, E.R. (1988) *The Relaxation and Stress Reduction Workbook*

PROGRESSIVE MUSCLE RELAXATION (PMR)

"Deep muscle relaxation, when successfully mastered, can be used as an anti-anxiety pill."

Martha Davis, Elizabeth Robbins Eshelman, Matthew McKay
The Relaxation and Stress Reduction Workbook (1988)

In his book, *Progressive Relaxation,* published in 1929, Edmund Jacobson describes a procedure of relaxing muscles that competes with the stress response. Stressful thoughts and circumstances produce muscle tension as part of the fight or flight response; this muscle tension can become chronic.

By becoming aware of the differences in the feeling and the appearance of muscles when they are tense versus when they are relaxed, an individual can exert control over stress-related muscle tension. This is important in mitigating the stress response in general, as well as reducing pain and other problems that result from chronic muscle tension.

This exercise usually takes 15 to 20 minutes. Like other relaxation techniques, you will get the most value by practicing it regularly. Find a comfortable place where you will not be disturbed. Close your eyes. Spend three minutes doing abdominal breathing. The procedure for each muscle or group of muscles is as follows:

- ✓ Tense each muscle for 10 seconds
- ✓ Imagine for five seconds what the muscle looks like as it is fully tensed
- ✓ Relax the muscle, letting go, letting go, letting go for 10 seconds
- ✓ Imagine for 5 seconds what the muscle looks like in its loose, limp, relaxed state

Focus on the following muscles, in this order:

- ✓ Forehead (frown)
- ✓ Nose (squeeze)
- ✓ Cheeks (lift)
- ✓ Mouth and jaw (big smile)
- ✓ Neck (head forward, head backward, head to right, head to left)
- ✓ Shoulders (pull upward)
- ✓ Chest (push out)
- ✓ Abdomen (pull in)
- ✓ Buttocks (press together tightly)
- ✓ Back (arch up and forward)
- ✓ Right arm (10 seconds each part); hand (clench), lower arm (hand down), upper arm (flex bicep)
- ✓ Left arm (10 seconds each part); hand (clench), lower arm (hand down), upper arm (flex bicep)
- ✓ Right leg (10 seconds each part); foot (curl toes), lower leg (point toes toward your nose), upper leg (clench)
- ✓ Left leg (10 seconds each part); foot (curl toes), lower leg (point toes toward nose), upper leg (clench)

Take two or three minutes to enjoy the feeling of deep muscle relaxation. Be aware of your breathing. Open your eyes and sit quietly for a minute or two.

In order to generalize this response, check your muscle tension levels throughout the day in a variety of circumstances. If one or more muscles are tense, let that be your cue to imagine a relaxed muscle and let go, let go, let go. I've found that when teaching children and adolescents this exercise, it often helps to focus on the arms and legs first, then mid body and finally on the head area. By relaxing the large muscles, the youngsters seemed better able to pay attention from start to finish.

THE RELAXATION RESPONSE

"Meditation is the gateway through which you arrive to the world of freedom."

Remez Sasson
Author of Visualize and Achieve

The relaxation response is a meditative technique that effectively reduces stress. Herbert Benson, a cardiologist, researcher and associate professor at Harvard Medical School, coined the term in his book, *The Relaxation Response,* first published in 1975.

The term refers to an inborn capacity of the body to enter a special state characterized by lowered heart rate, a decreased rate of breathing, lowered blood pressure and an overall reduction in the speed of the metabolic processes. The changes produced by this response counteract the harmful consequences and uncomfortable feelings of stress. This form of meditation has been an effective tool in treating medical conditions such as hypertension, angina, sleep disorders and chronic pain.

Benson, in his extensive and robust research on Transcendental Meditation. has identified four important components in the elicitation of the relaxation response – two of which, repetition and a passive attitude, must be present in order for this special state to occur. The four components are:

✓ A quiet environment
✓ Repetition of a word, a sound, a phrase, a prayer or a fixed gaze at an object
✓ A passive attitude of disregarding everyday thoughts and worries that inevitably come to mind, returning to your repetition
✓ A comfortable position

In his subsequent book, *Beyond the Relaxation Response: How to Harness the Healing Power of Your Personal Beliefs* (1984), Dr. Benson presents his findings regarding the advantage of using belief or faith-based words as mental devices. He notes that the more a person's beliefs are integrated into the procedure, the more likely one is to reap the advantages of the "Faith Factor."

For optimal benefit, the relaxation response should be practiced for 15 to 20 minutes twice daily on an empty stomach. After you've been regularly using this form of meditation, you will find that you have the ability to evoke mini relaxation responses when you choose to do so.

This can be an effective tool to combat stress and anxiety. Simply use your word or phrase on the out breath a number of times. Don't be discouraged if it takes a lot of practice before this starts to feel natural.

The steps as outlined by Dr. Benson are as follows:

Step 1
Pick a brief word, phrase or short prayer that is part of your belief system. The word or phrase should be easy to pronounce and easy to remember. If a belief based word does not come to mind, choose a word that evokes a neutral or positive response, such as one, peace or love. During the exercise you will be repeating this word or phrase as you exhale naturally.

Step 2
Choose a comfortable position, any position that will not disturb your thoughts and will not put you to sleep. Do not cross your legs.

Step 3
Close your eyes. Relax your muscles. Start with your feet, then your calves, thighs, and abdomen. Relax your head, neck and shoulders. Stretch and relax your arms and hands and let them drop naturally onto your lap.

Step 4
Become aware of your breathing and start using your word or phrase on the out breath. Breathe slowly and naturally without forcing the rhythm. Continue to repeat silently your chosen word or phrase always on the out breath.

Step 5

Maintain a passive attitude. Thoughts will inevitably enter your mind as you sit quietly repeating your personal phrase. You may even see mental images or patterns that distract you from your word. Remember, they do not matter. These lapses are natural. Respond to them in an unconcerned way. Don't try to force them out of your mind. Passively say to yourself "oh well" and then slip back gently to the repetition. Even if a thought or image persists from start to finish, just tell yourself that's okay. If you are distracted by an itch or tight clothing, go ahead and scratch or rearrange your clothing to become more comfortable.

Step 6

Continue for 15 to 20 minutes. Keep a watch or a clock handy and check it now and then. If the time has not elapsed, close your eyes and return to the repetition.

Step 7

When the time has elapsed, sit quietly with your eyes closed for a minute or two. Stop repeating your word or phrase. Allow your regular thoughts to enter your mind again. Open your eyes slowly and sit quietly for another minute or two.

SYSTEMATIC DESENSITIZATION

"Fears are educated into us and can, if we wish, be educated out."

Karl Menninger

Systematic Desensitization, also known as exposure therapy, is a highly effective method for overcoming fear and anxiety reactions to events, situations, persons or things. Joseph Wolpe, the South African psychiatrist, developed this procedure in the 1950's. Based on the classical conditioning model, this intervention is an effective treatment for phobias and anxiety disorders, as well as those fear responses that do not meet the criteria for a clinical diagnosis.

Sensitization is the learning process in which anxiety and/or stress symptoms become associated with a given stimulus, often a neutral one for which there is no basis for the fear; desensitization is the unlearning of that association. When a person experiences the stress response (discussed in another section), a common reaction is to avoid the situation that evokes fear or anxiety.

When you avoid something that scares you, those fearful feelings and the accompanying physical symptoms often diminish or disappear. Because the behavior of avoiding or escaping was so powerful in halting what is distressing, it becomes more likely that you will use the same response again when the situation or a similar situation presents itself. Avoidance has been reinforced, leading to more avoidance and to the increased strength of the connection between anxiety and the stimulus.

Let's use the example of public speaking. You have agreed to give a presentation, but just the thought of standing in front of an audience gives you heart palpitations, sweaty palms and the desire to run away. You decide to avoid the problem by canceling your commitment. After getting off the phone, all your symptoms quickly subside. What a relief!

The problem is that the more you avoid, the smaller your world becomes, restricting the number of choices available to you. To add to the difficulty, at some point just thinking about the fearful situation can evoke the fight or flight response. Then you start to anticipate when trouble might come. Alas, this problem can take over your life!

As Eleanor Roosevelt asserts, "You gain strength, courage and confidence by every experience in which you really stop to look fear in the face. You must do the thing you think you cannot do." To manage fear, you have to stop the avoidance. Fortunately, this can be done in a gradual, step-by-step way that won't overwhelm you.

Systematic Desensitization involves three major components: a hierarchy of anxiety-provoking situations or stimuli; the ability to generate a state of relaxation; and exercises where you pair the fear stimulus with the relaxed state. This can be done via imagery or in vivo (in the actual situation).

This approach works because relaxation competes with anxiety; when you are relaxed, you are not anxious. By pairing relaxation with whatever scares you, the association with the stimulus changes from fear to calm. The number of pairings for a successful outcome varies from person to person and from situation to situation. It's important to time the pairings close together, particularly for in vivo; if they are too far apart, the fear can regain strength.

Imagery and In Vivo Desensitization

In both types of desensitization, feared stimuli are arranged on a hierarchy. The exercises start with the stimulus or situation that evokes the least anxiety; in imagery, this is done by simply imagining the stimulus, and in vivo, this is done in the actual situation. When this stimulus no longer leads to an anxiety response because of repeated pairings with a relaxed state, then the next one on the hierarchy is targeted and the same procedure is followed.

Imagery Desensitization presents a number of plusses. It can be quite effective as a sole treatment; it is a way to prepare you to approach the actual situations with less discomfort; it is helpful in reducing anticipatory anxiety; and it is generally more accessible than some actual situations. For example, if you're afraid of flying, being on an airplane every day for two weeks may not be practical. In vivo, when done properly, is a very potent technique. I have found that using both types is especially helpful to many people.

The Steps

For both types of desensitization, you first develop a hierarchy. This hierarchy is based on Subjective Units of Distress (SUDS). The rating system can be 1 to 10 or 1 to 100. Your job is to list the fearful parts of what is being avoided. Then you rate them according to how much subjective anxiety they elicit. Consider the emotional, physical and behavioral symptoms you experience when faced with a given stimulus. There are two rating Subjective Units of Distress scales that are often used:

1 to 100 Scale	*1 to 10 Scale*	*Subjective Distress*
1 to 19	1 to 2	Low Anxiety
20 to 39	3 to 4	Medium Low Anxiety
40 to 59	5 to 6	Medium Anxiety
60 to 79	7 to 8	Medium High Anxiety
80 to 100	9 to 10	High Anxiety

Choose whichever scale you feel will be more helpful to you. Actually imagine and feel your response to each facet of your fear, and then assign the number that most closely approximates your subjective distress. Describe as fully as you can the specific situation.

For example, if you're trying to desensitize to dogs, one situation might involve a small dog on a leash 50 yards away in an open field = SUDS of 18. What are the elements that make one situation more fearful than another? This assessment is very important, so spend some time figuring out what the variables are.

The hierarchy should have around 15 situations, ranging in the intensity of anxiety from mild to high. Then arrange them in order according to the SUDS rating, starting with the least anxiety evoking, then the next and so on. This sequence may not correspond to how the events would occur chronologically. For example, if you are afraid of flying, a lower SUDS item might be eating lunch at the airport, while a higher one might be making reservations for the dreaded flight.

The Role of Relaxation

To bring about a relaxed state, you actually have a number of choices. I have discussed some of the most common and most effective relaxation strategies in another area of the techniques section. These include:

✓ Progressive Muscle Relaxation
✓ The Relaxation Response (a form of meditation)
✓ Abdominal Breathing and Imagery Relaxation

Choose the method that is best for you. Before starting each exercise, find a place where you won't be disturbed, then spend five to 10 minutes becoming deeply relaxed.

Putting Desensitization to Work: Pairing the fear stimulus with your state of relaxation

✓ Imagery Desensitization

Imagine yourself in the situation. Really be there. Be aware of all the elements that contribute to your distress. The vividness of your imagery is very important. Maintain this imagery for several minutes. Intermittently, while you are visualizing the fear stimulus, take some deep abdominal breaths. If your anxiety exceeds a 4 or 40 for a minute or so, return to your relaxation exercise or discontinue the imagery until your next planned session.

After several minutes of visualizing the target, take a break, relax and then do it again. When the targeted stimulus you are working on no longer evokes anxiety, you're ready to move on to the next target on the hierarchy. One of the terrific things about this process is that as it unfolds, even before you get to the higher anxiety stimuli, their SUDS ratings decrease. What a deal!

✓ In Vivo Desensitization

In vivo means you actually experience exposure to stimuli or situations you fear. Start with the least anxiety provoking situation. After becoming deeply relaxed, approach the first situation on the hierarchy. Try to abdominally breathe throughout the exercise. Stay in the situation for several minutes; if your anxiety exceeds the 4 or 40 rating for a minute or two, either revisit your relaxation exercise and then continue or try again in your next planned desensitization session. Repeat this exposure until it no longer evokes an anxiety response. Then move on to your next target. Generally, the time for each session for both types of desensitization is 30 minutes, unless your anxiety is too great.

An Example
Let's say that when you were a small child a dog jumped up on you and your heart beat right out of your chest. After that, you wanted nothing to do with dogs; then your fear generalized to cats and even small creatures. Fact is, now you stay away from areas where any animal might appear – and you're 33 years old! How do you get beyond something that has been going on for so long, is so much a part of you and has seriously restricted your choices? Answer: you commit to the process of desensitization. Your hierarchy might look like this:

Stimulus	*SUDS Rating*
Looking at a picture of a small docile dog	2 or 22
Looking at a picture of a large menacing dog	3 or 35
Watching a movie with a dog in a prominent role	4 or 40
Observing a small dog on a leash 100 feet away	4 or 40
Observing a large dog on a leash 100 feet away	4 or 43
Looking out the window at a friend's dog	4 or 46
Taking a walk in your neighborhood	5 or 54
Visiting the pet store and petting a dog	6 or 62
Going to a dog park where dogs are required to be on leashes	7 or 76
Sitting in a park area where there are children, dogs and cats	8 or 80

Stimulus	SUDS Rating
Holding a small dog for three minutes	8 or 80
Letting a small, unleashed dog jump on you	8 or 88
Petting a large, unleashed dog	9 or 91
Letting a large dog jump on you	9 or 95
Becoming a veterinarian!	?????

One of the first clients with whom I worked on desensitization was a five-year-old who was virtually housebound because of her fear of dogs. We actually performed most of the above steps, both in imagination and in vivo. She really did a super job. I got a call from her mother several years later to let me know that her phobia never returned. In fact, they had two large dogs now and my little client told her teacher she wanted to be a veterinarian. Sweet!

Some Pointers

- Desensitization takes practice, practice, practice. Have realistic expectations about how long this may take. If you are moving slowly, that's fine. Remember you are moving and not avoiding – that's the crucial part.
- Some people find it helpful to put the imagery desensitization on tape. Relaxation exercises can also be put on tape.
- When you start in vivo desensitization, you may want to have someone go with you for your sessions. For example, in the dog phobia, the child's mother joined us for many of the targets on the hierarchy
- This procedure is quite effective, even if the items at the top of your hierarchy evoke sheer terror.
- You need to come to terms with the possibility that you will experience some discomfort. Try to normalize that idea. Discomfort is a part of life. If you tell yourself that it's awful to experience discomfort, then you leave yourself with no room to be powerful on your own behalf. Instead tell yourself that it is just part of the deal, that by addressing its source, you won't let it get the best of you.
- Setbacks are another part of the learning curve. Normalize those in your self-talk. Expect setbacks to happen. Your response to them: "Oh well!"
- Be your own cheerleader in this process. Talk yourself into sticking with it. Tell yourself that this is the route to personal freedom and self-confidence.
- If you need help beyond what is described here, there are more extensive resources below. Also, many clinicians are well-trained to help you with this process.

Recommended Resources

The following books and audio cassettes by Edmund Bourne, Ph.D.

- ✓ *The Anxiety and Phobia Workbook* (2000). New Harbinger, Oakland, CA, paperback
- ✓ *Beyond Anxiety and Phobia* (2001) New Harbinger, Oakland, CA, paperback
- ✓ Audiocassettes on following fears: Flying, Giving a Talk, Driving on the Highway, Heights

ASSERTIVENESS

"Assertive behavior promotes equality in human relationships, enabling us to act in our own best interests, to stand up for ourselves without undue anxiety, to express honest feelings comfortably, to exercise personal rights without denying the rights of others."

Robert Alberti and Michael Emmons

Assertiveness is a proactive, positive set of beliefs and behaviors that helps an individual define the boundaries with other people. These boundaries pertain to the ownership of rights and responsibilities. It is distinguished from aggressive behavior at one end of the spectrum, which tends to be self-centered, destructive and alienating in relationships, and passive behavior at the other end of the spectrum, which tends to foster personal dependency, helplessness and inhibition. Becoming assertive is a giant step toward personal freedom and growth. It is an important component in managing the stress response.

Alberti and Emmons, in their excellent book on assertiveness, *Your Perfect Right* (1995), explain that assertiveness is learned and involves the following:

- ✓ Believing in and supporting equality in interactions with others
- ✓ Being your own decision-maker
- ✓ Believing in yourself regarding the judgments you make
- ✓ Establishing goals
- ✓ Behaving in ways that promote what you want
- ✓ Requesting assistance from other people when it is important to do so
- ✓ Communicating in an honest and forthright manner your thoughts, beliefs, feelings

✓ Having the ability to disagree openly and honestly

✓ Being able to say no when you mean no

✓ Refraining from treating others in noxious ways, such as manipulation

Manuel J. Smith, in the 1975 bestseller, *When I Say No I Feel Guilty*, outlines your rights in relationships with others:

✓ The right to evaluate your own thoughts, feelings, behaviors

✓ The right to determine your responsibility in assisting when others have problems

✓ The right to refuse to explain why you have behaved in a given way

✓ The right to change your thinking about any topic

✓ The right to fail

✓ The right to decide you are unsure of something or don't understand and communicate that

✓ The right to make choices that may not make sense

In *The Assertive Woman* (1995), Stanlee Phelps and Nancy Austin maintain the following are beliefs and behaviors of the assertive person:

✓ Belief that your importance is not a function of the opinions and comments of others and should not be measured by comparing oneself to others

✓ Belief that it is important to secure what you want and need

✓ Belief that you have a right to communicate your thoughts and feelings

✓ Belief that mistakes are a way to learn

✓ Deciding for yourself and thinking for yourself

✓ Having passion about possibilities and novel events

✓ Communicating without discomfort what you do well

DISPUTING

"The mind is its own place, and in itself, can make heaven of hell, and a hell of heaven."

John Milton

I certainly hope that by now I've convinced you that you have a choice about what goes on inside your head. You get to choose what you think, what you believe and what you expect to happen. Robust research has shown that disputing is a very effective technique to utilize in your quest to control your inner world. Disputing is arguing with disturbing beliefs, thoughts and assumptions about outcomes. It's about changing your interpretation and thus the consequent reactions you have to the adverse circumstances. It is represented by ABCDE model:

A = Adversity: The trigger or antecedent to your negative belief.
Example: You do not get the job you interviewed for at the prestigious Boston law firm.

B = Belief: Belief that automatically occurs in conjunction with the adversity.
Example: I am a failure and may never get a job. What made me think I could work for a law firm as prestigious as this? What an idiot I am.

C = Consequences: The usual consequences resulting from this belief.
Example: You feel deflated, disappointed, ashamed and scared.

D = Disputation: The argument disputing the erroneous belief.
Example: It often takes more than one interview to get hired. You remind yourself that you have had many of other jobs at which you excelled, that you have many professors who praised your accomplishments. You remind yourself of the reality that most new law school graduates have to interview with a number of firms before getting an offer.

E = Energy: The energy that occurs when one disputes successfully.
Example: You feel much better. You are optimistic that you can work somewhere that will be a great step in your career. You renew your search for other possibilities.

DISTRACTION

"Every thought is a seed. If you plant crabapples don't count on harvesting Golden Delicious."

Author Unknown

Your thoughts and imagery are your own private heaven or hell. You unquestionably get to decide what will go on between your ears. No one has the power you have to control what transpires in your sacred sanctuary. Knowing how to wield that control in order to design your optimal internal world makes all the difference.

Your thoughts are learned and have gained strength by repetition; by refusing, in a concerted, consistent and tenacious way, to allow certain thoughts, by distracting your focus from negative thoughts, images and beliefs and turning them to positive, motivating cognitions or activities, you can reshape your mental landscape.

Distraction methods are very effective ways to shrink the number, strength and amount of time you spend thinking and imagining all the bad things. Disputing (explained in another section) is a companion technique that debates the content and substance of your negative thinking. Together, these two are formidable techniques in your arsenal. Distraction reduces the occurrence of the thinking, and disputing questions the veracity and usefulness of the claims that remain.

For example, if you keep focusing on how fat you are, distraction is useful in diminishing the number of times you say that to yourself in a given day; it may also reduce the strength of the response you have to that particular thought or belief. Disputing is then used to question the veracity of your belief and the advisability of considering that this is so important to you.

Distraction is about saying "no" to one response and being ready to replace it with another, more adaptive response. This can be done by directly addressing the thoughts in your head or by opting for a competing external activity. The internal exercise I am going to discuss is one that many of my clients rave about: the Self-Control Triad.

The external approach involves switching to an action that competes with thinking, such as playing a sport, watching an engrossing or very funny movie, singing a silly song, playing a video game, or engaging in a hobby that holds your attention. The external distractions are often less accessible than the internal one, which you can have available to you whenever you need it and wherever you are.

The Self-Control Triad

My mentor at Boston College, the late Dr. Joseph R. Cautela, developed this technique in the early 1980's. I've been teaching this to people of all ages ever since then and with very heartening results. Thank you Dr. Cautela!

The Self-Control Triad has three major components: thought stopping, abdominal breathing and positive imagery. The idea is to strongly say stop to a thought, expectation, etc., then to switch to abdominal breathing to distract and relax you, and finally to replace the unwanted cognition with one that is positive and competes with the undesirable one. The steps to using the triad to your advantage are as follows:

✓ First, take an inventory of the cognitions that are problematic. This inventory will include negative thoughts, expectations, images, beliefs and the dreaded "shoulds."

For five days, keep a journal of all these cognitions. Have the journal handy so when an aberrant cognition surfaces you can write it down. Some cognitions will be more obvious to you than others. Keep track of how frequent each cognition is, how intense your response is to it (one to 10, 10 being most intense), how long each lasts and at what time it occurred.

Note if there is a specific trigger for that thought. For example, you have the fearful thought of going to the doctor's office and being told you have some disease. You have this thought 10 times in the five days. The intensity of response is eight to 10; it lasts an average of five minutes and occurred seven times in the morning and three in the afternoon. Several times it came to mind after listening to a health spot on the radio. At the end of the five days, you will probably have a pretty good inventory of what's going on upstairs.

✓ Thought Stopping

Thought Stopping was introduced by Robert Bain in his 1928 book, *Thought Control in Everyday Life*. Joseph Wolpe and others in the field of Behavior Therapy applied Thought Stopping as a technique to diminish anxiety and obsessive thoughts. This makes sense since negative thoughts are often antecedents to negative emotions.

Lots of people say stop to themselves when their thinking goes awry, but it does not get the job done. Believe me, I have heard it all. The catch is that the "STOP" has to be loud, strong and forceful – something that comes with a lot of practice.

To start the practice, make sure you are in a comfortable place where no one will disturb you. Close your eyes and yell ***STOP!*** in your head. Try to make it as loud as possible – as if you're hearing a rock band at full volume. Try to make it as forceful as if you saw a child or dog running into the street with a car coming. Measure both the loudness and the force on a one to 10 scale, with 10 being the highest. Don't be discouraged if you're at the low end on both as you begin this new learning process. Repeat the thought stop again and again.

When the loudness and the force are eight or above, you are ready to try it on an actual negative thought. If you continue to have difficulty with the loudness and force, record yourself yelling ***STOP!*** on an audio cassette. Listen to it and then try to replicate the stop in your head. Do this as many times as it takes to get the job done.

I will note here that some people have much better visual than auditory imagery. If this is true for you, you can use the image of a stop sign or a stop light with the auditory imagery or by itself. But keep in mind the visual images also need to be strong enough to compete with your strongest negative cognitions.

Choose a specific thought from your inventory that was not above 6 on the intensity of response rating. With your eyes closed, focus on that thought; make it as clear and as daunting as you can. Then yell ***STOP!*** inside your head until the thought is no longer present. Repeat this procedure five times.

✓ Abdominal Breathing

I have discussed abdominal breathing in its own section. Review this material and practice it for five minutes. When you are relaxed, close your eyes, think the negative thought, thought stop, and then switch to deep breathing. If the thought should come back on its own, thought stop, then breathe. Practice this sequence for five trials.

✓ Imagery

Which images or thoughts bring you strength, energy and joy? Spend some time thinking of the many possibilities. These can be beautiful places you've been, experiences you've had or would like to have, eating your favorite food, laughing with your friends, succeeding at your fondest goal, remembering all the good things about yourself, listening to music and so on.

You will need to have many positive images available in your repertoire because if you overuse one it loses its shine. So, variety is the spice of life in this exercise. Dr. Cautela had one image that he used for himself that definitely brought a smile to my face. He imagined he was a crew member (a psychologist, of course) on Star Trek! So use your imagination. It really can be quite a kick.

The effectiveness of these images or thoughts will very much depend on two variables, which you need to measure on the one to 10 scale: clarity of the image, and how reinforcing the image is to you at this time. These positive images or thoughts must be high-powered to compete with cognitions that have been driving you up a wall. Spend time on one specific image, getting the clarity and reinforcement to an eight or above. This can take practice, so be patient with yourself!

Putting It All Together
Now you're ready to practice the exercise as a whole.

Thought > Thought Stop > Breathe > Image

Think the thought or image. Make sure it's as clear and as strong as you can get it. Thought stop until the thought or image is gone. Deep breathe and then think the positive thought or image. Take time to enjoy the pleasure of this. If the negative image returns, thought stop and continue the whole sequence again. Do this sequence 10 times with 30 seconds between each trial.

Other Instructions/Information

✓ Practice two sessions per day, 10 triads per session.

✓ One session is with your eyes closed and one is with them open. This is because you will need to use the triad throughout your day when your eyes need to be open.

✓ Choose three positive images in the morning: one for each session and one to use on thoughts that come up outside of sessions.

✓ At any time during the day, if you experience a negative thought, immediately use the triad with your chosen positive image.

✓ Practice on thoughts that you really want to get rid of. The practice session can reduce the power of the negative cognition. Vary the negative cognitions you are targeting.

Not only can this be used to alter thinking patterns, it can also be helpful in situations that are confrontational to reduce the intensity of your reaction.

Chapter Eight

SOME FINAL THOUGHTS

I've said it once and I'll say it again: It's your little red wagon... you can push it, pull it or just stand and look at it. You – *and only you* – get to make the choice!

On one hand, you could choose to embrace the power of positive psychology and make a commitment to develop the core strengths detailed in this book. I've provided a map, some directions, a few signposts, and the proven tools and techniques to get you on your way. All you need to do is fill in the goals and dreams, study the map and get going along your own positive path!

On the other hand, you could choose just to stand and look at that vibrant red vehicle, with all the possibilities of the good life it represents, and simply do nothing with it. What a terrible shame that would be....

If your life isn't moving in the right direction, I urge you to accept the challenge to change it. If you convert the information contained in this book into an action plan, and stick to that plan, I know you can do it – because I've seen it done many, many times before!

Never underestimate your ability to change your life, and never forget that you are the one in charge of making that choice. Remember the words of Ben Franklin: "When you're finished changing, you're finished." If you have a question or simply need some words of encouragement, feel free to email me at ThePositivePath@cox.net, or visit my website at www.PositivePathLifeCoaching.com. I sincerely hope you find your own positive path to the good life!

Made in the USA
Lexington, KY
30 May 2014